The Heart Prepared

The Heart Prepared
Grace and Conversion
in Puritan Spiritual Life

Norman Pettit

Second Edition, with a New Introduction
by David D. Hall

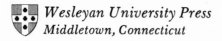 *Wesleyan University Press*
Middletown, Connecticut

Library of Congress Cataloging-in-Publication Data
Pettit, Norman.
    The heart prepared : grace and conversion in Puritan spiritual
life / Norman Pettit.—2nd ed., 1st Wesleyan ed. / with a new
introduction by David D. Hall.
        p.   cm.—(Wesleyan paperback)
    "Originally undertaken as a doctoral dissertation . . . at Yale
University"—P.
    Bibliography: p.
    Includes index.
    ISBN 0-8195-6224-6
    1. Puritans—Doctrines—History.   2. Grace (Theology)—
History of doctrines.   3. Conversion—History of doctrines.
4. Theology, Doctrinal—New England—History   I. Title.
BX9322.P4   1989
248.2′4—dc 19   89-5499
                                                               CIP

Manufactured in the United States of America

First Wesleyan Edition, 1989

Wesleyan Paperback, 1989

94 93 92 91 90   6 5 4 3 2

To Walter Jackson Bate, Friend and Tutor

Preface to the Wesleyan Edition

The Heart Prepared, first published in 1966 by Yale University Press, has long been out of print, and so it is with keen anticipation that I welcome the Wesleyan University Press edition. It not only makes the book available once again, but it also gives me a chance to reflect upon thoughts that first came to mind more than twenty years ago. My hope is that the second edition will find new readers. Those who knew the book in the past may be pleased to have it back.

This is a study of the interior life that deals with the conversion experience. It is concerned with the emergence and development of a theological notion: the concept of preparation for grace. In orthodox Reformed theology of the sixteenth century no allowance had been made for preparation. In strict predestinarian dogma the sinner was taken by storm—the heart wrenched from depravity to grace. Reprobates could neither anticipate salvation nor look to the inner self for signs of regeneration. Before the moment of effectual conversion, one was held to be spiritually void. Yet in the late sixteenth and early seventeenth centuries certain English clergy began to express the idea that sinners, although utterly depraved, might nevertheless "prepare" themselves for saving grace. In Puritan teachings, from the days of Elizabeth to the founding of New England, the notion of "an Heart Prepared" came to have momentous import. Puritan preachers, in both Old and New England, held that one must prepare the heart for salvation, that one must turn to God before saving grace may be achieved. Yet it was said, at the same time, that the unconverted could do nothing to effect their own conversion. In this realm no other system of spirituality so concerned itself with problems of fear, doubt, and despair. None has so closely described the struggles of the interior life.

The Heart Prepared attempts, therefore, to get at the roots of the religious imagination and to examine the thoughts of those who felt "the worm of conscience gnaw upon their hearts." It is an effort to describe the Puritan mind as both expansive and restrictive, imaginative yet dogmatic, and to examine that mind in the light of Reformed theology and biblical prescription. Above all, it is an effort to describe an introspective process, which in Puritan theology became a part of the conversion experience, and to point up the significance of such a process for the beginnings of New England life.

In first composing The Heart Prepared, it was my wish to show how broad in scope the Puritan mind could be, and how greatly men could differ on the use of biblical texts. I wished especially to point out the degree to which New England thought had been rooted in English divinity, to argue that the great Elizabethan divines, to whom the first generation on this continent owed so much, had set the tone, extending into the New World an older strain of piety. Finally, I wished to show how the New England mind, shaped in the motherland, had been reshaped according to the needs of the churches on these shores.

Unless the preachers themselves give another translation, all biblical citations are taken from the 1595 edition of the Geneva Bible. The Geneva New Testament first appeared in 1557. Three years later the whole Bible was printed, with a dedication to Elizabeth. Though never sanctioned for use in the Church, the Geneva Bible was the most influential of the English versions at this time. Of the eighty-five editions of Scripture issued under Elizabeth, sixty were made up from the Geneva edition of 1595. What is more, the marginal notes of this edition exerted considerable influence in the formation of Puritan views. In quoting from the Geneva Bible, as well as from all other original sources, I have modernized spelling and punctuation for clarity.

Special thanks are due David D. Hall, who has been kind enough to write the Introduction to this edition. I should like also to thank Peter J. Potter, associate editor, and Margaret Klumpp, editorial associate, Wesleyan University Press, for their help and guidance along the way. Looking back in time, I should like to acknowledge the debt I owe A. F. Thompson and Lawrence Stone, my tutors at Wadham College, Oxford, who first introduced me to the art of historical scholarship. To my tutor at Harvard College, Walter Jackson Bate, I should like to acknowledge once again the greatest debt I owe.

N.P.

Cambridge, Massachusetts
December, 1988

Introduction to the Wesleyan Edition

Norman Pettit's *The Heart Prepared* tells of the transfer of theological ideas from the old world to the new. The central concept is that of "preparation for salvation," which passed from the early Protestant reformers to late Elizabethan Protestants in England, and thence to the Puritan ministers who took part in the founding of New England.

All of these ministers and theologians were "Calvinists," which is to say that all of them agreed on certain premises about the relationship between man and God. Along the way, however, the Calvinist system grew and changed. By the end of the sixteenth century, and especially in Elizabethan England, this system included a richly elaborated psychology of religious experience. When certain English ministers described the Christian life they focused on the inward self, the self so aptly captured by that resonating word the "heart." Laying aside—though not forgetting—the logic of creeds and catechisms, these preachers declared that the men and women "elected" to salvation—those whom God had chosen of his own free will—would experience their redemption. Inwardly, the elect would come to feel transformed. Historians call this process "conversion." But to the ministers themselves it had no single name, although "work of grace" was a phrase in common use.

This work of grace was the doing of God alone. Divine mercy made it possible; the gift of grace was wholly free and without respect to human actions. Yet for the Puritan preachers Pettit describes in *The Heart Prepared* the work of grace also involved the willing, active self. The language of these preachers' sermons is a language of engagement. Men and women are asked to feel the curse of sin; they are summoned into action. There is much to do, and one must not sit idly by waiting for free grace. Repeatedly the ministers demanded that the people they addressed "reach out for the promises," "close with Christ," perform certain duties, engage in repentance. To give force to these commands, they quoted Scripture—for example, 2 Peter 1:10: "Wherefore the rather, brethren, give diligence to make your calling and election sure: for if ye do these things, ye shall never fall." Or they invoked Philippians 2:12–13: "Wherefore, my beloved . . . work out your own salvation with fear and trembling. For it is God which worketh in you both to will and to do of his good pleasure."

The more fully they developed this description of spiritual experience, the more two questions emerged: At what point in this process do I know when I am saved? Why strive so hard before I gain some sense of being saved? Lay men and women had to wonder (and sometimes despair) if they would ever gain assurance of salvation. They had to wonder if their struggle to repent of sin and become faithful Christians was in any way vital to salvation. These questions gained a new importance when the founders of New England decided in the mid-1630s to restrict church membership to persons who could describe the work of grace in a public avowal. So determined were the colonists to purify their gathered congregations that they required a "relation" of spiritual experience of everyone who wished to enter the church covenant.[1]

1. This development is described in Edmund S. Morgan, *Visible Saints: The History of a Puritan Idea* (New York: New York University Press,

As Pettit tells us in *The Heart Prepared,* the tensions spring-
ing from this demand exploded in the Antinomian controversy
of 1636–1638. Anne Hutchinson, a charismatic woman and a
member of the newly founded Boston congregation, accused the
ministers in New England of misleading the people by teaching them to reason they were saved if they performed godly
duties and engaged in repentance. She questioned whether this
was preaching "works" and not "free grace." Hutchinson had
an important ally in John Cotton, her minister in Boston.
Speaking in the technical language of theology, Cotton argued
that no "conditions" were attached to the covenant of grace,
and that faith was "passive" prior to the stage of justification—
that is, the moment when the sinner was accepted before God
on the basis of Christ's righteousness. Moreover, he demurred
at using "sanctification"—the godliness that people manifested
after they had been accepted before God—as the basis for assurance of salvation. He wanted to make sure that no one confused or connected the striving that the preachers called for
with the event of free grace.

When Cotton and his fellow ministers debated the relationship between justification and sanctification, they were also
debating whether "preparation for salvation" was required of
the faithful. As his colleagues declared in rejecting Cotton's
position: "But there must be some saving preparatives wrought
in the soule, to make way for faith, and our union with Christ.
For wee must be cut off from the old *Adam,* before wee can
be grafted into the new. . . ." To such reasoning Cotton replied, "To works of creation there needeth no preparation;
the almighty power of God calleth them to be his people. . . .
And by calling them to be so, hee maketh them to bee so."[2]

1963), a book that strongly influenced Pettit's account of the relationship
between church membership and the doctrine of preparation.

2. David D. Hall, ed., *The Antinomian Controversy, 1636–1638: A
Documentary History* (Middletown, Conn.: Wesleyan University Press,
1968), 177. This collection of documents includes Mrs. Hutchinson's statements as well as Cotton's argument for "passive" faith.

Historians have often been unsympathetic to the ministers who opposed John Cotton and who labeled Mrs. Hutchinson an Antinomian. Did these "legal" preachers, as she in turn labeled them, bend the logic of the Calvinist system by giving too much credit to the stage of preparation? Did they institute a shift from piety to moralism by insisting on the "practical syllogism," or the principle that visible saints may reason they are saved on the basis of behavior?[3] Perhaps without intending it, were they hinting there was more that man could do, and more freedom for his actions?

So Perry Miller argued in a brilliant essay, " 'Preparation for Salvation' in Seventeenth-Century New England." In this essay Miller extended the interpretation he had laid out in *The New England Mind: The Seventeenth Century*, where he proposed that the Puritans developed a distinctive "covenant theology" that enabled them to insist on conditions—as in those on each side of a contract—individuals must fulfill in the process of salvation. Miller painted the New England ministers as in search of ways to modify the "strict" doctrine of election. Not only, therefore, did they liken the relationship between man and God to a contract, but they also advanced the concept of "preparation for salvation" as a strategy for obliging everyone to perform moral duties—for only afterwards, and long afterwards at that, would the elect know that they were different from the nonelect. In so acting, the ministers in New England were responding, Miller argued, to their New World situation, acknowledging a responsibility for social order that they had been able to evade while in England. Miller went on to propose that this doctrine of preparation for salvation, improvised to meet new needs, got out of hand

3. Hall, *Antinomian Controversy*, 58, 76, 182. A full and sympathetic interpretation of the "legal" preachers that establishes their orthodoxy is found in William K. B. Stoever, *"A Faire and Easie Way to Heaven": Covenant Theology and Antinomianism in Early Massachusetts* (Middletown, Conn.: Wesleyan University Press, 1978).

as the ministers increasingly appealed for preparatory actions. By Cotton Mather's generation, at the outset of the eighteenth century, these appeals had "steadily enlarged the field of such behavior." It even seemed to Miller that Mather had begun, "though in the most tentative fashion, to suggest that whoever would prepare himself would almost certainly go to heaven!"[4]

Not until the Epilogue of *The Heart Prepared* does Norman Pettit fully manifest his dissent from this interpretation. So great was Miller's authority at the time *The Heart Prepared* was first published in 1966, and so awesome *The New England Mind,* that to disagree took special courage. Yet Pettit broke with Miller's analysis in three different ways: by dissenting from Miller's gloss on covenant as contract; by locating the concept of preparation as of earlier origin among Reformed (Calvinist) theologians of the sixteenth century; and by noting that Scripture held the germ of the idea. Pettit's training as a literary historian lies behind his assertion that the "religious imagination" in early New England was nurtured on the Bible. When the ministers elaborated their psychology of spiritual experience, when they appealed to the affective self or heart, they did so in response to Scripture. *The Heart Prepared* therefore tells a story quite different from Miller's tale of improvisation and decline. Yet it also owes to Miller the perception that "preparation for salvation" was contested in the Antinomian controversy.

The process of revising Miller continues to the present day.[5]

4. Perry Miller, " 'Preparation for Salvation' in Seventeenth-Century New England," in *Nature's Nation* (Cambridge, Mass.: Harvard University Press, 1967), 50–77; this essay was originally published in 1943. Miller's *The New England Mind: The Seventeenth Century* was published in 1939; its sequel, *The New England Mind: From Colony to Province* (Cambridge, Mass.: Harvard University Press, 1953) incorporates the argument of " 'Preparation for Salvation.' "

5. For the details of this revision, consult Michael McGiffert, "American Puritan Studies in the 1960's," *William and Mary Quarterly,* 3d Ser., 27 (1970): 36–67; David D. Hall, "Understanding the Puritans," in *The State of American History,* ed. Herbert J. Bass (Chicago: Quadrangle

In recent years a major change of thinking has occurred about
preparation, assurance, and the Puritan vision of the work of
grace. *The Heart Prepared* antedates this change of thinking,
and some of its judgments have been modified or challenged.

One step toward a better understanding of preparation and
the work of grace occurred when Robert Middlekauff reap-
praised the preaching of the three Mathers—Richard, Increase,
and Cotton. Acknowledging that publicly Cotton Mather spoke
the language of preparation and exhorted sinners to seek
Christ, Middlekauff discovered that Mather actually "rejected"
preparation as a stage that individuals, unaided, could perform:

> Mather announced his disenchantment with the language
> of preparation in order to point out the dangers he saw
> in the entire conception. Believing that preparation had
> yielded "inconceivable prejudice" to the attempts of the
> Lord to save the souls of men, he did not hesitate to scrap
> the whole scheme from its psychological assumptions to
> its vocabulary of stages and steps.[6]

Almost in passing, Middlekauff noted that New England's
"preparationists" always said that men and women were able
to perform "evangelical preparation"—certain steps or stages
of experience that seemed to precede conversion—only with
the help of the Holy Spirit. No steps they took on their own
had any direct bearing on salvation.[7]

This important observation was seconded by Brooks Holifield, who insisted that no minister in seventeenth-century
New England believed that human actions could influence or

Books, 1970), 330–49; David D. Hall, "On Common Ground: The Coher-
ence of American Puritan Studies," *William and Mary Quarterly*, 3d Ser.,
44 (1987): 193–229.

6. Robert Middlekauff, *The Mathers: Three Generations of Puritan
Intellectuals 1596–1728* (New York: Oxford University Press, 1971), 233–
34, and see 238–39.

7. Ibid., 241–42, 61.

cause the bestowal of grace. When the willing, active self participated in the process of salvation, it did so only because God enabled preparation to occur. Holifield was uncomfortable with the very term "preparationist" because it implied that the New England ministers compromised the doctrines of election and free grace. In two respects, moreover, he clarified the significance of the sacrament of baptism. Pettit had suggested that "baptismal efficacy," or the concept that the sacrament planted certain seeds of grace, enabled the ministers to overcome the difference between "works" and "grace" and introduce a stage of preparation. Holifield has demonstrated, however, that no New England minister regarded the sacrament as efficacious. And in contrast to the Miller-Pettit interpretation, he proves that the ministers in New England agreed with one another about the meaning of baptism.[8]

Thanks to certain recent publications we have learned much more about ordinary people and how they experienced the work of grace. Many testimonies survive in two notebooks, one that Thomas Shepard kept in Cambridge and another that John Fiske kept in Wenham. The full text of Thomas Shepard's private journal has also been published.[9] These new sources, as well as others long familiar to historians of Puritanism, tell us that the colonists often felt disheartened. They pleaded their unworthiness; they spoke of themselves as sinners lacking any hope that God would spare them from his anger. Yet they voiced their dependence on the risen Christ, clinging to verses such as Matthew 11:28: "Come unto me, all ye

8. E. Brooks Holifield, *The Covenant Sealed: The Development of Puritan Sacramental Theology in Old and New England, 1570–1720* (New Haven, Conn.: Yale University Press, 1974).

9. George Selement and Bruce C. Woolley, eds., *Thomas Shepard's "Confessions,"* Colonial Society of Massachusetts *Publications,* 58 (Boston, 1981); Robert G. Pope, ed., *The Notebook of the Reverend John Fiske, 1644–1675,* ibid., 57 (Boston, 1974); Michael McGiffert, ed., *God's Plot: The Paradoxes of Puritan Piety, Being the Autobiography and Journal of Thomas Shepard* (Amherst, Mass.: University of Massachusetts Press, 1972).

that labor and are heavy laden, and I will give you rest." They
repented but did not dare to assume that repentance gained
them favor in God's sight.[10]

In the main, the flow of experience did not coincide with
the crisp sequence outlined by the clergy in their sermons. Nor
did the work of grace ever seem to end, or assurance become
certain. Assurance was offset by uncertainty, as people continued to struggle against sin even after gaining some hope
of election. Pettit, sensing these complexities, tells us in *The
Heart Prepared* that no single model of conversion prevailed.
Other historians prefer to speak of "paradox" as part of the
pilgrim's journey and discern a pattern of "renewed conversions," a phrase that Thomas Shepard applied to himself.
Pursuing this insight, the historian Michael McGiffert defines
conversion as a "process," as contrasted with a "settled condition"—a process "patterned by a dynamic relation of hopeful
and fearful emotions, interacting and interpenetrating."[11] The
point of sharpest strain, the main source of tension, was assurance of salvation—craved, yet never granted absolutely.

Assurance was the central issue in the Antinomian controversy. When John Cotton and his fellow ministers debated
the relationship between justification and sanctification, they
were dealing with the felt need for an answer to the question,
"Am I saved?" Moreover, they were dealing with a problem
that had rarely troubled John Calvin. Here is not the place
to rehearse Calvin's concept of assurance or to explain why
the issue became so important within late Elizabethan Puritanism.[12] What matters is that by the middle of the seventeenth

10. These kinds of statements are repeated in Selement and Woolley,
Thomas Shepard's "Confessions." An important study of these texts is
Charles Lloyd Cohen, *God's Caress: The Psychology of Puritan Religious
Experience* (New York: Oxford University Press, 1986).

11. McGiffert, *God's Plot*, 25–26.

12. Anyone who is interested in these questions can profitably consult
R. T. Kendall, *Calvin and English Calvinism to 1649* (Oxford: Oxford
University Press, 1979), and especially an unpublished dissertation, Lynn

century, the New England clergy shared with many other Protestants a conception of the Christian life as a journey that required an incessant, never-ending struggle against sin. In his book *The Practice of Piety,* Charles Hambrick-Stowe describes this journey in a way that takes account of Scripture, as Pettit did before him. Hambrick-Stowe observes that conversion was not an "isolated and distinct moment in a person's life," but part of a "larger pilgrimage." He reiterates that the New England ministers "consistently rejected the idea that an unregenerate sinner could achieve preparation for conversion." But his most important task is to sketch a different meaning for "preparation," a redefinition that makes it a series of spiritual exercises—from daily prayer and meditation to worship on the Sabbath—by which Christians must prepare constantly and all their lives for final union with the risen Christ.[13]

The progress of Puritan studies has changed the way we think about the issues Pettit addressed in *The Heart Prepared.* Yet in prose that remains fresh and clear, Pettit teaches us the enduring lesson that Puritanism drew on the resources of the literary imagination. It did so, he informs us, because Puritanism was a religion of experience. His book unfolds for us a powerful scenario—conversion or the work of grace—as imagined by a group of writers who were deeply influential in America. Always, these writers understood religion as engaging the affective self. And always they looked back to Scripture. These are propositions that give classic stature to *The Heart Prepared.*

David D. Hall

Boston, Massachusetts
January 1989

Baird Tipson, Jr., "The Development of a Puritan Understanding of Conversion" (Yale University, 1972).

13. Charles Hambrick-Stowe, *The Practice of Piety: Puritan Devotional Disciplines in Seventeenth-Century New England* (Chapel Hill, N.C.: University of North Carolina Press, 1982), 76, 149–241.

Contents

Preface to the Wesleyan Edition   vii

Introduction to the Wesleyan Edition   xi

1. Preparation and the Problem of the Heart   1

2. Continental Reformed Theologians   22

3. The English Preparationists   48

4. The American Preparationists   86

5. Early Criticism and the Antinomian Controversy   125

6. Later Criticism: To the Halfway Covenant and Beyond   158

Epilogue   217

Bibliography   223

Index   237

The Heart Prepared

1

Preparation
and the Problem of the Heart

Seventeenth-century New Englanders examined their hearts
with an intensity now quite alien to the American mind. The
image of the heart, the biblical metonym for the inner man,
held a central position in their total conception of the spiritual
life. The heart could be "proud" or "humble," "stony" or
"fleshy," the source of perpetual corruption, a jealous and
indifferent barrier to grace, or the final realm of understanding,
the ultimate dwelling place of God. When they touched their
hearts, they touched their deepest faith. If they could deceive
others with their tongues, they could never deceive themselves
in their hearts. Beyond the voice, behind the conscience, the
heart told them the truth about themselves and their relation
to God. Only there could self-examination be effective. Only
there could God's will be known. What assurance of faith they
possessed, however weak, had to be discovered in the inner
man, for it was written: "Let the hidden man of the heart be . . .
before God a thing much set by" (I Peter 3:4).

This deep concern with the common depravity and potential
holiness of the human heart prevailed in all of Puritanism. No
other facet of Puritan spirituality so dominated the written
expression of the interior life. But in the sermon literature of
early New England the image of the heart took on special

significance; for if in theory there was nothing one could do
to bring on, or even to anticipate, regeneration, piety in New
England demanded that the heart be put in order for the coming
of the Spirit. Through introspective meditation, within the
depths of the self, it was possible and indeed necessary to prepare the heart for salvation.

When we consider that Puritan thought in sixteenth- and
seventeenth-century England derived from the strict dogmatics
of Reformed theology, it seems extraordinary that a concept of
preparation should have emerged at all. In other schools of
theology similar processes were not unusual; but in Reformed
theology, to which most English churchmen adhered, preparation was heretical. It was, in fact, forbidden by Reformed dogmatics; for the Reformed understanding of St. Paul had led to
an extreme emphasis on the utter depravity of man and his
inability in any way to influence God or to predispose himself
for saving grace. Huldreich Zwingli (1484–1531), to whom this
great body of orthodox Reformed thought owed much, had
conceived of God's movement toward man as absolutely arbitrary. Man could neither calculate nor expect God's dealings.
As in Paul's own conversion, the fallen creature was wrenched
from sin to grace by the predestined, inscrutable will of God.
In salvation there could be no cooperation; otherwise God
would cease to be supreme. "The elect are the children of God,"
wrote Zwingli, "even before they believe."[1] And when Calvin
published his *Institutes* in 1536, the Zwinglian tradition had
been well established.

In Scripture conversion is described in two ways: as man's
voluntary return to God and as God's turning man to Him. In
the Old Testament, God in some passages exhorts man to return, while in others He turns him to Himself by changing his

1. Zwingli, *Opera,* ed. M. Schuler and J. Schulthess (8 vols. Zurich,
1828–42), *3,* 426. "Rursus electi eligebantur antequam in utero conciperentur;
mox igitur ut sunt filii dei sunt, etiamsi moriantur antequam credant aut
ad fidem vocentur."

heart. In Hosea 14:1 man is exhorted, "return unto the Lord thy God." In Jeremiah 31:18 it is written, "turn thou me, and I shall be turned." In the New Testament, Peter tells the Jews, "Repent ye therefore, and be converted" (Acts 3:19), while Paul tells the Romans, "it is not of him that willeth . . . but of God that showeth mercy" (Rom. 9:16). Yet Paul presents the Philippians with the paradox, "work out your own salvation with fear and trembling. For it is God which worketh in you both to will and to do of his good pleasure" (Phil. 2:12, 13).

Throughout the history of Western Christendom theologians of various schools have tended to prefer those proof texts which fit their total doctrinal stance and to suppress those which do not. The earliest English churchmen, standing as they did in the shadow of continental Reformed theology, had for the most part based their conception of conversion on the Pauline message, "It is not of him that willeth . . . but of God that showeth mercy." They had emphasized divine sovereignty, human depravity, and irresistible grace. All is done on God's part, nothing on man's. But as early as 1570 certain English divines began to ask whether or not there might indeed be something man could do, so to "return unto the Lord" as Scripture had demanded. In time they began to express the idea that man, although utterly depraved, might somehow predispose himself for saving grace; and this was the attitude of mind that developed in English divinity, especially among theologians of the "Puritan" party, to become a part of the New England Way.

The words "Puritan" and "Puritanism" are difficult, if not impossible, to define. But here we must attempt as close a definition as possible for a clear understanding of the problem at hand and of the mind from which preparation emerged. The evangelical strain has always been a part of Christian tradition, and this perhaps could be called "Puritan" in its broadest sense. Historical Puritanism, however, as we have come to know it, began under the reign of Elizabeth in the middle of the sixteenth century and lasted roughly until the end of the seven-

teenth. The term "Puritanism" itself first came into common
use in England about 1564 to describe that side of English Reformed thought which had been reluctant to accept surviving
"popish" practices.[2] As continental Reformed theology became
more influential in England, hostility to Rome increased; and
after the return of the Marian exiles, anti-Catholic feeling ran
high. By 1570 radical Protestantism strongly felt the restrictions of ecclesiastical conservatism, and Thomas Cartwright
had gathered a following to challenge the authorities of the
Church. They were "Puritans" in the stricter sense, in that most
of those in the presbyterian *classes* wanted both to purify the
Church of relics and to alter the established form of Church
government. It was in this brief period that the term "Puritan"
most accurately described those to whom it was applied. But the
so-called "Puritans" or "spiritual preachers," with whom we are
concerned, were not normally associated with this radical group.
They were English churchmen, some returned exiles, who were
determined to preach the revival of "true religion" within the
established Church. After the restoration of Protestantism under Elizabeth in 1558 they had gathered into a "spiritual
brotherhood" which launched, as it were, the second phase of
the English Reformation.[3] Their seat of learning was Cambridge, where they were primarily concerned with conformity;
and in most cases they were willing to compromise on ceremonial and ecclesiastical issues for the sake of Church unity. They
remained in the Church because they considered separation too
drastic, and because they were willing to wait until the Church
itself was reformed.

The point to be emphasized is that from 1558 these Puritan
divines preached within the pastoral tradition of the English
clergy, acquired a large popular following, and continued to
debate with their fellow churchmen as to what the Church

2. John Brown, *The English Puritans* (Cambridge, England, 1912), p. 1.
3. See William Haller, *The Rise of Puritanism* (New York, 1938), chap. II.

should be.[4] There was no normative Anglicanism at this time from which to break away. Indeed, it was not until after the establishment of the Church under Laud, in the reign of Charles I, that the term "Anglicanism" was to become applicable.[5] Such early Puritan pastors as Richard Greenham, Richard Rogers, Arthur Hildersam, and William Perkins all preached within the same tradition as Lancelot Andrewes and George Herbert. It was a tradition, above all, to be assessed in terms of the influence of Reformed theology on the English clergy.

Important for our purposes is the way these Puritans interpreted that theology, how they modified it, and what they contributed in terms of emphasis.[6] At Cambridge in the 1580s and 1590s, when the "godly brethren" joined for the exposition of Scripture, their purpose was to discover the "true sense" of the Bible. This meant that while they followed the general

4. H. C. Porter, *Reformation and Reaction in Tudor Cambridge* (Cambridge, England, 1958), p. 261.

5. It might even be argued that "Anglicanism" in a normative sense did not become a reality until after the Restoration and the "Great Ejection" of St. Bartholomew's Day, 1662. See Sydney E. Ahlstrom, "Theology in America: A Historical Survey," in *Religion in American Life,* ed. James Ward Smith, *1* (Princeton, 1961), 238–39.

6. See Charles H. and Katherine George, *The Protestant Mind of the English Reformation, 1570–1640* (Princeton, 1961). The Georges have said that there was no distinctly Puritan point of view in this period in that all English churchmen agreed on essential points of doctrine. But Puritanism, it should be remembered, was not a doctrine. Rather, it was an interpretation of doctrine ultimately determined by Reformed convictions. And this interpretation has come to be known as Puritan spirituality. In the words of Louis Bouyer:

> Spirituality is distinguished from dogma by the fact that, instead of describing the objects of belief as it were in the abstract, it studies the reactions which these objects arouse in the religious consciousness. . . . Dogmatic theology, therefore, must always be presupposed as the basis of spiritual theology, even though the latter concerns itself with the data of the former only under the relationship that they entertain with the religious consciousness [*The Spirituality of the New Testament and the Fathers* (New York, 1963), p. viii].

approach laid down by orthodox Reformed theology, they in
no sense assumed that the last word had been said. And what
they sought to convey, as we shall see, was something quite
different: not an overwhelming sense of man's insignificance,
but an increasing awareness of the loving, willing side of human
nature, or the need, above all, for "purity of heart."[7] That they
should be branded "Puritans" for these concerns was never
entirely to their liking. William Perkins, for one, lamented
that "the pure heart is so little regarded, that the seeking after
it is turned to a by-word: those that most endeavor to get and
keep the purity of heart . . . are so much branded with vile terms
of Puritan and Precisians."[8]

Historical Puritanism, then, was a form of piety within the
English Church which, if centered on church order, vestments,
and externals, was essentially dedicated to the revival of "true"
religion. As such, it took with high seriousness the notion that
Adam's fall had left his descendants totally depraved. Where
the conforming churchman tended to ignore the more extreme
forms of predestinarian dogma, the Puritan felt compelled to
face the problem directly. He had always to keep in mind that
the harmony of the universe could be found only in the disparity between man's absolute impotence and God's unconditional sovereignty. Therefore it is truly remarkable that in
time he was able to strike such a delicate balance between the
needs of religious enthusiasm and the demands of a rigorous
predestinarianism. The early English Reformer William Tyndale, who died in 1536, had been convinced of the blinding
power of grace as a lightning flash, in accordance with Paul's
conversion; but the Puritan preachers of the Elizabethan
Church were able to find a closer bond between man and God.
Grace, as they conceived it, gently linked man to God in such a
way that if man never knew the precise moment it had occurred,
he would certainly know the process through which it had been
attained.

7. Porter, p. 270. See Ahlstrom, "Theology in America," p. 240.
8. William Perkins, *Works* (3 vols. London, 1626), *3*, 15.

Above all, the Puritans tried to effect in others the pattern of regeneration they themselves had experienced.[9] Since rarely had this happened in the manner of Paul, but more frequently through the faintest beginnings, they had necessarily to be concerned with other possibilities. Was the *ordo salutis* a set procedure, inevitably initiated by a sudden realization of faith; or could conversions be variable, both empirically and biblically? When they turned to Paul's relation of his own conversion, or to the Reformed interpretation of Pauline theology, they saw that grace came, to be sure, as a sudden seizure. But when they turned to Paul's preaching, to the teachings of Jesus in the Gospels, or to the Old Testament itself, they discovered that faith could come in other ways; that it might be "weak" at first, and that it was possible to be prepared for its coming. As members of an evangelical, proselytizing, and reforming movement, these Puritans were concerned not merely to inform of salvation but to exhort to it;[10] and to uphold the Pauline conversion as normative would surely discourage potential believers. Paul had neither sought nor asked for God's redemptive love. He had been against Jesus from the start. Moreover, when he finally experienced regeneration, it was as an actual event, as a moment in time on the road to Damascus.

> And so it was, as I made my journey and was come nigh unto Damascus about noon, that suddenly there shone from heaven a great light round about me. So I fell unto the earth and heard a voice saying unto me, Saul, Saul, why persecutest thou me? . . . So when I could not see for the brightness of that light, I was led by the hand of them that were with me, and came unto Damascus. . . . Then I said, Lord, they know that I prisoned and beat in every Synagogue them that believed on thee. [Acts 22:6, 7, 11, 19]

After his conversion, Paul believed that because he had persecuted Jesus, the new life could have no relation to his

9. Haller, chap. II.
10. George, p. 58.

strivings or desires. But it is important to remember that he
did not uphold his own conversion as normative. The first Reformers, particularly Zwingli, assumed from the experience of
Paul that if grace came, it would come as it had to a confirmed
sinner. But the doctrine Paul himself had preached was that
faith could be "weak" as well as "strong." "Him that is weak
in the faith receive unto you" (Rom. 14:1); for "if thou shalt . . .
believe in thine heart . . . thou shalt be saved" (Rom. 10:9).

However much the Puritans preached rigid predestinarian
concepts, their own ministerial enthusiasm led them to insist
that a "weak" faith, or the "endeavor to apprehend," the "will
to believe with an honest heart," was as much as most Christians
could hope for.[11] Salvation need not depend on the strength
of faith, as even a "seed" of grace could save. "If ye have faith
as much as is a grain of mustard seed," said the Gospel, "nothing
shall be impossible unto you" (Matt. 17:20), and many took
this text as the basis of their exhortations to faith. As they
looked with greater frequency to God's mercy, rather than to
his majesty, the way for preparation was opened; for Paul
himself had warned the Corinthians to be "ready" lest he find
them "unprepared" (II Cor. 9:3, 4). "This yet remember," said
Paul, "that he which soweth sparingly shall reap sparingly;
and he that soweth liberally shall reap also liberally. As every
man wisheth in his heart, so let him give: not grudgingly, or of
necessity; for God loveth a cheerful giver" (II Cor. 9:6, 7).

In the first Book of Samuel the Israelites are exhorted, "Prepare your hearts unto the Lord" (I Sam. 7:3). In the Book of
Job, Zophar advises, "If thou prepare thine heart, and stretch
out thine hands toward him . . . then truly shalt thou lift up
thy face without spot" (Job 11:13, 15). And in Luke's Gospel,
Jesus warns, "Be ye prepared therefore . . . for the Son of man
will come at an hour when ye think not" (Luke 12:40). But
in other passages from Scripture these exhortations are counter-

11. Perkins, 2, 208–09.

acted by the dictum that God, not man, prepares the heart for reconciliation: "Lord, thou has heard the desire of the poor: thou preparest their heart" (Psalm 10:17). In still others the meaning is left ambiguous: "The preparations of the heart are in man, but the answer of the tongue is of the Lord"; and "The heart of man proposeth his way, but the Lord doth direct his steps" (Prov. 16:1, 9).[12]

The question to be answered, then, was how these biblical passages, with their apparent contradictions, should be interpreted not only in the light of experiential religion but against a background of Reformed dogmatics. If, according to Reformed thought, man cannot even anticipate salvation, should preparation be preached at all? And if preparation could be reconciled to some degree with Reformed theology, to what extent was it the work of man or God? The earliest Puritans could agree neither on the nature of preparation nor even on its absolute necessity; yet the scriptural idea of the heart prepared, whether from God or man, gradually came into its own. As the Puritans never consciously separated experiential from biblical religion, but always assumed they were one and the same, the tendency was to move toward those proof texts which could best be correlated with individual experience.

✠

This movement in Puritanism toward experiential immediacy was exemplified most strikingly by a renewed interest in the doctrine of the Holy Spirit. The earliest Puritans were determined to show that grace came not from God as a removed creator but through a personal experience of the direct opera-

12. In the Geneva Bible these passages from Proverbs are accompanied by marginalia which read: "He dirideth the presumption of man, who dare attribute to himself any thing, as to prepare his heart or such like." Yet the textual ambiguity remained uncorrected until 1611, when the authorized version was made to read: "The preparations of the heart in man, and the answer of the tongue, is from the Lord."

tion of His Spirit. This meant, among other things, that grace
was no longer an external something which descended from
above, as in orthodox Reformed thought, but an "indwelling"
of the Spirit which demanded "entertainment" in the heart.
From the time of Richard Rogers, who wrote in the 1570s, an
increasing interest in the doctrine of the Holy Spirit allowed
for a kind of enthusiasm which orthodox Reformed theology
had not known. Where the early English Reformers had accepted the Word of God without qualification, or had simply
found "careless rapture" in the experience of Scripture itself,
the Puritans believed that as they read the Bible the Holy
Spirit was at work, illuminating the Word and enlightening
their hearts. Thus the assistance of the Spirit was considered
essential for a saving knowledge of Scripture, uniting experiential and biblical religion in one.[13]

When it came to putting down the experience for others,
however, they were faced with the problem of how a man could
know that it was the Spirit, and not his fancy, which spoke to
him. Those who tried to describe the experience often fell back
on the analogy of sense perception. For one teacher of the faith,
when the Spirit was at work, the Word "warmed" his heart and
converted him.[14] To another the Spirit gave a sense of freedom,
working "liberty . . . in the heart, making it free and causing
it to rejoice, and making it confident toward God."[15] For still
another the experience could never be adequately described:

> If you ask one what it is the saints know, which another
> man knows not, I answer you fully he himself cannot tell
> you. For it is certain as to that impression which the Holy
> Ghost leaves upon the heart of a man, that man can never

13. Geoffrey Nuttall, *The Holy Spirit in Puritan Faith and Experience*
(Oxford, 1946), pp. 3–4, 21, 23.

14. Richard Sibbes, *Works*, ed. Alexander Grosart (7 vols. Edinburgh,
1862–64), *3*, 434.

15. John Forbes, *How a Christian Man May Discern the Testimony of
God's Spirit* (London, 1616), p. 42.

make the like impression on another; he may describe it to you, but he cannot convey the same image and impression upon the heart of any man else.[16]

In early Puritanism, then, from about 1570, we find an increasing emphasis on the work of the Spirit coming by degrees, and on man's duty not to "grieve" the Spirit.[17] "Give him entertainment," it was said, "let us give him way to come . . . when he knocks by his motions. . . . Grieve not the Spirit by any means."[18] But could the heart be laid bare, as it were, to receive the impression? Could it be submitted to the operation of the Spirit in advance? Here was an interest not dogmatic in a theoretic sense but primarily experiential. It was an interest experience had forced, and which, perhaps only experience could resolve.

✠

The questions whether experiential religion was simply expressed in terms of covenant theology or whether covenant theology opened the way for experiential religion are open to debate. Probably both were true. Certainly covenant theology provided a theological consistency for experiential notions; and in this respect it was an essential ingredient for the emergence of preparation. Indeed, if all Puritans upheld predestinarian doctrine over synergistic error, whether Protestant or Roman, these convictions had been expressed within the framework of covenant theology from the start.

According to the Reformed interpretation of the Pauline message, God had made a covenant of works with Adam requiring absolute personal obedience, but Adam's rebellion had left mankind in ruins. Therefore, God was pleased to make another covenant, this time with Abraham (Gen. 15:17; 17:2,

16. Thomas Goodwin, *Works*, ed. John C. Miller (12 vols. Edinburgh, 1861–66), *4*, 297.
17. Nuttall, p. 139.
18. Sibbes, *5*, 370.

4, 7). The importance of Abraham's covenant in Pauline
theology was that God for the first time had made a covenant
with man on the basis of faith, and that the covenant promises
extended to his seed: "For the promise that he should be the
heir of the world, was not given to Abraham or to his seed
through the law, but through the righteousness of faith" (Rom.
4:13). This meant for Paul that "They which are the children
of the flesh are not the children of God: but the children of the
promise are counted for the seed" (Rom. 9:8); and Reformed
theologians were able to justify infant baptism, as the antitype
of circumcision, on the grounds that the children of the regenerate were among the seed of the covenant. By virtue of
creation they stood in an organic relation to God which needed
only re-creation to restore perfection. Such re-creation was provided by the new covenant; through Christ, as prophesied in
Jeremiah. Since Israel had broken its covenant time and again,
the New Testament must fulfill the Old: "Behold . . . I will
make a new covenant with the house of Israel . . . I will put my
law in their inward parts, and write it in their hearts; and will
be their God, and they shall be my people" (Jer. 31:31, 33).

While covenant theologians never said that saving grace
could be inherited, they insisted that God honored his creation
in spite of man's innate depravity. Moreover, from the time of
the earliest Reformers, these covenant convictions provided a
biblical argument for retaining the reprobate children of regenerate parents within the Church. The children, as the seed
of the covenant, were to be given the benefit of the doubt until
such time as they experienced or failed to experience conversion. And when it was further assumed that a child might even
possess grace without being conscious of it, this allowed for
an introspective element in Reformed theology which went
hand in hand with the rigors of predestination.[19]

It was not, however, until the Puritans combined covenant

19. Peter Y. De Jong, *The Covenant Idea in New England Theology*
(Grand Rapids, 1945), p. 59.

notions with the needs of experiential religion that the assumption was fully realized. The early English Reformers had been preoccupied solely with the disparity between the regenerate and the unregenerate and with the requirement of grace as an instantaneous illumination. They were not, therefore, concerned with exhorting the "covenant seed" to examine themselves for signs of grace on the basis of an external relationship. In Puritan thought, on the other hand, the baptized were expected to look for the beginnings, or first "signs," of regeneration. Upon God's promise of the new covenant, it was assumed that they would search diligently for such evidence. If God's will was always omnipotent, still He looked to the inner man for the "new heart" required in the new covenant. If God alone sought out those to be taken, man had always to "choose" God by entering the covenant voluntarily. And the more the English Puritans turned toward voluntarism, the higher became their conception of baptism, with greater possibilities for man's doing something of his own.

During what might be called the "first phase" of the English Reformation, William Tyndale had mentioned the covenant in various tracts. But he wove the covenant idea so thoroughly into strict predestinarian concepts that the promises were virtually smothered. Richard Greenham, on the other hand, was among the first in the post-Marian period to apply covenant ideas to the needs of practical divinity. Greenham, who began preaching in 1571, saw the advantages of the covenant promises, which he said should be used "for the stirring up of ourselves" in order more surely "to tie us to God."[20] Others at this time who concerned themselves with covenant notions were Arthur

20. Richard Greenham, *Works* (London, 1612), pp. 589–90. According to the Danish theologian Jens G. Møller, "Within two decades or so after the return of the exiles the covenant idea seems in England to have become almost exclusively the preserve of the Puritans. . . . In fact Anglican theologians seem to avoid this concept of the covenant. One reason for this may be found in the fact that the covenant is essentially God's covenant

Hildersam and William Perkins. Perkins, who preached his
first public sermon in 1584, made extensive connections between covenant theories and practical religion. The covenant,
said Perkins, is "absolutely necessary for salvation." Since all
must enter it freely, "every man hath a calling to search into
himself." If God's ways are beyond man's knowledge, all can
gain at least some assurance of their covenant standing first
"by descending into their own hearts" and then by turning
up toward "God's eternal counsel."[21] Thus Perkins put the
heart at the center of the covenant relationship.

From Perkins, as well as from Hildersam, others learned the
rudiments of covenant theology, adding their own emphasis on
voluntarism. Do not begin with predestination and election,
they now advised, but "go first to thine heart and then to those
deep mysteries afterwards"; for "if you look to God the Father,
we are Christ's by donation, if you regard Christ by himself,
we are his by purchase . . . if we regard ourselves, we are his by
voluntary acceptance of the covenant of grace."[22] Through a
careful analysis of Scripture they discovered that man must
enter the covenant not by "mere assent" but with "real obedience" and with a "lively motion of the heart," and that he must
"stir up and watch over his heart at all times."[23] Although
faith must come from God, man might "beg" for grace as well;
he might turn his mind from the eternal decrees toward genuine responsibilities in the inner self—responsibilities on which
a fully developed concept of preparation would soon be built.

✝

with the individual man: neither Church nor Tradition is needed to
establish the bond between God and his faithful servant." Møller, "The
Beginnings of Puritan Covenant Theology," *Journal of Ecclesiastical History, 14* (1963), 57–58.

21. Perkins, *1*, 73; *3*, 419; *1*, 290.

22. Sibbes, *4*, 182; *5*, 308.

23. John Preston, *The Breastplate of Faith and Love* (London, 1632),
p. 239.

The notion of the heart prepared thus emerged within a scriptural frame of reference. It was not a mystical conception. It did not derive from the Neoplatonic idea that man, through an effort of the will, may move from one level of spiritual activity to another until at last he becomes one with God. Augustine had said, "We ascend thy ways that be in our heart, and sing a song of degrees" (*Confessions*, Bk. 13, Cap. 11). But this notion of preparatory ascent did not provide the image of the heart that the Puritans had in mind. This side of Augustinian piety, carried on by the great medieval mystics, had been virtually discarded by the Reformers, who held more closely to the conviction that salvation comes from God alone, and that man cannot ascend by his own will to a state of union with Him. In Reformed theology man is essentially the object of God's descending Spirit, and to this conception the English churchmen adhered. Mystical preparation, in its classic form, belongs to another tradition. In Puritan thought, preparatory activity must be examined in terms of the Law and the Gospel.[24]

In the Old Testament, as interpreted by Paul, man gained righteousness through adherence to the Law of God as handed down at Sinai (Exod. 20). In the New Testament, righteousness by the Law is abolished, as man is saved by grace through faith alone, being "justified freely by His grace through the redemption that is in Christ Jesus" (Rom. 3:24). Yet the Law, in the days of the Gospel, retains its "use," which is to lead the soul to Christ. Its ceremonial and judicial aspects no longer apply,

24. The great histories of mysticism by Dean Inge, Rufus Jones, and Evelyn Underhill (to mention only the most accessible) deal with another genre of religious thought and life, a tradition that in its Western forms owes much to Plato and Plotinus. It has important roots in Hellenic categories and modes of thought. It could and did appear in all branches of the Church and outside the Church altogether. Mystical thinkers did emerge in parts of English church life touched by Puritanism, and there are mystical passages even in Puritan literature; but these are exceptional rather than normative.

but its moral function remains efficacious. The moral Law, by the threat of damnation, convinces man of his sins, brings him to despair, and forces him to see that Christ is his only hope for salvation; for God does not allow man to partake of Gospel grace without some foregoing sense of bondage. This convicting work of the Law drives the soul to Christ; while righteousness by the Law no longer applies: "For I through the law am dead to the law, that I might live unto God" (Gal. 2:19). Natural man, in sinful lusts, is kept under the domain and bondage of the Law until, in conversion itself, the Law kills sin. Once sin is dead, man is then freed from the Law's tyranny; for the Law is "our schoolmaster to bring us to Christ, that we might be made righteous by faith" (Gal. 3:24).

In orthodox Reformed theology this foregoing sense of bondage is greatly emphasized, but it is reduced in time to the moment of conversion itself. God proceeds immediately from one extreme to another, so that man is virtually wrenched by the Law into Gospel grace. In the Zwinglian tradition no allowance is made for a period of extended time, under the Law, when man may be said to "return" to God or to do anything of his own volition.[25] "The Word of God is so sure and strong," wrote Zwingli, "that if God wills, all things are done the moment that he speaks his Word." Paul, Zwingli points out, was "thrown to the ground and rebuked"; therefore grace comes only "when you find that the Word of God . . . crushes and destroys you, but magnifies God himself within you."[26]

Under such conditions, all who looked to the scriptural exhortations to prepare for grace were confronted with a genuine

25. In this connection it should be remembered that the "preparationist" problems posed by the question, "Was there not something man could do?" have to do with the *interior* life. The problem of how strictly or in what way unconverted or unregenerate persons could be held in obedience to the Law in their *outward* behavior was another and much debated question.

26. Zwingli, "Of the Clarity and Certainty of the Word of God." Printed in *The Library of Christian Classics*, Vol. 24: *Zwingli and Bullinger*, ed. G. W. Bromiley (Philadelphia, 1953), pp. 68, 82, 94–95.

dilemma. Indeed, for the great University divines who founded the Puritan tradition, this blanket condemnation of human response under the Law presented immeasurable problems. As "spiritual" preachers, "physicians of the soul," and builders of faith, how could they urge on all men the biblical question, "What must I do to be saved?" without violating this rigid discipline derived from Reformed dogmatics? In short, how could they encourage the doubtful, who had never been taken by storm, to seek assurance of salvation? At first, to be sure, they had no set solution for the problem; but the more they directed their preaching toward the experience and practice of religion, the less concern they showed for the rigors of theory.[27] As an early Puritan remarked, divinity should tend "more principally . . . to the sanctification of the heart than to the informing of the judgment."[28] If men followed the workings of the Spirit in their hearts and looked to the inner self for signs of grace, perhaps this was the beginning of the Christian life.

Those who preached preparation and believed it to be consistent with predestination were concerned with the problem of a possible period in time before conversion that was neither wholly the work of the Law nor entirely beyond man's control. Although natural man, under the Law, did not have the power to make the Gospel effectual or to choose Christ out of the power of his nature, he could respond to the Law in a gradual way and need not be constrained all at once. By preparation they meant a period of prolonged introspective meditation and self-analysis in the light of God's revealed Word. In this process man first examined the evils of his sins, repented for those sins, and then turned to God for salvation. From conviction of conscience, the soul moved through a series of interior stages, always centered on self-examination, which in turn were intended to arouse a longing desire for grace.

27. Haller, chaps. I, II.
28. John Downame, *Guide to Godliness* (London, 1622), Epistle Dedicatory.

In this preparatory process the soul had first to experience contrition and humiliation. Contrition is the moment of awareness, when a man perceives sin and is separated from its corruptions. Humiliation follows, when he submits to God and is divorced from vanity and pride. The preparationists maintained that contrition and humiliation were not in themselves saving graces but preliminary steps, and that while God takes away all resistance, this cannot be done without man's consent. The period of preparatory meditation on sin and depravity was intended to "soften" or "break" the heart, forcing man to realize his need for grace. Such preparatory humility, they said, had been demanded by God through Isaiah: "I dwell in the high and holy places with him also that is of a contrite and humble spirit, to revive the spirit of the humble, and to give life to them that are of a contrite heart" (Is. 57:15). Moreover, the Psalmist had written, "O Lord . . . thou delightest not in burnt offering. The sacrifices of God are a contrite spirit: a contrite and a broken heart" (Psalm 51:15, 16, 17). A stony heart, the preparationists believed, would continue to resist grace, while a broken or fleshy heart would be "lovingly teachable" and willing to entertain God. According to the prophet Joel, unless a man seek righteousness by rending his heart, he will never turn toward God: "Therefore also now the Lord saith, turn you unto me with all your heart . . . and rend your heart and not your clothes, and turn unto the Lord your God." (Joel 2:12, 13)

No point in New England theology was more significant for religious introspection than how much a man could do under the Law to predispose himself for saving grace, or how much through preparation he could dispose God to save him. From the earliest settlement sound conversions had been few; and as piety seemed to wane, all were exhorted to prepare. Yet all were told, at the same time, that no matter how much they prepared, no matter how thoroughly they searched beneath the surface of human appearances, God's mercy could be denied in the end. The prepared heart, while a necessary prerequisite to the conversion experience, was no guarantee of salvation. The lost soul could be left in utter confusion, between preparation and conversion, in "horror of heart, anguish and perplexity of spirit," even in the "very flames of hell."[29] Uncertainty of outcome could lead, and often did, to an inner tension and agony of soul disruptive in a new society; for if preparation was preached to encourage sound conversions in some, it provoked critical questioning from others. Was there an inherent logic between preparation and predestination, or were they mutually exclusive? Did the concept comply with biblical prescription according to Reformed interpretations, or did it run against it? And what of the consequences, the possibility of error? Was there danger of leading the unregenerate first into pride, then into despair, putting grace at a further remove? These questions and others like them aroused a series of searching controversies which virtually molded the New England mind.

To strict predestinarians preparation was a veritable doctrine of works, elevating natural abilities and cheapening grace. Contrition and humiliation, they maintained, were not antecedents to conversion but consequents of the conversion experience itself. In 1637 at Massachusetts Bay, Mistress Anne Hutchinson, John Wheelwright, and the Reverend John Cotton opposed the preparationists on the grounds that they were teaching a "Covenant of Works" rather than the "Covenant of Grace." Our "drowsie hearts," they said, cannot awaken unless Christ makes an opening for himself. Moreover, if contrition and humiliation are not in themselves signs of grace, they asked, how can one ever find assurance of faith? Far from being a comfortable doctrine, it was bound to lead to despair. Far from

29. Thomas Hooker, *The Application of Redemption* (London, 1659), Bk. 10, p. 413.

bringing the reprobates in, it was sure to keep them off. But
if these objections were doctrinally sound, the founding divines
were not moved. They sent all save one, John Cotton, beyond
the borders of the realm.

With the downfall of the Hutchinsonians the preparationists
felt compelled not only to defend their doctrine but to advance
it as dogma. In time it became an established prerequisite for
full church membership as well as an integral part of New
England theology. But as the century wore on, it never ceased
to be a source of controversy. As certain individuals began to
demand membership in the church regardless of a preparatory
experience, and as others lost interest in the intricacies of
religious introspection, the necessity of the heart prepared continued to be severely criticized. Yet this earlier withdrawal into
the interior self to prepare the heart for grace had been the
message of the founding divines. This intensely personal anticipation of salvation had, for the most part, guided the aesthetic
of Puritan expression in early New England. That it has not
been discussed by previous scholarship in full detail, nor examined for its total significance, is perhaps a serious oversight.
Its origins, emergence, and development should be considered
in their proper light.

✛

As we concern ourselves with the emergence of preparation,
and particularly with its importance for early New England,
two main questions should be kept in mind: to what extent did
preparation, as an outgrowth of experiential religion and
covenant theology, become an "ability" on man's part as a
wedge into grace; and to what extent, in its fully developed
form, could it be described as a barrier to grace? In other words,
was preparation merely an inroad into predestinarian assumptions, or did it also have the reverse effect of making the standards of grace too high?

The answer to these questions depends to a large extent on

the men who preached the concept, on whether they emphasized the nearness or remoteness of the covenant seed. The Puritan divines who immigrated to New England were determined to establish the covenant ideal of a pure church. By 1640 they were limiting full membership to those who had consciously experienced regeneration. Some American divines held firmly to the double covenant, with a clear-cut line between "visible saints" and those in "federal holiness." Therefore, even if they themselves were eager to fill the churches with saints, they had always to demand extensive proof of regenerate status; and if the "elect seed" failed to provide such proof, inadequate preparation might be singled out as the cause. How many ministers, then, felt compelled to demand additional preparation, lest faith seem too easy? And how many began to realize that the whole trend toward personal responsibility, out of which preparation emerged, might serve simply to confine the unregenerate to their lost condition? Those New England divines who taught that there was no certain connection but only a probable connection between baptism and regeneration, between federal holiness and grace, were involved in a perpetual dilemma; and their exhortations to prepare the heart were always subject to scrutiny, not only from others but from themselves as well.

2

Continental Reformed Theologians

Any discussion of preparation in Reformed theology, and particularly in Puritanism, must begin with a close look at early Reformed views against a background of Patristic and Scholastic thought. Indeed, the concept of a preparatory period before saving grace in which man is assigned a part to play of his own had long been a matter of dispute in orthodox Christianity. Before the Pelagian Controversy, which followed the appearance of Augustine's *Confessions* in the year 400, Christianity did not especially concern itself with an initial step toward salvation. The earliest Fathers of the Primitive Church, from Aristides to Clement of Alexandria, appear to have had no clearly formulated theology based on an exact exegesis of Paul. In general they tended to emphasize the atonement through Christ's death, with no specific interest in the antithesis of Law and Gospel, or merit and grace.[1] Clement, for one, upheld "free-will of the soul," and argued that God rewards those who prepare to seek him: "He gives to those who desire and are in deep earnest"; "He provides for those who seek, He supplies to those who ask, and He opens to those who knock."[2] For the majority of the Fathers, it would seem, Adam's Fall did not

1. W. T. Whitley, ed., *The Doctrine of Grace* (London, 1932), p. 378.
2. Titus Flavius Clemens, *Works*, ed. and trans. G. W. Butterworth (New York, 1919), Par. 10, p. 289.

entirely deprive man of his freedom of will; nor did Adam transmit total depravity or "original sin" to his descendants. Rather, man had inherited what might be more accurately described as "original corruption." In keeping with the Hebraic tradition, the Fathers may be said to have adopted the view that the Fall of Adam had left no more than a stain or blemish on mankind. Therefore, man, while in need of divine assistance, might be allowed to begin the process toward righteousness of his own free will. What is more, man could be said to have retained the power to resist grace if and when it was offered.[3]

In opposition to this Augustine held more closely to the Pauline view that Adam's descendants had virtually lost their power of free choice; when Pelagius challenged this thesis with a vigorous defense of the more commonly held Patristic view, Augustine argued on the basis of Paul that man, after the Fall, could no longer act of his own in matters that affected his redemption. ("For by grace are ye saved through faith; and that not of yourselves: it is the gift of God" Eph. 2.8.) God's mercy cannot be merited, said Augustine, but must be a gift, freely given. Moreover, since we sin by necessity and cannot turn toward the good without divine aid, grace not only precedes free will but actually creates it. Hence the initial step toward salvation is decisive, as it determines whether the grace to turn the will or the will to hold on to grace comes first.[4] According to Augustine, it is error to think that "our seeking, asking, knocking is of ourselves, and not given to us; for this is also of the divine gift . . . that we ask, seek, and knock."[5] The will to turn, in short, comes only from God.

Clearly, then, the question of whether in the first movement toward salvation man prepares himself or is prepared by God is

3. Harry A. Wolfson, *Religious Philosophy* (Cambridge, 1961), pp. 160–61.

4. Ibid., pp. 161–62.

5. Augustine, "On the Gift of Perseverance", chap. 64; *Nicene and Post-Nicene Fathers*, ed. Philip Schaff (New York, 1887), 5, 551.

related to a central issue in the Pelagian Controversy. What is more, it is a question to which the late Medieval Church returned in the period preceding the Reformation. Although Augustine's triumph had made a profound impression on the Western Church, in the eleventh, twelfth, and thirteenth centuries certain Pelagian or "semi-Pelagian" problems were again opened for consideration; and this, to a large extent, was a result of the Aristotelian revival. Indeed, until the emergence of Scholasticism, the Church had not been compelled to take an official stand on the question of preparation, for it was not until men began to concern themselves with the Aristotelian notions of "form" and "matter" that the concept of a process which may be called *praeparito* or *disposito* had fully to be considered.[6]

Of particular concern to Medieval theologians was the fact that Aristotle had conceived the universe in its natural state to be composed of unformed matter. Such matter, the philosopher had said, must receive its form through a process of generation in order to become complete. It was not long, therefore, before scholastics began to draw analogies between the Aristotelian notion of *generatio* and Christian conversion. With the revival of interest in the *Physics,* theologians argued that sanctifying grace may be associated with form, while man and his soul may generally be thought of as matter. And if matter must "move toward" form in the Aristotelian pattern, should there not, they asked, be some process by which man is disposed for saving grace?[7]

St. Thomas Aquinas (1225–74), the greatest of all scholastics, was among the first to deal with the question in terms of its Pelagian implications: he did this by joining Aristotelian premises with Augustinian hypotheses. In his *Summa Theologica* he asserted that matter cannot of itself move toward form, but must be moved, as in Aristotle's system, by a supreme

6. Charles S. Singleton, *Dante Studies 2* (Cambridge, 1958), pp. 44–46.
7. Ibid., pp. 46–47.

"mover." Therefore it follows, said Thomas, that "man's preparation for grace is from God, as Mover, and from the free-will
as moved." Moreover, this movement may come about in either
of two ways, depending upon the nature of the "gift" from
God. If grace is taken as a "habitual gift" which precedes
effectual conversion, then "a certain preparation of grace is
required for it, since form can only be in disposed matter." But
if grace is taken as an immediate "help from God" to "move
us to good," then "no preparation is required on man's part,
that, as it were, anticipates the Divine help." In both cases,
however, "every preparation in man must be by the help of
God moving the soul to good." It is in this sense only, Thomas
insisted, that "man is said to prepare himself, according to
Prov. 16:1: 'It is the part of man to prepare the soul.' "[8]

For Thomas, then, God may convert the soul in two possible
ways. He may allow man, under the grace of help, to anticipate
divine salvation and so play a preparatory role in which "it is
not necessary to presuppose any further habitual gift in the
soul." This first way, which Thomas calls "imperfect preparation," is extended in time as the soul is gradually brought to
Christ. In the second way, or "perfect preparation," God may
bring about an immediate preparation for conversion that is
"simultaneous with the infusion of grace." This is the moment
of conversion as Paul knew it on the road to Damascus.[9]

> A certain preparation of man for grace is simultaneous
> with the infusion of grace. . . . But there is another imper-
> fect preparation, which sometimes precedes the gift of
> sanctifying grace, and yet it is from God's motion. . . .
> Since a man cannot prepare himself for grace unless God
> . . . move him to good, it is of no account whether anyone

8. St. Thomas Aquinas, *Summa Theologica*, trans. Fathers of the English
Dominican Province (3 vols. New York, 1947), *1*, Pt. I–II, Quest. 112, Art. 3,
resp., p. 1142; Art. 2, resp., p. 1141.
9. Ibid., Quest. 109, Art. 6, resp., p. 1127; Quest. 112, Art. 2, Rep. Obj. 1,
p. 1141.

arrive at perfect preparation instantaneously, or step by step. For it is written (Ecclus. xi.23): 'It is easy in the eyes of God on a sudden to make the poor man rich.' Now it sometimes happens that God moves a man to good, but not perfect good, and this preparation precedes grace. But He sometimes moves him suddenly and perfectly to good, and man receives grace suddenly. . . . And thus it happened to Paul, since, suddenly when he was in the midst of sin, his heart was perfectly moved by God to hear, to learn, to come; and hence he received grace suddenly.[10]

Here, as can plainly be seen, Thomas points to the very crux of the issue at hand—to the critical question which later arose in Reformed theology—what is the temporal nature of conversion? For Thomas, as for Reformed theologians after him, regeneration could be conceived of as a moment in time; but it was "of no account" to the great scholastic "whether anyone arrive . . . instantaneously or step by step." Thus, what was of "no account" to Aquinas in the thirteenth century would eventually distinguish the Puritan preparationists from the strict Reformers. Indeed, although the "steps" themselves were never described by Thomas, it need hardly be said that they anticipate Puritan formulations.

Yet it would not be correct to say that the Puritans looked to the *Summa Theologica* for their concept of preparation. Nor did they subscribe to Scholastic distinctions between "habitual" and "sanctifying" grace. Thomas, it should be remembered, was primarily concerned with a problem that Aristotelian postulates had posed for Christianity—the "disposition of matter" and its "due disposition for the form." Seldom in Puritan thought were preparatory activities to be discussed in these terms. The motions of the Holy Spirit, for example, were rarely to be compared to the movement of form toward matter. If anything, Puritan spirituality wished to avoid mechanical metaphors.

10. Ibid., Quest. 112, Art. 2, Rep. Obj. 1, 2, p. 1141.

Important for our purposes is the Thomistic recognition of
the two ways that grace may be attained, "instantaneously" or
"step by step," for this distinction became an issue of immense
concern in the minds of continental Reformed theologians.

✠

In spite of general agreement among Reformers that the
divine act must precede man's, there was much confusion over
God's method in altering the will, or the nature of the "calling"
itself. While all Reformed theologians were deeply concerned
with the fact that Paul had been overcome by grace in one
effectual call, they were also aware that he had preached "repentance toward God, and faith toward our Lord Jesus Christ"
(Acts 20:21). The question that came to their minds, therefore,
was whether Paul had implied that repentance precedes faith,
is simultaneous or synonymous with it, or follows after. In one
important episode during Paul's preaching the Lord had
opened the heart of Lydia, "a seller of purple," before she was
converted (Acts 16:14). And in this case the internal, or effectual
call, was preceded by an external call, or a call to repentance.
If we assume, however, that the *ordo salutis*—from the call or
vocation through justification, sanctification, and glorification
—deals with the effective call only, the external call can hardly
be considered one of its stages. As long as the external calling
does not become an internal or effectual call through the direct
operation of the Spirit, it has only a preparatory significance.
Thus some Reformed theologians spoke of the external call as
part of a general revelation of the Law and not the Gospel,
meaning that men must first acknowledge, fear, and honor God
as their creator.[11] Such an interpretation equated the external
call with a call to repentance in that man must respond to God's
offer of salvation before grace is achieved. This view, in their
estimation, complied with Paul's teaching that the Law is "our

11. Louis Berkhof, *Reformed Dogmatics* (2 vols. Grand Rapids, 1932), 2,
43–44.

schoolmaster to bring us to Christ, that we might be made righteous by faith" (Gal. 3:24). It was also in accord with Paul's rejoicing that the Corinthians had "sorrowed to repentance. . . . For goodly sorrow causeth repentance unto salvation" (II Cor. 7:9,10). But the point it left obscure was the extent to which preparatory repentance is the work of God or man. God might open the heart, as with Lydia; but what of the duties demanded from man in anticipation of the promises? "Amend your lives," the Apostle Peter had said, "for the promise is made unto you, and to your children, and to all that are afar off, even as many as the Lord our God shall call" (Acts 2:38,39).

Furthermore, if the external calling, accompanied by repentance, is general in that it comes to all men who hear the Gospel preached, then it is inconsistent with strict predestination, particular atonement, and with Pauline restrictions on the power of the will, for Paul had said election lies "not in him that willeth . . . but in God that showeth mercy" and God "hath mercy on whom he will, and on whom he will he maketh hard hearted" (Rom. 9:16, 18). If, in Paul's words, the potter has power over the clay "to make of the same lump one vessel to honor, and another unto dishonor" (Rom. 9:21), how may man be exhorted, "Harden not your hearts" (Heb. 3:8) and "Quench not the Spirit" (I Thes. 5:19)?

For a concept of preparation to emerge from Reformed theology in which man would be assigned a part to play, the emphasis had to shift from the effectual to the external call. The emphasis had also to shift from God's initiative in the external call to the human response which the call itself implied. Zwingli had asserted that faith comes only as an effectual call, or that repentance is synonymous with faith achieved, and many theologians followed his views to the letter.[12] Others, however, became concerned with the importance of the external call, along with its implications for preparatory activity,

12. Whitley, p. 213.

and their views on preparation were bound to be determined by the degree to which they could reconcile man's part in the external call with particular atonement. If man hears the call to repentance, he must certainly respond. But if man is depraved and utterly passive, what can he be asked to do? With these considerations in mind, and with an eye to the consequences for Puritan thought, we must examine the Continental theologians who took sides on the issue and whose influence on the English Reformation can be measured with some degree of accuracy.

Writers on the English Reformation have not always agreed on the influence of Continental Protestantism, but the great body of theological and documentary evidence would indicate that its influence was great.[13] At one time it was generally held that the Reformation in England received its greatest inspiration from the Medieval reformer John Wycliffe (1320?–84).[14] But later historians began to doubt whether Wycliffe and other pre-Reformation reformers could have provided the theological concepts that English divines shared with Continental theologians.[15] In this respect John Colet (1467?–1519) holds a some-

13. For a close analysis of Continental influences see Frederick J. Smithen, *Continental Protestantism and the English Reformation* (London, 1927). See also *Zurich Letters*, ed. Parker Society (Cambridge, England, 1842), and *Original Letters Relative to the English Reformation*, ed. Parker Society (2 vols. Cambridge, England, 1846), for extensive correspondence between Continental Reformers and English divines.

14. For the Wycliffe interpretation see A. F. Pollard, *Cambridge Modern History* (Cambridge, England, 1903), 2, 478. Pollard writes: "In so far as the English Reformers sought spiritual inspiration from other than primitive sources, there can be no doubt that, difficult as it would be to adduce documentary evidence for the statement, they, consciously or unconsciously, derived this inspiration from Wiclif."

15. See Thomas M. Lindsay, *History of the Reformation* (2 vols. Edinburgh, 1907), 2, 358. Lindsay states that the question that divides Medieval reformers, such as Wycliffe, from Reformation thinkers, is how man may

what dubious position. On the eve of the Reformation he was among the first native Englishmen to abandon Scholastic and allegorical interpretations of Scripture for textual exegesis itself. As early as 1497 he had delivered a course of lectures at Oxford on the Epistle to the Romans in which he clearly adhered to a strict Augustinian interpretation of Paul. Moreover, he had expressed dissatisfaction with the conditions of the Church, lamented the loss of its primitive quality, and recognized the need for making Scripture intelligible to the people. Yet from all that can be gathered from his thought, it is almost certain he would have considered the Lutheran Reformation excessive.[16] What is more, the extent to which his views radically altered the theological climate at Oxford cannot be accurately judged. If there were certain periods in pre-Reformation England when men were sympathetic to Church reform, the lines along which such reform would be carried out had yet to be decided. Until the ideas of Luther, Zwingli, and Calvin were disseminated in England, the course theology would run remained obscure.

After the split with Rome in 1531, Continental theology began to make itself felt. Henry VIII, though anti-Lutheran, allowed Lutheran theologians to come to England so that he might gain support for his antipapal policy. In 1538 the Lutheran Myconias, in cooperation with Thomas Cranmer (Archbishop of Canterbury, 1533–55), drew up the *Thirteen Articles* which he based on the Augsburg Confession. Although these

---

achieve saving grace. The Medieval solution, he points out, is by imitation of Christ, while the Reformation answer is justification by faith. "In their answer to this test question," he writes, "the English divines are at one with the Reformers on the continent, and not with Wyclif."

16. Sidney Lee, *Dictionary of National Biography* (Oxford, 1950), *4*, 777–84. For a full discussion of Colet's departures from Erasmian humanism and his close adherence to Augustinian piety, see Eugene F. Rice, Jr., "John Colet and the Annihilation of the Natural," *Harvard Theological Review*, *45* (1952), 141–63.

did not satisfy Henry, who replaced them a year later with the *Six Articles,* Luther's views gained official recognition for the first time. And here it is significant to note that neither the Augsburg Confession nor the Lutheran Formula of Concord (1580) makes any mention of preparation for conversion.

Early in 1547, shortly after Henry died, Protector Somerset and Edward VI openly favored Protestantism; and English Protestant divines who had been in exile on the Continent returned to assume high positions in the Church. Among them were men who had lived in Zurich and Geneva as well as Lutheran Germany. Many Continentals came, too, either through invitation or for refuge from persecution. It was at this time that Zurich and Geneva began to exert more influence than Wittenberg; and orthodox Reformed theology gained ascendancy as visits and letters were freely exchanged.[17] It was at this time, moreover, that English Reformed theology took the course it would follow for the next hundred years.

✠

At least three Continental Reformed divines stand out clearly for their immediate influence in England: Peter Martyr (1500–62), Heinrich Bullinger (1504–75), and John Calvin (1509–64). Martyr's reputation was high among English Reformers in the reign of Henry VIII. In 1547, when Edward VI came to the throne, he was invited by Thomas Cranmer to lecture at Oxford.[18] Before that he had held the chair of theology at Strasbourg, where he was a close friend of Martin Bucer (1491–1551). (Without compromising their thought we may say that Martyr and Bucer preached the same doctrine: their combined views, at least, were accepted by Cranmer as compatible with the proposed Prayer Book of 1552.[19]) Bucer, invited to Cambridge

17. Smithen, p. 23.
18. Ibid., pp. 106–19.
19. Joseph C. McLelland, *The Visible Words of God* (Grand Rapids, 1957), pp. 38–39.

in 1549, remained in England until his death in 1551. When in
1553 Martyr was forced to leave, on the eve of Cranmer's
martyrdom, many churchmen followed him into exile. One
of these, John Jewel, the final reviser of the *Thirty-Nine Articles*
under Elizabeth, later wrote back to him from England in
1562: "As to matters of doctrine, we have pared everything away
to the very quick, and do not differ from you by a nail's
breath."[20]

Martyr's reputation, however, had always to contend with a
continued interest in Bullinger and with increasing concern
for Calvin. Heinrich Bullinger, who succeeded Zwingli as chief
pastor of Zurich in 1531, was the first to state clearly the idea
that all of religion should be considered in terms of man's
covenant relationship to God. While Zwingli had emphasized
the covenant primarily to retain infant baptism, Bullinger
believed that "true religion is none other thing than a friend-
ship, a knitting, and an unity (or league) with the true, living,
and everlasting God."[21] Bullinger's *Decades,* first published
in 1552, came out in three English editions: 1577, 1584, and
1587. He himself had frequently advised the English Reformers,
and he was their chief correspondent in Edward's reign.

Calvin, too, had been eager to give advice, writing not only
to Cranmer but to the King as well.[22] Indeed, by the time the
Church had been restored under Elizabeth in 1558, both Bullinger and Calvin were considered high authorities. By 1586
the Convocation of Canterbury had declared that "Every minister . . . shall . . . provide . . . Bullinger's Decades in Latin or
English . . . and shall every week read one sermon in said
Decades";[23] and in 1587 Calvin's Catechism was ordered by

20. Quoted in Philip Schaff, *The Creeds of Christendom* (3 vols. New
York, 1877), *1*, 603.
21. Heinrich Bullinger, *Decades: Fifty Godly Sermons* (London, 1587),
p. 232.
22. Smithen, p. 65. *Original Letters, 1,* 704 ff.
23. Heinrich Bullinger, *Decades,* ed. Parker Society (5 vols. Cambridge,
England, 1849), *1*, viii.

statute to be used in the Universities.[24] Bullinger's *Decades,* in fact, was used as a manual by the Elizabethan clergy until the time Calvin's *Institutes* became the accepted textbook of theology at Oxford and Cambridge.[25]

In Martyr, Bullinger, and Calvin, then, we have three strong influences on the English Reformed mind. For our purposes, their interpretations of Reformed theology should indicate which avenues were left open for a concept of preparation. Although a recent scholar has said that Martyr's theology was "practically identical" with Bullinger's, that Bullinger's views were "wholly acceptable" to Calvin, and that Calvin's and Martyr's teachings were virtually "identical,"[26] it is hard to accept this statement as final. As we shall see, on the critical problem of the external and effectual calls they can hardly be said to exhibit one mind. It is here that we must look for the beginnings of preparation, for it is here that a concept of preparation must either gain a foothold or be totally denied.

Martyr, without the least hesitation, rejected all thought of an external call involving repentance before faith. "The thing is not to be understood that men may first repent," he said. "First it is apprehended by faith: afterward followeth a sound repentance." From faith, which is the gift of God, "proceedeth the efficient cause of repentance . . . otherwise if there is no faith, repentance is not available." Those who allow for repentance before faith "seem to have taken the name out of Holy Scripture." He then cites several passages from which the concept could be derived. "In the 51 Psalm it is read; 'A sacrifice to God is a troubled spirit, a contrite heart.' In the 147 Psalm: 'Who healeth them that be broken in heart, and bindeth up

24. Smithen, p. 48.
25. Schaff, *1*, 566.
26. McLelland, pp. 37, 279.

their contritions.' Isaiah in the 66 chapter saith that God will
have respect unto them that be of an humble and contrite
spirit." From these passages, Martyr observed, it is assumed
that "man for obtaining salvation his heart after a sort should
be broken, and that he should use this contrition."[27] But the
matter is otherwise, as the words of the prophet were intended
merely "to detest the suspicion of the Jews"; for they "neglecting
the inward piety of the mind trusted only to the outward ceremonies." Those who believe on scriptural evidence that grace
involves preparation, or that "a man may of himself prepare
himself to the obtaining of righteousness," should remember
that "it is no upright dealing to cite some places of scripture
and to . . . leave unspoken other some. Let them go therefore
and see what Ezekiel says in the 36 chapter, 'I will take away the
stony heart out of your flesh, and I will give you an heart of
flesh' " (Ezek. 36:26).[28] Thus, by following Zwingli, Martyr
denied the external call, or repentance before faith, on the
grounds that it opened the way for Pelagian free will; and we
have only to look at one of the earliest examples of an English
Reformer's conversion to find a clear statement in line with
these views.

William Tyndale, a leading Reformer under Henry VIII and
the first to translate the Bible into English from the original
tongues, had officially adopted Zwingli's theology sometime
between 1528 and 1530.[29] To Tyndale's mind, as well as to
Zwingli's and Martyr's, the call to salvation could be effectual
only. The uncalled, he said, cannot be prepared, either by God
or themselves, when "the devil possesses their hearts" and "they
themselves can do no good." Until God has "poured the Spirit of
his grace into our souls, to love his laws, and hath graven them

27. Peter Martyr, *The Common Places* (London, 1583), pp. 203–04, 213.
28. Peter Martyr, *Commentaries on the Epistle of Paul to the Romans* (London, 1558), pp. 399, 381 b.
29. Edward I. Carlyle, *Dictionary of National Biography* (Oxford, 1950), *19*, 1353.

in our hearts . . . we know not God."[30] For Tyndale the arche-
typal conversion experience was that of Paul on the road to
Damascus. Without anticipation or preparation of any kind
man is suddenly seized, after which he repents for his sins.
Until the Lord has shed his grace, without warning, on the
predestined few, we cannot know in which direction to turn.
"And why God giveth it not every man, I can give no reckoning
of his judgments," said Tyndale. "But well I wot, I never
deserved it, nor prepared myself unto it, but ran another way
clean contrary in my blindness and sought not that way; but
he sought me and found me out."[31]

Here Tyndale clearly follows the Zwinglian tradition to
which Martyr adhered—a tradition which had set the tone for
much of Reformed theology. The elect, or those predestined
for salvation, are chosen by God who "giveth it not every man."
Having been chosen, as Zwingli observed, "even before they
believe," they may run "another way" and yet be fully converted the moment grace descends. The majesty of God, through
His eternal decrees, has determined a time that can neither be
anticipated nor prepared for; and only those who have known
this moment, in all its glory, may thereafter count themselves
among the elect. Conversion, for Zwingli, was essentially a
"sign" of election; and as a sign it could have nothing to do with
human expectation. But in Zwingli's successor, Bullinger, we
find another attitude entirely, an attitude which showed a
growing concern for man's relationship to God on quite another
level of experience.

✠

Bullinger first came into contact with Zwingli in 1527 and
later accompanied him to the Disputation at Bern. Generally

---

30. William Tyndale, *Prologue upon the Epistle of St. Paul to the
Romans*, 1533, p. 316. *An Answer unto Sir Thomas More's Dialogue*, 1531,
ed. Parker Society (Cambridge, England, 1850), Bk. IV, p. 174.

31. *An Answer*, Bk. IV, p. 192.

speaking, it could be said that he fell in line with Zwingli's
Reformed ideals. Therefore, when in 1531 Zwingli was killed
at the second battle of Kappel, Bullinger was chosen to suc-
ceed him as pastor of the Grossmünster at Zurich.[32] But Bullinger did not follow his predecessor in at least one important
respect: unlike Zwingli, who held that the baptized were not
necessarily of the elect and should have a decidedly external
relationship to the Church with no particular claim on saving
grace, Bullinger put into the forefront of his theology the
biblical promises to the covenant seed. "In the 30 of Deut.,"
he wrote, "Moses saith, 'The Lord thy God shall circumcise
thy heart, and the heart of thy seed, that thou mayest love the
Lord thy God.'" And now, he went on to explain, it is through
Christ that "our mother Sarah gendereth us into liberty. She
is the mother of us all. Of that mother we have the seed of
life."[33] God's people, or the baptized descendants of Sarah and
Abraham, are those who now "do acknowledge Christ." And
for them, Bullinger maintained, faith may be achieved through
an "unfeigned turning to God." Although "many have made
faith a part of repentance," he said, "I will not stand in argument whether faith be a part of repentance, or doth by any
other means depend upon it. It seemeth to me a notable point
of folly to go about to tie matters of Divinity to precepts of
logic."[34]

Thus Bullinger virtually discarded the low Zwinglian conception of baptism. For the baptized conversion is not a sudden
seizure followed by repentance in one continuous motion but
involves a "turning" toward the divine will, an acknowledgment of sin, and a desire for reconciliation with God in anticipation of the promises offered. To this end, Bullinger and those
who followed him could use with great effect the vast prophetic
arsenal of the Old Testament, through which man is called back

32. Smithen, p. 66.
33. Bullinger, *Decades: Fifty Godly Sermons,* pp. 297, 361.
34. Ibid., p. 566.

to his covenant obligations. Furthermore, although Bullinger never believed that salvation may be inherited, or that man may merit grace through repentance, he was quick to point out that Paul had made a distinction between repentance and faith: "repentance toward God, and faith toward our Lord Jesus" (Acts 20:21). "Unto penitents," said Bullinger, "faith in God and the merit of Chirst is most of all and especially needful. In which sense it is, I think, that many have made faith a part of repentance, which as I do not greatly deny, so yet do I see that St. Paul made, as it were, a difference between faith and repentance, when in the 20 of the Acts he saith that he 'witnessed both to the Jews and Gentiles the repentance that is toward God, and faith in Jesus Christ' . . . Therefore repentance and faith seem to be diverse, not that true repentance can be without faith, but because they must be distinguished and not confounded." In his *Decades* he wrote: "We in this disputation of ours will use Repentance for a converting or turning to the Lord . . . an unfeigned turning to God, whereby we being of sincere fear of God . . . do acknowledge our sins." And this acknowledgment, he said, must include "grief conceived for sins committed . . . mortification and the beginning to lead a new life, and . . . the change, correction, and amendment of the life from evil to better." Yet "sincere fear" does not mean "servile dread of punishment" but a "careful study mixed with love and honor of God." Nor does repentance "of itself obtain grace or forgiveness of sins," even as "the bare acknowledging of a disease is not the remedy for the same." Rather, "The acknowledging of sin is a certain preparative unto faith, as the acknowleding of a disease doth minister occasion to think upon a remedy." It is not the fear of God, however sincere, not the sorrow conceived, however great, not the love for Christ, however deep, that make us acceptable to God. Rather, these preliminary motions "prepare an entrance and make a way for us to Christ himself." Penitent sinners have their sins remitted not for repentance as a "work" but as it "comprehendeth the

renewing of man . . . which delivereth us to Christ our physician
that he may heal our diseases."[35] And these same sinners, before they may be healed, before the promises are theirs, must
look first to the inner man, and open their hearts to God:

> We do then make our confession to God privately when
> we disburden our hearts before God, open the secrets of
> our hearts to him alone. . . . This confession is necessary
> to the obtaining of pardon for our sins. For unless we do
> acknowledge our own corruptions and unrighteousness,
> we shall never by true faith lay hold on Christ. . . . He is
> the physician to whom alone we must discover and open
> our wounds. . . . He alone doth look into our hearts . . .
> to him alone therefore we must disclose our hearts.[36]

Here, then, we have one of the clearest and earliest acknowl-
edgments by a major Reformed prophet of the need to put
the heart in order for salvation—perhaps the first decisive
description of the heart in preparation. It portends much for
later developments in Puritan thought. God will heal the sick,
says Bullinger, as the sinner turns in anticipation, for "They
that are whole need not a physician, but they that are sick"
(Luke 5:31). The sick, to be sure, must make a beginning before
the healer can intervene; but such a beginning is an act of
acknowledgment, not of cooperation. Man, in acknowledging
his sins, does not yet stand again in the covenant, which only
God can renew. Rather, he stands before God's face. As one of
Abraham's seed, his anticipation of the promises, his contem-
plation of the future, forms the basis for preparatory acknowledgment. When Bullinger says we must "open the secrets of
our hearts," he means that we must confess to our present depravity in the light of future salvation; and while such preparation is not decisive, it is something we can do of our own. When
we "disburden our hearts" we acknowledge the promises to be

35. Ibid., pp. 361, 566, 562, 565, 567.
36. Ibid., p. 572.

meaningful; we begin anew and are ready to accept the covenant of grace. This, for Bullinger, is not merit but sheer anticipation of our renewal in Christ. It is, to his mind, the one disposition of the heart which allows us to lay hold on "true faith."

✛

Needless to say, Bullinger's conception of conversion can hardly be reconciled with Martyr's; yet both expressed themselves in terms of Reformed theology. Although the two did not meet until 1543,[37] after 1549 they frequently exchanged ideas; and throughout their correspondence one is struck by a cautious, almost conscious avoidance of topics touching on predestination. "In the treatment of that subject," wrote Martyr to Bullinger in 1553, "I have been specially on my guard. . . . I so treat it as to follow the Holy Scriptures as closely as possible."[38] At no time, it appears, did they publicly clash; yet each interpreted Scripture according to his own convictions: one in terms of God's inscrutable will, and the other in terms of the covenant bond with God. Both were read by the English clergy; both were taken seriously; and since their influence can scarcely be doubted, their convictions should clearly be kept in mind.

✛

In Calvin's *Institutes*, on the other hand, we find an interpretation not wholly in keeping with either Martyr or Bullinger. Nevertheless, for the emergence of preparation from Reformed theology, Calvin's position adds a significant dimension. Unlike Martyr, Calvin allowed for the external as well as the effectual call. But unlike Bullinger, he was not concerned with man's voluntary acknowledgment of the covenant bond. Calvin, it is generally agreed, was not a covenant theologian,

37. McLelland, p. 277.
38. *Original Letters*, 2, 506.

in that covenant concepts were never the organizing principle of his theology. Yet neither was he rigidly Zwinglian, in that his conception of conversion involves a wider range of experience than sudden transformation. While he held that man is totally depraved, and can do nothing of his own to prepare for grace, he did not deny preparation as such. Nor did he dismiss the biblical exhortations to preparation as "useless."[39]

If, unlike Bullinger, Calvin held no conception of preparatory repentance, still he did not insist that grace comes suddenly. Indeed, the very perversity of the heart suggested to him that it must be constrained by God in advance: because the heart is depraved, "deceitful above all things, and desperately wicked" (Jer. 17:9), Solomon prayed, "May the Lord incline our hearts unto him" (I Kings 8:58). And here, according to Calvin, we are shown the "stubbornness of our heart," the "perverse bias of the heart," which can be corrected only by that which "constrains it to obedience." Thus David asked God, "Unite my heart to fear thy name" (Psalm 86:11), and "Incline my heart unto thy testimonies" (Psalm 119:36); so that God, in Calvin's words, by way of preparation, "directs, inclines, and governs our hearts" toward salvation.[40]

---

39. See Everett H. Emerson, "Calvin and Covenant Theology," *Church History*, 25 (1956), 136–42. Emerson says quite rightly that Calvin was not preoccupied with conversion as a sudden transformation, contrary to what Perry Miller would have us believe. Mr. Miller, in *The New England Mind*, writes of the Puritan preparationists: "Had the mechanism of regeneration been phrased exclusively in the blunt language of Calvin, as a forcible seizure, a rape of the surprised will, there would have been no place for a time of preparation" (Cambridge, 1953, 2, 56). But Mr. Miller is confusing two concepts here. A "forcible seizure" does not necessarily imply a "rape of the surprised will." Admittedly Calvin saw grace as a seizure, but conceived in terms of gradual constraint, not sudden disruption. Thus he could and did allow for a time of preparation in the external call, when God prepares man for effectual conversion. Unlike the convenant theologians, however, he did not emphasize human anticipation in preparation. He was more concerned with conversion as an accomplished fact than as an experience per se.

40. *Institutes of the Christian Religion,* trans. John Allen (2 vols. Philadelphia, 1936), *1*, Bk. II, Cap. III, Par. IX, 325; Par. X, p. 327.

Calvin's belief that God may prepare the unregenerate, even by constraint, marks an initial break with the Zwinglian position, for, as we have seen, Zwingli, Martyr, and the strict Reformed school held firmly to a sudden, if not violent, transformation in conversion. Moreover, Calvin set himself off in still another respect by refusing to dismiss the biblical exhortations to preparation as "superfluous." Since the operations of God are twofold, "externally by His Word" as well as "internally by His Spirit," both, said Calvin, must be taken into consideration. If the Holy Spirit alone can begin the internal, or effectual work, by "bending . . . our hearts toward righteousness," we cannot, for this reason, discount the importance of the Word. Thus, in Calvin's opinion, the biblical exhortations to preparation in the external call "ought not . . . to be esteemed wholly useless." Though ineffectual, they confound the conscience and "shake off sloth"; so that "who can dare to reject them as superfluous?" "Christ, though he pronounces that 'no man can come to him, except the Father draw him' [John 6:44], yet himself neglects not the office of a teacher, but with his own mouth sedulously invites those who need the internal teachings of the Holy Spirit to enable them to derive any benefit from his instructions."[41]

Through the external operation of the Word, said Calvin, God frequently requires "newness of heart;" for it is written: "Circumcise yourselves to the Lord, and take away the foreskins of your heart" (Jer. 4:4). If elsewhere God declares this to be His own gift, "A new heart also will I give you" (Ezek. 36:26), still the exhortation is part of His ways. And here, as in many other passages, Calvin recoils from the classic Reformed position, moving toward Luther's view of the mysteries of God's counsels (*Deus absconditus*):

> But it will be said, what can a miserable sinner do if the softness of heart, which is necessary to obedience, be denied

41. Ibid., Bk. II, Cap. V, Par. V, p. 347; Bk. II, Cap. III, Par. VI, p. 320; Bk. II, Cap. V, Par. V, p. 347; Bk. II, Cap. V, Par. V, p. 348.

him? I ask, what excuse can be pleaded, seeing that he cannot impute the hardness of his heart to anyone but himself. . . . Who art thou, O man, that wouldest impose laws
upon God? If it be his will to prepare us by exhortation
for the reception of this grace, by which obedience to the
exhortation is produced, what have you to censure in this
economy?[42]

Thus, while the exhortations to self-preparation are by no
means efficacious, Calvin refuses to discard them. They are,
in his opinion, part of God's preparation of man. "I deny,"
he said, "that God is cruel or insincere to us, when he invites
us to merit his favors, though he knows us to be incapable of
doing this." Although the Psalmist exhorts, "Harden not your
hearts" (Psalm 95:8), still, wrote Calvin, "it is absurd to infer
from this passage that the heart is equally flexible to either
side; whereas 'the preparation' of it is 'from the Lord'"
(Prov. 16:1).[43] However, since God works externally
through the Word, as well as internally through the Holy
Spirit, everything contained in the Word belongs to His "economy"; and if, in the conversion experience, the Word con-
tributes toward a beginning, the exhortations to preparation
cannot be condemned as "superfluous." In short, the external
call, while not an integral part of the *ordo salutis,* is still to be
reckoned with. For the emergence of preparation in Puritan
thought it points toward untold consequences.

Like Bullinger, then, Calvin allowed for the external call,
which he also interpreted as a preparatory period before saving
grace. But unlike Bullinger, he denied that man in preparation
could do anything of his own. Being "previously prepared,"

42. Ibid., Bk. II, Cap. V, Par. V, p. 347.
43. Ibid., Bk. II, Cap. V, Par. X, p. 353, Par. XI, p. 356. Although the
Geneva Bible reads: "The preparations of the heart are in man, but the
answer of the tongue is of the Lord"; Calvin's interpretation is more in
keeping with the King James version: "The preparations of the heart in
man, and the answer of the tongue, is from the Lord" (Prov. 16:1).

said Calvin, does not mean that man has his "own share" in the work. There can be no "flexibility of the human heart" other than that "supplied by the grace of God," as God alone can take away the "stony heart" and give the "heart of flesh" (Ezek. 36:26). In fact, if the issue is ever to be resolved, Calvin declared, "Let us hold this as an undoubted truth, which no opposition can ever shake—that the heart is so thoroughly infected by the poison of sin that it cannot produce any thing but what is corrupt; and always remains enslaved by its inward perverseness." Where Bullinger had allowed for a high degree of efficacy in baptism and so was able to insist that Abraham's seed could effectively anticipate the promises, Calvin, like Zwingli, denied that baptism could in any sense be a cause of salvation. He saw it as an "outward sign," token, or "symbol," which testified that children of believers are members of the church; but in no sense could regeneration be said to begin in baptism. Indeed, "many which are children of the faithful," he wrote, "are counted bastards, and not legitimate, because they thrust themselves out of holy progeny through their unbelief."[44]

44. Ibid., Bk. II, Cap. III, Par. VI, p. 321, Cap. V, Par. XIX, p. 366; Bk. IV, Cap. XIV, Par. XVI; Cap. XVI, Par. IX. John Calvin, *Corpus Reformatorum* (Brunswick, 1882), 76, 76. For an extensive examination of Calvin's views on baptism, see Egil Grislis, "Calvin's Doctrine of Baptism," *Church History*, 31 (1962), 46–65. For a full discussion of Paul's teachings on baptism, see H. G. Marsh, *The Origins and Significance of the New Testament Baptism* (Manchester, 1941), pp. 128–94. According to Marsh, several contradictions in Paul's own views account for later disagreement on the issue:

> The belief in the close connection of baptism with the reception of the Spirit was widely held in the early Church, and it is not surprising to find that it had a prominent place in the teaching of Paul. ['For by one Spirit are we all baptized into one body.' I Cor. 12:13.] Yet the deciding factor in Paul's own case in bringing about communion with Christ was the Christophany at Damascus and not the rite of baptism. . . . We may say that in his teaching of the connection of the Spirit with baptism Paul was following the current doctrine of the Church. Allowance must be made, however, for the certainty that this belief, as every other

Where Bullinger had said that in preparation "we must disburden our hearts" and "open the secrets of our hearts" to God, Calvin never wavered from his conviction that before grace the heart "cannot produce any thing but what is corrupt." Where Bullinger maintained that the "confession" of the heart is "necessary to the obtaining of pardon for sins," otherwise "we shall never by true faith lay hold on Christ," Calvin held firmly to the belief that we can only be "constrained" to obedience, that the heart is "enslaved by its inward perverseness." Calvin's image of the heart in preparation is ever one of coercion and restraint, where Bullinger's is one of repentance and acknowledgment. Nowhere in Calvin is man allowed to anticipate in the sense of Bullinger's "unfeigned turning . . . mixed with love and honor of God." For Calvin there is no divine offer to which the heart must respond, but only God's omnipotence, through which the heart, though invited to prepare, is compelled toward grace.[45]

✢

which the apostle received, underwent a change in the light of Paul's personal experiences. [p. 137]

Nevertheless, Marsh concludes:

We may recall also Paul's words in Galatians 3:29: 'If ye are Christ's, then are ye Abraham's seed, heirs according to promise.' The phrase 'if ye are Christ's' must be interpreted by the sense of the preceding verses, where we have: 'For as many of you as were baptized into Christ did put on Christ.' (3:27) From this it is clear that 'if ye are Christ's' is to be explained as expressing the result of the baptismal experience, and understood in this way there is a fresh meaning in the reference to Abraham's seed and those who are heirs according to the promise. [p. 193]

45. As early as 1550 a dispute arose between two English Reformers over Calvin's and Bullinger's points of view. Although not enough is known to show the full scope of the argument, it at least indicates an early awareness of their differences. Bartholomew Traheron (1510?–58?) and John Hooper (d. 1555) had both lived with Bullinger at Zurich, Traheron in 1537 and Hooper from 1547 to 1549. In 1546, however, Traheron went to Geneva, where he gradually abandoned Bullinger's views for Calvin's (A. F. Pollard,

In Martyr, Calvin, and Bullinger, it is safe to say, we have major representatives of three attitudes of mind from which Puritan thought could draw: that grace comes only as an effectual call, with no preparatory disposition of the heart; that grace, while entirely a matter of seizure, may nevertheless involve preparation through divine constraint of the heart; and that grace follows the heart's response to God's offer of the covenant promises in preparatory repentance. In England the problem was recognized by the Articles of the Church, as drawn up in 1552, 1563, and finally into the *Thirty-Nine Articles* of 1571; but it was not entirely resolved. The Articles themselves had been designed primarily to refute the Roman Catholic position, especially as it had been drafted by the Council of Trent from 1545 to 1563. Trent, itself an effort to defend Rome against the Reformers as well as an attempt to reconcile conflicting views within Roman Catholicism, had condemned theologians who held man passive in conversion along with those who said he could act of his own to get salvation without divine aid. The Council was content to affirm both free will and the necessity of grace without attempting to reconcile them, and without trying to solve the problem of the influence of grace upon free will.[46] Thus, in the language of Trent, man

---

*Dictionary of National Biography, 19, 1075). When by 1550 both Traheron and Hooper had been back in England some time, the Reformer John Ab Ulmis wrote Bullinger of their different attitudes "respecting God's predestination of men." He asked Bullinger not to "set them at variance, or bring them into collision by letter," closing with the remark that "this is a profound secret which you must not disclose or mention to a single individual" (*Original Letters*, Letter 193, 2, 402–07). But two years later the dispute was common knowledge; and Traheron himself wrote Bullinger requesting his opinion "respecting the predestination . . . of God." He ended by reminding his former master that "the greater number among us, of whom I own myself to be one, embrace the opinion of John Calvin as being . . . most agreeable to Holy Scripture" (*Original Letters*, Letter 154, 1, 325).*

46. N. P. Williams, *The Grace of God* (London, 1930), pp. 94–95, 63.

could prepare for grace with little concern for the line dividing
his part from God's:

> While God touches the heart of man by the illumination
> of the Holy Ghost, neither is man himself utterly inactive
> while he receives that inspiration, for as much as he is also
> able to reject it. . . . Whence it is said in the sacred writings:
> "Turn ye to me, and I will turn to you" [Lam. 5:21]. . . .
> and finally, "Prepare your hearts unto the Lord" [I Kings
> 7:3].[47]

The *Thirty-Nine Articles,* on the other hand, drew a clearer
distinction between man's role and God's. As opposed to the
ambiguities of the Council of Trent, the *Articles* were more
emphatic on the subject of preparation. Man in his fallen state,
said the *Articles,* may not in the strict sense be said to dispose
himself for grace, as whatever activity there may be in the
regenerative process must come entirely from God:

> The condition of man, after the fall of Adam, is such that
> he cannot turn and prepare himself by his own natural
> strength and good works to faith and calling upon God;
> wherefore we have no power to do good works, pleasant
> and acceptable to God, without the grace of God by Christ
> preventing us, that we may have a good will, and working
> with us when we have that good will.[48]

The earliest Puritans, writing at this time, were immediately
aware of the problem yet to be solved. Indeed, their entire
conception of the interior life was largely an attempt to define
man's role in the face of God's initiative. In some respects their
views were decidedly close to Bullinger's; in others, they held
more rigidly to Calvin's or Martyr's; yet in every respect they

47. Schaff, *Creeds,* "The Canons and Decrees of the Council of Trent," 2,
92-94.
48. In Edward H. Browne, *An Exposition of the Thirty-Nine Articles*
(New York, 1870), p. 261.

had always to reconcile their own experiential knowledge with the facts of dogmatic predestinationism.

The problem, as they saw it, can be broken down roughly into four major considerations, all of which have a direct bearing on the Puritan attitude toward preparation. First they looked to the Law as a general revelation and concerned themselves with its efficacy in the external call. How close, they asked, does the Law actually bring a man to Christ? This led them, in turn, to the question of initiative; whether the efficacy of the Law is wholly God's work or somehow man's as well—perhaps the most significant point in the development of their views on preparation. They then turned to the temporal nature of the change itself. How sudden, gradual, or imperceptible a transformation is involved from initial awareness of the Law to final assurance of saving grace? And finally they sought to measure the degree to which regeneration involves man's affective nature; whether it is merely a grasping of man by God as a logical necessity, or must include anticipation, acknowledgment, and response. These four considerations, while not necessarily separable, together gave rise to a preoccupation with preparation which put its mark on Puritan thought from the start.

3

The English Preparationists

Richard Greenham, pastor at Dry Drayton, Cambridgeshire, has been called the "patriarch" of Puritan divines and the first great teacher of the "spiritual brotherhood."[1] Born about 1535, he entered Pembroke Hall, Cambridge, in 1559, took the B.A. in 1567, and was installed at Dry Drayton in 1570. There he kept the door open to undergraduates, always ready to offer spiritual advice. There he preached for twenty years, occasionally coming to Cambridge to "lecture" at St. Mary's, where his sermons were taken down and copied for circulation. In 1599, several years after his death, his works were collected and edited by Henry Holland, appearing in five editions before 1612;[2] and in these early writings we have a good indication of the pattern Puritan expression would follow.

Greenham complained that sermons were becoming "glassy, bright and brittle . . . so cold and so humane, that the simple preaching of Christ doth greatly decay." Therefore he had set himself "to edify the heart and conscience . . . to quicken affections to embrace true godliness." Beginning in the tradition of Calvin, he at first concerned himself with the perversity of the human heart and the necessity of divine constraint. "So corrupt is the heart," he wrote, that "it must have much tempering and

1. Haller, *Rise of Puritanism*, p. 26.
2. Alexander Gordon, *Dictionary of National Biography, 8*, 520–21.

great ado to bring it to God. . . . Our heart is a wandering thing; it is like the mill that is ever grinding, still setting us a work with more commandments than ever God gave us. If we follow God's way there is some end, but if we follow our own way there is an endless maze." In our corruption, he said, we must know that God "refuseth the service of the proud, because then . . . we are unprepared by pride to receive any mercy." Therefore, the Lord "humbleth his children before that he honoreth and crowneth them with his graces."[3]

Once Greenham had established this fact, however, he then went on to say that if the Lord "worketh all," yet "is it attributed to men"; for "God is not pleased but with voluntary offering," and man must yield to the covenant of his own accord.

> I mean not that yielding which the Lord by his threatening or judgments as by strong hand getteth of us, which is no voluntary submission but a violent subjection and constraineth us rather than allureth us to obey the will of the Lord: but I mean that willing humbling of ourselves before the face of God which cometh from an heart bleeding at the conscience of its own unworthiness.[4]

When the Psalmist cried, "I have applied mine heart to fulfill thy statutes" (Psalm 119: 112), said Greenham, he "began in his heart"; for "here is the beginning of all goodness, here is the root of religion, and here the foundation of our faith must be laid." It is not the "refraining from outward actions," not the "restraining of the outward man," we must look to; rather, it is "the heart we must travail about and care for . . . to make our beginning there." If we are "troubled in our hearts with hardness" but are "desirous of softness," we need not be "discomforted"; for God will "spare us" and be "gracious unto us," according to the prayer of Hezekiah: "The good Lord be merciful toward him that prepareth his whole heart to seek the Lord

3. *Works*, pp. 26, 700, 704, 269–70.
4. Ibid., pp. 448, 271.

God, the God of his fathers, though he be not cleansed according to the purification of the sanctuary" (II Chr. 30:18, 19).[5]

In the space of a few paragraphs, then, Greenham clearly indicates the problem that preparation presented for Puritan thought. At first he insists that man must be constrained from above, that God alone can humble the sinner before he is ready for grace: "Yea, before the Apostles received that great gift, the sending down of the Holy Ghost upon them, they were humbled with the Laws, they were shaken with a great wind, and after so solemn a preparation, they were endued with the sweet graces of the Spirit." But for fear of discouraging the unconverted, he then exhorts to voluntary submission—to begin at the heart and prepare for grace according to biblical prescription: "Hereof it came to pass that many of the Kings and people in the Books of Chronicles . . . prepared their hearts, as Hezekiah, Josiah, and others." For those who did not prepare, "all was in vain." Therefore, says Greenham, "the first thing . . . is preparation." Before we can enter the covenant, "we must labor to circumcize the foreskin of our hearts" as commanded in Jeremiah. With the help of the Word we must turn to God in advance: "As we cannot see our face but in a glass, so we cannot see our hearts without the Word. And if in the Word we will see our hearts, then we must bring them to the presence of God. . . . If we bring ourselves to God's presence we shall be greatly humbled."[6]

Here, as elsewhere in Greenham, the question of initiative hangs in the balance. At first we are told that we must be "humbled with the Laws" before we can do anything. Now we are told that "if we bring ourselves to God's presence we shall be greatly humbled." The extent to which man is given a part to play of his own, then, stands in direct relation to the efficacy of the Law. Though man is utterly depraved, he must submit voluntarily and "stir up" himself to lay hold on the covenant

5. Ibid., pp. 271, 487–88.
6. Ibid., pp. 269–70, 487, 706, 561.

promises. So long as he turns toward God in the prophetic tradition, so long as he yields of his own accord, God will be gracious. In this respect man is not "shaken with a great wind," not grasped by God through the Law as a logical necessity, but encouraged to anticipate and respond. In short, man's affective nature is of the greatest importance.

Nowhere, however, does Greenham attempt to reconcile the biblical exhortations with divine constraint. As in Calvin, God's "ways" are not to be questioned. But others who followed Greenham in the Puritan tradition were not content to let the paradox stand. If the Dry Drayton pastor was the first to state the problem for Puritan thought, Richard Rogers was among the first to try to deal with it.

✢

Richard Rogers, born about 1550, was the son of a joiner at Chelmsford, Essex. In 1565 he was sent by a patron to Christ's College, Cambridge, where he was granted the B.A. in 1570, the year Greenham became pastor at Dry Drayton. During his time at Cambridge he often heard Greenham preach, and more than once he was given a meal at the pastor's charitable table. After proceeding to the M.A. in 1574, he returned to Essex, where from 1577 he served as lecturer at Whethersfield. Before his death in 1616 he had written, among other things, the famous *Seven Treatises*, considered to be the first complete expression of the spiritual life in Puritan thought. First published in 1592, it was reissued seven times before 1630 and had considerable effect on the rising generations of Puritan divines.[7]

In the preface to the *Treatises* Rogers stated his desire to present divinity in such a way that men would be neither "cast down with needless fear" nor "destitute of encouragement to walk forward in an heavenly course."[8] And in this respect his thought was much in line with Greenham's. But unlike Green-

7. William A. Shaw, *Dictionary of National Biography, 17*, 138.
8. *Seven Treatises* (London, 1610), "Preface to the Reader."

ham he did not exhort to preparation only to remind his readers of their inabilities. Rather, he began with experience itself, from which he moved toward effectual conversion.

In order to "anatomize and describe the heart," said Rogers, we must know that it is "overspread with unbelief and prone to evil"; for this is the "nature and disposition of the heart . . . since the fall of our first parents . . . before there be any work of grace in it." But the evil of the heart, he insisted, does not limit the variety of ways in which it may be transformed. Conversions themselves are variable. All men are not sensibly constrained. Indeed, the greatest difficulty in conversion is knowing whether it has taken place at all. While the heart must be "cleansed and changed," the alteration itself may be imperceptible. "That which most troubleth the weak about this matter," said Rogers, "is that this change of the heart, and renewing thereof, is so hardly seen and so meanly felt within them, that they cannot satisfy themselves. . . . Now idle motions and vain thought and fantasies much trouble them . . . they cannot be rid of them; now they fear they believe not . . . they fear that they are not renewed and changed at all."[9] This uncertainty he then attributes to the subtle, almost indiscernible motions of the Holy Spirit. While Greenham had virtually nothing to say about the temporal nature of the change, for Rogers it was all-important.

In the conversion process, he holds, man is neither wrenched from sin to grace nor violently constrained by divine coercion but is "secretly drawn, he cannot tell how, by the unspeakable work of the Spirit." Since "we cannot discern or set down the very moment when faith is wrought," we must look to the "Works" of the Spirit. If we know, for example, that in the "First Work" we are "pricked in the heart by the preaching of the Law," we may rest assured that God "provideth for His that they, by seeing and feeling the desert of their sins, may

9. Ibid., pp. 95, 103.

have an appetite thereby to seek mercy and forgiveness." In the "Second Work" the Lord takes man into consultation and "guideth his heart to enter into further consideration with himself, of and about his present estate, and draweth him to consult what to do in that extremity." Then, in the "Third Work," man must strive for self-humiliation. And this "unfeigned humbling of himself before God," says Rogers, marks the "beginning of all goodness and grace which man feeleth in himself." "For being thus humbled he is now easily to be persuaded . . . and though he do not yet believe that his sins are pardoned, yet he believeth that they are pardonable, and that they may be pardoned, which is a great lightening and easing of the heart." So that finally, in the "Fourth Work," God through His Spirit "kindleth" in man "an especial desire," a "hungering after mercy," at which point his heart becomes "full of relenting and sorrow for displeasing God" and is now "an heart of flesh, not of stone, in which saving grace may be planted and received."[10]

Through an awareness of the various "Works" of the Spirit, then, man may take part in the process leading up to the moment of assured grace. As he anticipates each "Work," he participates in the experience itself. Moreover, his response at each step carries him on to the next. The Law is no longer a "solemn preparation" for the "sweet graces of the Spirit," as in Greenham, but a "Work" of the Spirit. Man is not "shaken with a great wind" but responds to the initial "prick" of the Law to make way for the succeeding "Works." And this "prick," for Rogers, is the full extent of the Law's immediate efficacy in the external call. ("Now when they heard this, they were pricked in their hearts and said . . . men and brethren, what shall we do?" Acts 2:37) Indeed, man is assigned so much to do under the prick of the Law, before he "feeleth" grace, that Rogers takes into account the dangers his notions imply.

10. Ibid., pp. 10–20.

> But what then? [Some will say] do you affirm that these
> things can do any man good without faith . . . or that any
> thing is accepted of God which he doth (as his desire to be
> forgiven, his hungering after it, his humiliation . . . con-
> fession of sins) all these being without faith? . . . Or if not
> so, do ye then say that we ourselves must thus prepare our-
> selves to receive faith? But that is to attribute free will unto
> man, being yet in the estate of misery and bondage and
> unrenewed as being without faith.[11]

To these hypothetical questions Rogers answers; "although
none of these be faith, yet I say that they are not without it."
Since "it be hard to determine when faith is wrought," there
may be "some true measure of saving faith" in preparation. But
"some true measure," he has to confess, is not saving faith
itself. Thus he calls these preparatory works "the weakest
measure of faith," or a state in which the sinner, though he
"longeth and almost fainteth for God's mercy," cannot be "assured of it." Through weakness and want of experience the
sinner cannot as yet "call God Father," though he cannot
"suffer the contrary thought to have any place in himself."[12]
Therefore, in the workings of the Holy Spirit, Rogers sees a
connecting link between God's part and man's, between divine
initiative and human endeavor. Although man is not assigned
"abilities" in the natural state, he is given a part to play of his
own as he responds to the Spirit in the external call. For Rogers
the facts of regeneration along experiential lines take precedence over prescribed theological dogma. Where Greenham
saw "violent subjection" and "voluntary submission" as irre-
concilable opposites, Rogers let experience itself determine the
process of conversion. What is more, he upheld Lydia's conversion as the foremost scriptural example of the process: "And
a certain woman named Lydia, a seller of purple, of the city of

11. Ibid., p. 20.
12. Ibid., pp. 20–21, 25–26.

the Thyatirians, which worshiped God . . . whose heart the Lord opened, that she attended unto the things which Paul spake" (Acts 16:14). In Lydia, as one who "worshiped God," whose heart the Lord then "opened," and who finally came to believe, the change itself was barely perceptible. She was neither suddenly transformed nor gradually constrained, but inwardly moved. At each step her response to the workings of the Spirit put her that much closer to salvation. At each step her desires, or affective nature, could be efficacious without diminishing God's initiative.[13]

In the light of all this, there can be little doubt that Richard Rogers and Richard Greenham point to a crucial concern for later developments in Puritan thought. As the first of the spiritual divines to express themselves fully in writing, each, it should be emphasized, was determined to uphold the necessity of divine initiative in the conversion process. Yet each was concerned to show that man may be allured to God without sudden transformation. Moreover, when Greenham called for "voluntary submission," as opposed to "violent subjection," and for the "willing humbling of ourselves," as opposed to that which "constraineth us rather than allureth us," it is evident that he favored the language of Bullinger to that of either Martyr or Calvin. And when Rogers elaborated on the "Works" of the Spirit, it is clear that he sought to provide for such voluntary "humbling" and to allow for human participation in a realm of activity where man could be said to respond to what allured him.

Puritan spirituality, it is safe to say, virtually began as an attitude of mind essentially concerned with rigid dogma. But if sinners were to be exhorted to the religious life, the concept of self-involvement had to be made a part of that life, and the

13. Ibid., p. 26.

idea of conversion had to encompass more than brute recognition of a preordained sign. Indeed, the very fact that spiritual preachers began to think of regeneration as a process, rather than as a moment in time, meant that conversion itself no longer implied immediate assurance of final election. Man, in the course of introspection, had to search for evidence of grace. Perhaps, in time, he could gain some inkling of salvation. But rarely could he claim election without the agony of doubt. St. Thomas had said that the first movement in the soul is "not indeed of coercion, but of infallibility," and that if God intends the one "whose heart He moves" should attain to grace, he will "infallibly attain to it."[14] But if Puritan preparationists were willing to abolish the notion of coercion, they were never without doubts about infallibility.

✠

Among Greenham's and Rogers' contemporaries or immediate successors at Cambridge were Laurence Chaderton (1536–1640), John Dod (1549?–1645) and Arthur Hildersam (1563–1632). They were all preachers of Puritan bent, and all were connected by a common purpose—the revival of "true religion" in what they considered to be the best Reformed tradition. As teachers they were never part of a formal organization or group, but the goal they shared was to train younger men in the ways of practical divinity. All lived far into the next century, beyond the founding of Massachusetts Bay. Devoted disciples, both in England and America, owed much to their inspiration. Chaderton, though he published little, had a great personal influence on those who heard him or studied under his direction. From 1570 he was fellow at Christ's College, and for fifty years he lectured at St. Clement's Church. In 1584 he was chosen master of the newly founded Emmanuel College, where he presided for forty years. Dod, who lived to become the "chief

14. *Summa Theologica*, Quest. 112, Art. 3, p. 1142.

holy man" of the spiritual brotherhood, was fellow of Jesus College and University Preacher until 1585. Like Chaderton, however, his literary efforts were slight; so that the influence of both must be judged in terms of legend.[15]

In Arthur Hildersam, on the other hand, we have a man of considerable stature as a theologian. What is more, he was the first spiritual preacher of noble blood, an inheritance from his mother's side. His parents were zealous Roman Catholics who had designed him for the priesthood. But after a thorough grounding in Protestant principles at his grammar school, he deserted the family faith and was disowned. At Christ's College he was supported by a distant relative, the Earl of Huntington, who entered him in 1576, while Chaderton was still a fellow. But in 1583, when he came up for a fellowship himself, for some unknown reason it was refused. By 1587 he had left the University for good, having been vested by his noble relatives with the benefice of Ashby-de-la Zouch. There, for almost forty years, he preached to the people of Leicestershire, while his influence on the rise of Puritanism never faltered. Unlike Chaderton or Dod, he was a Puritan of strong nonconformist views. The only member of the spiritual brotherhood to be frequently suspended, he had often to rely on his followers for support; and for his undoubted influence on many of these his thought deserves special attention.[16]

With Hildersam, in fact, the steps leading up to effectual conversion were given full elaboration for the first time. Beginning with the work of the Law in the external call, he alluded to the covenant promises themselves and emphasized throughout what man must "do" before conversion. Ever careful to insist that regeneration "to speak properly be the mighty work of God," he nevertheless proclaimed that "we may ourselves do much in this work, yea . . . we must be doers in it ourselves

15. William Hunt, *Dictionary of National Biography*, 5, 1050; Haller, p. 54.
16. Gordon, 9, 833–35; Haller, p. 55.

or else it will never be well done." If we would "do what we might," said Hildersam, "our hearts would be much softer and better able to mourn for our sins than they are";[17] for "our hearts are like instruments, ever out of tune; we must either . . . take some pains to set them in tune, or we shall never make good music in the ears of God." With David we must be able to cry, "Mine heart is prepared, O God, mine heart is prepared" (Psalm 57:7).[18]

Like Rogers, Hildersam took into consideration the varieties of religious experience, striving at the same time for a sense of order to which the individual conversion may be related. His purpose, like that of most early Puritans, was not so much to impose a rigid pattern as to establish guideposts along the way. But unlike Rogers, he began with far greater emphasis on fear of the Law. What Rogers calls the "First Work" of the Spirit or the "prick" of the Law Hildersam calls the "Spirit of bondage." "Ordinarily," he said, "the Lord useth by the Spirit of bondage and legal terrors to prepare men to their conversion"; for Christ was sent to preach the Gospel to such as had the "Spirit of bondage" (Rom. 8:15). This first constraining, however, is a warning as well as an effectual act. Man, in order to free himself from "legal and desperate fears," must "seek and labor for godly sorrow, for an afflicted and humble heart." In effect, "the best way to prevent the Lord from afflicting and humbling our souls with his own hand," Hildersam maintained, is to "humble and afflict our own souls"; for it is written: "Godly sorrow worketh repentance unto salvation not to be repented of" (II Cor. 7:10).[19]

Now when God as an angry judge strikes and afflicts the soul with sorrow for sin . . . Oh that sorrow is terrible, and

---

17. Arthur Hildersam, *The Doctrine of Fasting and Prayer, and Humiliation for Sin* (London, 1633), pp. 110–11.
18. *Lectures upon the Fourth of John* (London, 1629), p. 445.
19. *The Doctrine of Fasting*, pp. 88–89, 92–93, 99.

intolerable, when he smites the heart, he so sets it on as no
man is able to abide it. . . . And the best way to prevent the
Lord from wounding and afflicting our souls is to smite and
afflict our own hearts for our sins. The way to prevent those
intolerable and everlasting sorrows which God in His fury
will bring upon wicked men is to work our hearts to this
godly sorrow ourselves, and to humble our own souls.[20]

We have only to look to Scripture, said Hildersam, to find
"wherein we are to be the principal agent ourselves"; and here,
for the first time in Puritan literature, man is given a specific,
almost exclusive, sense of responsibility for the state of his
soul. Indeed, it would be hard to find a statement more explicit
in intention, or one more firmly rooted in the Hebraic exhortations to return to the covenant God. In Scripture, Hildersam
declared, we read that David "chastened" his soul (Psalm 69:10).
Of Josiah it is said that he did "humble" himself before God
(II Chr. 34:27), and of Manasseh that he "humbled himself
greatly before the God of his fathers" (II Chr. 33:12). "Yea
God's people are commanded in the day of their fast," Hildersam points out, "to afflict their own souls" (Lev. 23:27). In Joel
they are told to "rend" their hearts (Joel 2:13), and in Jeremiah
to "break up" their "fallow ground" (Jer. 4:3). We must therefore "examine our hearts seriously and impartially . . . labor
to find out, and call to mind our sins . . . lay them to our hearts
and so consider and weigh with ourselves the heinousness of
them"; for "to know in general . . . that thou art a sinner will
never humble thee aright; thou must know thy sins in particular, or thou canst never truly repent." Moreover, he who is
"truly humbled," says Hildersam, mourns for the "evil of sin"
rather than for the "evil of punishment." He mourns for sin
not so much in respect to himself as in respect to God. "Saving
sorrow" is therefore called "godly sorrow," or sorrow that
"respecteth God." It is opposed to "worldly sorrow" that "re-

20. Ibid., p. 100.

specteth only the . . . miseries that sin maketh us subject unto."
"Sound and saving humiliation," Hildersam asserts, "useth to
begin in this legal compunction and terror, which hath respect
only to the misery that sin brings us to. And not one of a
hundred do ever come to mourn for sin in respect to God, till
they have first learned to mourn for sin in respect to themselves.
This prepareth, maketh way for, and draweth in the other."[21]

For Hildersam, then, man first responds out of fear, then
sorrows for himself, and finally repents for offending God.
These are the three essential steps in his preparatory process.
We must first bring our hearts to a "religious fear," he says, and
after that we must "do something" more, or else we cannot
profit by the "promise of God."[22] Thus Hildersam, unlike
Bullinger, makes fear of punishment the primary response.
Repentance and humiliation come after. Where Bullinger believed that initial fear should not imply "servile dread of
punishment" but a "careful study mixed with honor and love
of God," Hildersam puts fear of punishment first, before "godly
sorrow" may be achieved. Yet we must remember that man
does not remain in fear throughout, and here Hildersam allows
for anticipation on man's part as well as for forceful constraint
on the part of God. In short, he modifies Calvin's conception
of constraining preparation in at least one important respect:
for if man is seized by the "Spirit of bondage," he must act in
turn as the "principal agent." If the Law prepares him for a
clear sight of sin, he must prepare himself for effectual conversion. Through "unfeigned repentance," a favorite phrase of
Bullinger's, he must turn toward God in anticipation of the
promises.[23] After initial fear of the Law, he must take it upon
himself to afflict his own soul, he must teach himself to sorrow
for sins against God, and he must repent and humble himself

21. Ibid., pp. 110–11, 119–20, 133–38.
22. *Lectures upon the Fourth of John*, p. 446; *CLII Lectures upon Psalm
LI* (London, 1635), p. 30.
23. *Lectures upon the Fourth of John*, p. 446.

before effectual conversion, both to escape God's anger and to acknowledge the covenant.

What Hildersam never makes clear, however, is the spiritual condition of man in preparation: whether he is still thoroughly reprobate or perhaps somewhere between reprobation and regeneration. In other words, Hildersam does not commit himself on the efficacy of the preparatory stages themselves. This point is also unclear in Rogers, where man in preparation is considered neither to have faith nor to be entirely "without it." In effect, Puritan divines had yet to take a clear stand on man's spiritual status in the preparatory phase. If a reprobate, could man desire grace as well as fear the Law? Or are all desires God-given, indicating some kind of regenerative condition? Few Puritans, if any, could offer a satisfactory solution; but of those who tried, William Perkins was perhaps the most articulate of his age.

�﹢

While Elizabeth reigned, the Puritan imagination flourished; and William Perkins contributed more than his share to its most formative period of development. Born in 1558, the year the Queen came to the throne, he died in 1602, just a few months before her death, so that his life and her reign span the same period. Although several years older than Hildersam, Perkins did not go up to Christ's College until 1577, a year after Hildersam. There he came immediately under the influence of Chaderton, and he often found his way to Dry Drayton, where he conferred with Greenham. From these two men Perkins learned the rudiments of practical divinity, what he himself would practice in his pastoral career. With Chaderton's backing he was elected fellow of Christ's in 1584 and soon became lecturer at Great St. Andrews, where ever-increasing crowds flocked to hear him. Like Hildersam, he was destined to become a leading Elizabethan Puritan divine. Until his death at the age of forty-four he was by far the most popular preacher at the University. No less than eleven editions of his collected works were put up for sale in London between 1600 and 1635, and for a century after his death his treatises and sermons were widely read in both England and America.[24]

Perkins was not only a forceful preacher but a great literary stylist. Moreover, he took advantage of his gift with one clear goal in mind: to check error and reassert the basic tenets of Reformed theology. Accordingly, he launched his career with several vigorous attacks on those whom he called "semi-Pelagian Papists," or all churchmen who "ascribe God's predestination partly to mercy and partly to man's foreseen preparations."[25] While "the doctrine hath been for divers hundreds of years that the will can do it, and the doctrine of the Papists now is that the will, so it be stirred up by God, can do it . . . the certain truth is that the will cannot." The "new and fleshy heart," he maintained, is the "gift of God." We can do "nothing but sin" before regeneration. The conversion of a sinner is a "creation," and "no sinner can prepare himself to his own creation."[26]

> When a man is dead, chafe him and rub him, put aqua vitae into him to warm him at the heart. When this is done, take him by the hand, pluck him up and bid him walk. For all this he will not stir the least joint, neither can he. All chafing and rubbing, all speach and persuasion, and all helps in the world be in vain. . . . Even so, no persuasion offered to the mind, nor good desires to the will, are of any moment till the image of God standing in holiness . . . begin to be restored.[27]

The will to become regenerate, Perkins insisted, is the "effect and testimony of regeneration begun." It cannot proceed from

24. James B. Mullinger, *Dictionary of National Biography*, *15*, 892–95; Louis B. Wright, "William Perkins: Elizabethan Apostle of 'Practical Divinity,'" *Huntington Library Quarterly*, *3* (1940), 171–96; Haller, p. 64.
25. *A Golden Chain* (London, 1597), p. 7.
26. *Works, 1*, 730–33.
27. Ibid., *1*, 733–34.

man until the heart is "mollified and framed by God to that which is good." The "bodily sick" may will to be healed, as they are alive; but the "spiritually sick" are "dead in their sins" and can neither "think, nor will, nor desire their conversion."[28]

There can be no doubt, then, that Perkins was determined to deny any ability on man's part to bring about his own conversion. And in this respect he held firmly to the orthodox Reformed position. Yet he was also an exponent of experiential religion, a preacher of practical divinity, and, most important of all, a covenant theologian. He knew from experience, as did Rogers, that few men could draw a firm line between reprobation and regeneration. Moreover, he had inherited from Greenham a concern for the biblical promises and for the scriptural exhortations demanding voluntary submission to the covenant of grace. To provide for these concerns, he therefore turned to the concept of a "weak faith" in which, he said, "men believeth the promise truly" though "perplexed with many doubtings." But where Rogers was undecided on the efficacy of a weak faith, and where Hildersam would not commit himself on man's spiritual status before effectual conversion, Perkins maintained that a man who "doth but begin to be converted" is "even at that instant the very child of God," though "inwardly he be more carnal than spiritual." What desires for faith a man may have are actually the first signs of regeneration; for "as there be divers ages in the life of man, so there be divers degrees and measures of true faith." "Mark then," said Perkins, "though as yet thou want firm and lively grace, yet art thou not altogether void of grace, if thou canst unfeignedly desire it. Thy desire is the seed, conception, or bud of that which thou wantest. 'If any man thirst, let him come to me and drink' " (Rev. 21:6).[29]

From this we might assume that man in preparation must first have the "seed" of grace, which is a "true faith" though

28. Ibid., *1*, 734.
29. *A Golden Chain*, p. 129; *Works, 1*, 637–39.

not a "strong faith." As the seed of the covenant, he might even have the seeds of grace through baptismal regeneration; for once the seed is planted, says Perkins, man's "sighs and groans" for a lively faith will be "truly in acceptation with God." But for Perkins the term "preparation," in a strict sense, does not apply to this condition. What Rogers and Hildersam group under the general heading of "preparation," Perkins breaks down into two categories. The "beginnings of conversion," he says, must be "distinguished." Some are "beginnings of preparation"; some are "beginnings of composition." Beginnings of preparation are "such as bring under, tame, and subdue the stubbornness of man's nature without working any change at all." Of this sort are "accusations of conscience," "fears and terrors," and "compunction of heart"—all arising from the ministry of the Law. Though they "go before to prepare a sinner for his conversion following," yet they are "no graces of God" but merely "fruits of the Law." A "reprobate," says Perkins, "may go this far." "Beginnings of composition," on the other hand, are "all those inward motions and inclinations of God's Spirit that follow after." Here the will or desire to become fully regenerate is "the effect of regeneration begun."[30]

Thus Perkins took into account man's affective nature before effectual conversion without diminishing the efficacy of the Law and without assigning "abilities" to man in his natural state. Although man in "preparation" as such is given a lower spiritual status than in Rogers or Hildersam, man before effectual conversion is given a higher one. In "preparation" man as "reprobate" is seized by the Law; but in "composition" he begins to prepare himself for saving grace with the help of the Spirit. Not yet effectually converted, his thirst for grace and his anticipation of the covenant promises allow him a part to play of his own. Indeed, he is able to "return unto the Lord" as Scripture demanded.

30. *Works, 1,* 638–41; 2, 13.

Unlike Hildersam, Perkins never offered an alternative to divine coercion. Man is not exhorted to humble and afflict his own soul to avoid God's doing it with His own hand. More-over, coercion by "legal terrors" must always precede God's offer of the promises; so that the Spirit may not begin to work until the "stubbornness of man's nature" has been thoroughly subdued. Where Rogers had emphasized the Law as the "Work" of the Spirit which merely "pricked" the heart into awareness of sin, Perkins held more closely to Calvin's idea of forceful constraint. And from this it is possible to assume that in the last two decades of the sixteenth century, when Calvin's *Institutes* was required reading at the universities, certain Puritan divines were made to be more aware of the Calvinist strain in Reformed theology than at an earlier period. Yet Perkins, like his predecessors, was also determined to preserve the covenant ideals which Bullinger had so carefully compiled; and this he did through the notion of "composition." In the "beginnings of composition," with the aid of the Spirit, man may look to God for the promise of everlasting life. In short, he may pre-pare himself for a "lively faith," though "perplexed with many doubtings."

✛

We saw in Richard Rogers the beginnings of a renewed interest in the Holy Spirit as the principal agent in saving grace. Through the "workings" of the Spirit man was obliged to respond in various stages by which he progressed from reproba-tion to regeneration. But what remained in doubt, as we have noted, was the line where reprobation left off and regeneration began. This, in turn, left in doubt the extent to which man could cooperate in the process; and as some spiritual divines became more concerned with the drawing activities of the Spirit and less concerned with the "terror" of the Law, the problem gave rise to several considerations.

If it is assumed, let us say, that the Spirit is given to us in some degree as reprobates, must we not obey the "motions" of the Spirit? For how else can it be said that we resist or "grieve" the Spirit, but that the Spirit is more eager to draw us than we are to respond ("Grieve not the Holy Spirit of God." Eph. 4:30). If, then, we are to be stirred up by the Spirit, must we not, to some extent, stir up ourselves? For how else may we "entertain" the Spirit in our hearts? If the Spirit, in short, is the principle of the holiness of our actions, are we not, in a sense, the principle of our actions as well?

✠

These concerns, among others, were later taken up by Richard Sibbes, who brought to bear the richest imagination of all. Indeed, Sibbes was unique among spiritual preachers, perhaps the most original of his time. Like many of his predecessors, he was a man of humble origins; but unlike most he lived to become one of the truly great English divines. The eldest son of a wheelwright, he was born in 1577 at Tostock, Suffolk, and in 1595 was sent as a sizar to St. John's College, Cambridge. As an undergraduate he listened to Perkins' sermons, but he owed his conversion to Paul Baynes (d. 1617), who succeeded Perkins at Great St. Andrews in 1602. By 1610 he had been granted the B.D., and in 1617 he was chosen preacher at Gray's Inn, one of the prize pulpits in London. There his sermons were taken down, frequently printed, and widely sold as classic examples of spiritual divinity. Soon his fame spread, and in 1626 he returned to Cambridge as master of St. Catherine's Hall, a post he held in addition to his lectureship at Gray's Inn.

As a Puritan Sibbes was never eager to provoke conflict with the authorities, although by 1615 he had been sufficiently non-conforming to lose the lectureship of Holy Trinity, Cambridge, to which he had been appointed in 1610. In 1633, however, he was allowed to return to Holy Trinity with a crown appointment to its perpetual curacy; and there he preached until his death two years later. Of his countless sermons, only those in

The Bruised Reed and Smoking Flax were published during his lifetime; but within the next few years Thomas Goodwin and Philip Nye issued several editions, many of which found their way to America.[31]

We find in Sibbes a highly sensitive, quite poetic mind, in which the doctrine of the Holy Spirit is fully developed. Moreover, it is developed with a minimum of concern for the rigors of dogma. Sibbes, more than any other Puritan divine, spoke for spiritual warmth. If divinity were cold, scholastic, or dogmatic, he maintained, few would feel the need for a change in heart. But if divinity could "warm" the heart, it mattered little what in theory man should not be allowed to do to effect his own salvation.

Unlike Perkins, Sibbes made no distinction between the "beginnings of preparation" and the "beginnings of composition." Reprobates, he maintained, might immediately respond to the Spirit and so desire grace without excessive preliminary constraint. While some need violent conversions and must be "pulled out of the fire with violence . . . because their will is nought, and thereupon usually their conversion is violent"; others, though reprobates, may be made responsive to the "sweet motions" of the Spirit. These "we must bring on gently and drive softly," for they are "like glasses which are hurt with the least violent usage," and if "gently handled" will "continue a long time." Those who turn toward God in obedience will receive the full benefits of the Spirit; those who resist are lost. Therefore, "The Holy Ghost is given to them that obey, to them that do not resist the Spirit of God. For in the ministry of the Gospel the Spirit is given in some degree to reprobates. It is offered, it knocks at the hearts of the vilest persons. . . . They have gracious motions offered them, but they do not obey them. Therefore the Spirit seizeth not upon them, to rule in them. . . . The Spirit is given to them that obey the sweet motions of it."[32]

31. Gordon, *18*, 182–83; Haller, p. 66.
32. *Works, 1*, 53, 25.

As reprobates, said Sibbes, we have "many motions by the
Holy Ghost"; so that if we are to have the Spirit of Christ, we
must "labor to subject ourselves unto it." "Turn not back those
blessed messengers," he implores, "let us entertain them" so
that the Spirit may "dwell and rule in us." But in order to do
this, in order to entertain the Spirit before effectual conversion,
we must become as a "bruised reed . . . sensible of sin and
misery." Seeing no help in ourselves, we must be "carried with
restless desire" to have saving grace. From the depths of our
desires, this "spark of hope" will then become a "smoking flax"
which Christ will not quench ("A bruised reed shall He not
break, and smoking flax shall He not quench, till He bring
forth judgment unto victory." Matt. 12:20). Upon some hope of
mercy from "the promise and examples of those that have
obtained mercy," we must "hunger and thirst after it."[33]

What is more, this bruising of the Spirit is never forced on
us against our will. It may be thought of "either as a state into
which God bringeth us, or as a duty to be performed by us";
but "both," Sibbes insists, "are here meant." We must "join
with God in bruising ourselves"; we must "lay seige to the
hardness of our own hearts and aggravate sin all we can."
Then "conviction will breed contrition, and this humiliation,"
all of which must precede effectual conversion. Yet we should
be careful, Sibbes warns, not to "press too much and too long
this bruising"; for we may "die under the wound." If we
remember that "none are fitter for comfort than those that
think themselves furthest off," there is ground for "true hope."[34]
While some might say, "If Christ will not quench the smoking
flax, what need we fear any neglect on our part?" Sibbes asserts:
"Who, if he knew before it would be a fruitful year, would
therefore hang up his plough and neglect tillage?" Who, if
he felt the nearness of grace, could afford to neglect his heart?
Indeed, "The heart of a Christian is Christ's garden, and his

33. Ibid., *1*, 25, 43-44.
34. Ibid., *1*, 47.

graces are as so many sweet spices and flowers, which his Spirit blowing upon makes them to send forth a sweet savor. Therefore keep the soul open for entertainment of the Holy Ghost, for he will bring in continually fresh forces to subdue corruption."[35]

This, perhaps the most poetic image of the heart in Puritan literature, embraces the full range of Sibbes' views on the regenerative process. Grace, he maintains, "sometimes is so little as is indiscernible to us." The Spirit "sometimes hath secret operations in us, which we know not for the present." Therefore we, still "mingled with corruption," are unable to tell when God's work begins. But we cannot, for this reason, "stay our turning unto God till we feel him saying to our hearts, 'I am thy God.'" "His work in bruising" and "our work in bruising ourselves" must go hand in hand. We must "beg the Spirit" that God would "alter our hearts" and "discover his love to us"; we must "labor . . . to have our heart kindled with the love of God." Yet in all of this we are essentially "reprobates." While the outcome remains in doubt, "there goes somewhat of ours together with somewhat of God's."[36]

For Sibbes, unlike Perkins, the efficacy of the Law has slight significance. Man's "bruising" he would prefer to call the "inferior work of the Spirit." Such terms as "legal terror" and "fear of punishment" have little place in his vocabulary. "Some divines, too many indeed," he says, "hold that the Holy Ghost only works . . . as it were, without . . . not upon the soul as an inward worker." But this, Sibbes believes, is "too shallow a conceit for so deep a business"; as the Spirit works "more deeply than so." The "Spirit of love," as preached in the Gospel, must be prized above the "Spirit of bondage." "It is not enough," he says, "to have the heart broken," for "a pot may be broken in pieces, and yet be good for nothing; so may a heart be, through terrors and sense of judgment, and yet be

35. Ibid., *1*, 74–75.
36. Ibid., *1*, 59, 47, 265; *4*, 198, 181.

not like wax, pliable." True "tenderness of heart," he holds,
is first wrought by an expectation of God's love;[37] and here,
without the least hesitation, he singles out natural abilities.

To prepare for God's love, says Sibbes, "let us not neglect
natural tenderness." Although we cannot "bring ourselves under the compass of God's kingdom by it," yet we can "get our
hearts the sooner to be tender" and so prepare ourselves to
"yield to the motions of the Holy Ghost." When the Spirit
moves and man yields, "this shows there is a tender heart";
while a hard heart "beats back all" and, "as a stone to the
hammer," will not yield to any "motions of God's Spirit." "As
when things are cold we bring them to the fire to heat and melt,"
Sibbes says, "so bring we our cold hearts to the fire of the love
of Christ." What is more, in the words of God to Josiah we
see that "tenderness of heart and humbling of man's self go
both together." ("Because thine heart was tender, and thou
didst humble thyself before God . . . I have even heard thee
also, saith the Lord." II Chr. 34:27) Therefore, we must first
make ourselves "low" to provide a "spiritual emptiness" which
may be filled with the Spirit of God. "In that measure we empty
ourselves," says Sibbes, "in that measure we are filled with the
fullness of God"; for "as all the water that is upon the hills
runs into the valleys, so all grace goes to the humble."[38]

For Sibbes, unlike most before him, man's natural abilities
are barely distinguishable from the work of the Spirit. In com-
menting on Psalm 27:8 ("When thou saidst, seek ye my face;
mine heart answered unto thee, O Lord, I will seek thy face.")
Sibbes concludes that "the heart and conscience of man is
partly divine, partly human." Therefore, when David cries,
"O Lord, I will seek thy face," it comes, Sibbes maintains, both
"from his heart root" and "from the heart grounded upon the
command and encouragement of God." Yet God remains the
sole initiator of saving grace. Sibbes wants not so much to exalt

37. Ibid., *4*, 225; *6*, 33.
38. Ibid., *6*, 33–34, 41, 44, 51.

natural man as to emphasize the indiscernible nature of divine activity. Only through the closest analysis of experience itself, he holds, can we tell where God's work begins. "If we will ever think to stand out resolutely," he says, "we must labor for experience and diligently observe God's dealings." Experience "breedeth patience and hope"; experience of a truth "seals a truth." In natural man since the Fall "there is so much left . . . that he draws to that which is good." There is "this general foundation of religion in all men," so that "all men from the principle of nature draw to that which is good." But in drawing and cleaving to God, man can go only so far. There is still sufficient distance between corrupt nature and divine grace so that "a great deal of preparation" is required.[39]

Although there is nothing in preparation "to bring the soul to have grace," says Sibbes, yet it "brings the soul to a nearer distance than those that are wild persons." While nature cannot work above its own powers, "as vapors cannot ascend higher than the sun draws them," yet we must prepare ourselves, we must "study experience" to know when God "by His Spirit . . . doth open . . . our hearts." We must "dig deep," we must "lay a sincere foundation" through "a deep search of our hearts and ways by sound humiliation." A man who is sincere in "doing that which is good" will have "a heart prepared with diligence." We must "enter deeper and deeper into ourselves"; we must "empty ourselves of self-confidence that we may be vessels for grace."[40]

Such preparation, for Sibbes, is not a prerequisite to salvation for its own sake, conceived merely in terms of everlasting life. Nor does he exhort to preparation out of fear of punishment, which for Hildersam was a major consideration. Rather, his focus of attention is the covenant promise of divine love— God's pure, unselfish love for man. Since both the Old and New Testaments "runneth upon love," we must "work upon

39. Ibid., 6, 114–15; 7, 69, 86.
40. Ibid., 7, 195; 3, 252, 241, 18, 21.

our hearts a disposition to see God's love." Love is the "firstborn
affection"; it "breeds desire for communion with God." And
when our natural love for God, through preparation, is joined
with His love for us, through grace, we may then reflect this
love back to Him again. "For being as we are," says Sibbes,
"we can never love God till we see in what need we stand for his
favor and grace." Indeed, the first love must be a love of dependence, which comes as an "issue of the heart." We must
"look to the heart, look to the beginning, to the spring of all
our desires . . . that is, the heart. The qualification of that is
the qualification of the man. If the heart be naught, the man is
naught. . . . Therefore look to the heart. See what springs out
thence."[41]

Then, too, we must "beg . . . a heart able to discern spiritual
favors, to taste and relish them." Grace, though virtually indiscernible at first, may be more readily discerned if conceived
in terms of sense experience; so that preparation, for Sibbes,
is not only a self-emptying, or even a "love of dependence,"
but the cultivation of a "taste," a heightened sensitivity to
"spiritual favors" which will allow us to "relish spiritual
things." In spiritual life "it is most necessary that the Spirit
should alter the taste of the soul"; and "a heart able to discern
spiritual favors" will be receptive to such alteration.[42]

Hence "works of preparation make not a Christian"; but "by
these a Christian is prepared to be wrought upon by God's
Spirit." And here Sibbes turns, as did Rogers, to the biblical
example of Lydia's conversion. Certainly "she had some religion
in her," Sibbes comments, "though yet she was not ripened in
the true religion." From "such kind of places as this," he says,
we have occasion to speak of "works of preparation." We do not
"sow among thorns"; we "purge before cordials"; yet "we grant
no force of a meritorious cause in preparations to produce such

41. Ibid., 3, 23, 248; 7, 60; 4, 195; 2, 218.
42. Ibid., 3, 25, 107; 2, 238.

an effect as conversion is." Preparation is only "to remove the hindrances and to fit the soul for conversion." Since the Spirit will not be effectual in a "rude, wild, and barbarous soul," to those who use the "talents of their understanding and will," God "discovers Himself more and more." Lydia, says Sibbes, "was religious in her kind," yet her heart had to be "further opened" before she could be saved. Then, as soon as she believed, "the Spirit of God blowing upon the garden of her heart, where the spice of grace was sowed, stirred up a sweet scent of faith."[43]

In this highly experiential process, where man's part and God's seem always to blend, Sibbes insists that it is "over-curious to exact the first beginnings of grace"; for grace "falls by degrees, like the dew indiscernibly." God "offers no violence to the soul," but works "sweetly yet strongly, and strongly yet sweetly." The "stream is but changed," the "man is the same." Moreover, if God deals with men "propounding mercy by covenant and condition," His covenant is "always a gracious covenant." He not only gives grace freely but "helps us in performing the condition by His Spirit." While God "looks upon us in our resolutions and preparations," He also "works our hearts to believe and repent"; so that "we are the principle of our actions, as they are actions, but the Holy Ghost is the principle of the holiness of the actions." In all of this, says Sibbes, "acknowledgment" is the key word, when the will and affections yield to the entertaining and the owning of the "thing known." And when the thing known is the covenant bond, we are indeed "the principle of our actions"; we are God's by "voluntary acceptance of the covenant of grace."[44]

Of all the preparationists Sibbes was by far the most extreme in terms of the abilities he assigned to natural man. But if

43. Ibid., 5, 7; 6, 522–523, 534.
44. Ibid., 7, 221, 119; 3, 107, 314; 4, 122; 5, 308.

reprobates "from the principle of nature" could naturally turn toward "that which is good," their effectual turning was always conceived within a highly developed doctrine of the Holy Spirit. Moreover, such turning was inevitably expressed in terms of the covenant relationship. Thus Sibbes could concern himself with the "heart root" (which he said had survived in man since the Fall) if only to distinguish it from "the heart grounded upon the command and encouragement of God." In other words, he could take into account man's natural desire to seek divine light, as the "root" in the "garden" of his heart, yet insist that effectual preparation could not begin until "sweet spices and flowers" had begun to blossom. This effectual change, wrought by the breath of the Spirit, then allowed the heart to "send forth a sweet savor" or to return the warmth and love that had caused "Christ's garden" to grow. And man, with his soul opened for "entertainment" of the Holy Ghost, could acknowledge the covenant relationship with God.

Yet Sibbes, although he lived to see a covenant community founded in New England, was never clear on the extent to which "reprobates" had a claim on grace as heirs to the covenant promises. While the seeds of faith must be planted in "Christ's garden," no connection is made between the event itself and God's promise to the "seed" of Abraham. Nor are we told precisely when the implantation occurs. Perkins, in his day, had confined the seeds of grace to the "beginnings of composition," and only then after considerable constraint by the Law. Neither he nor Sibbes after him thought of regenerative growth in terms of baptismal efficacy. But with two slightly later divines, John Preston and William Ames, we find a significant change in emphasis which points directly back to Bullinger. In fact, on the eve of American colonization we find that preparation is discussed specifically in terms of baptismal regeneration. This aspect of covenant theology, so forcefully stated in Bullinger's phrase, "Our mother Sarah gendereth us into liberty . . . of that mother we have the seed of life," is now clearly associated with preparatory activity; and the degree to which it alters the concept deserves careful analysis, as an examination of Preston's thought will show.[45]

✠

John Preston was born the son of a poor farmer at Upper Heyford, Northamptonshire, in 1587. In his youth he was adopted by a wealthy relative who sent him first to Northampton grammar school and then to King's College, Cambridge. In 1604 he matriculated with a diplomatic career in mind but later turned to philosophy as well as medicine. Then in 1611, while a fellow of Queen's, he heard a sermon from John Cotton which altered the course of his life. He read Calvin, took the

45. Bullinger, *Decades*, p. 297. In the New Testament the word "regeneration" is used in connection with baptism in Titus 3:5: "according to his mercy he saved us by the washing of regeneration and renewing of the Holy Ghost." In Titus 3:7 those saved through the "washing of regeneration" are said to become "heirs according to the hope of eternal life." Therefore, Puritan divines who spoke of baptismal efficacy had scriptural support for their stand. Although Paul does not mention baptismal regeneration elsewhere, it is implied in I Cor. 12:13: "For in one Spirit were we all baptized into one body." In this passage, writes H. G. Marsh, "it should be noted that the reception of the Spirit and the act of baptism are so closely linked together in Pauline thought that they may be regarded as simultaneous experiences." Marsh goes on to say:

It is true that Paul connects baptism with real and very vital experiences, but it is true also that according to other passages in his writings these same experiences are described as realized in a way that appears to have little connection with the rite of baptism. . . . Since in Paul's theology the doctrine of justification by faith is prominent . . . baptism was really superfluous from such a standpoint. Any emphasis on this side of the work of the baptismal act would have led to a confusion of the work of faith and the work of the sacrament.

Nevertheless, Marsh concludes:

While some scholars have held that Paul interpreted the rite symbolically, others have maintained with equal assurance that he regarded it as the actual means by which experiences vital in the Christian life were obtained. [*The Origins and Significance of the New Testament Baptism*, pp. 132, 135, 134, 128]

degree of B.D. in 1620, and became dean and catechist of
Queen's. In 1622 he succeeded John Donne as preacher at
Lincoln's Inn, and the same year, on Chaderton's resignation,
was made master of Emmanuel.

Like Sibbes, whom he greatly admired, Preston trod the line
between conformity and nonconformity, and as chaplain to
Prince Charles he was able to influence the crown on behalf of
his Puritan friends. When in 1625 James I died and Charles
came to the throne, Preston immediately obtained a general
preaching license for the much suspended Arthur Hildersam,
who at Cambridge had "come often to his chamber." But when
Laud put a stop to efforts of this kind, Preston lost influence
at court; and Hildersam, to whom he owed much, was again
forbidden to preach. By now Preston's health was broken. His
lungs diseased, he died in 1628 at the age of forty-one. John
Dod, the aging holy man of the spiritual brotherhood, read
his funeral sermon; and Richard Sibbes, among others, began
to edit his posthumous works.[46]

What Perkins called the "beginnings of preparation," Preston
called "outward preparation"; and what Perkins called the
"beginnings of composition," Preston called "inward preparation," putting both categories back under the heading of "preparation." Preparatory activity, he said, may both precede the
assistance of the Spirit and follow it as well; but in all of this
he was primarily concerned with preparation only where the
Spirit is present, or the covenant relationship established.[47]

Indeed, where Perkins held that preparation under the Law,

46. Samuel Clarke, *The Lives of Sundry Modern English Divines* (London, 1651), pp. 473–520; Gordon, *16*, 308–11. In 1615 Preston had begged
Hildersam for a copy of his *Lectures upon the Fourth of John*. On receiving
it he wrote back: "When I went about to take out some things for mine own
use briefly, I could not almost tell what to leave out . . . I hope it will be
a good help to Ministers when they read it, and bring the method of doctrine and use into more credit" (Letter quoted in Clarke, pp. 382–83).

47. *The New Covenant, or Saints Portion* (London, 1630), p. 394; *Remains*
(London, 1637), pp. 193–196.

without the Spirit, was a "foundation of grace," for Preston the Law is "not a schoolmaster," it "teacheth no man," unless the Spirit "put an edge upon it" to "prick the heart." He allows for preparation under the Law by itself, but only for those whom he says "shall never be saved." This is, so to speak, preparation for damnation; while true preparation is the work of the Spirit. What is more, as soon as man has the Spirit, says Preston, "at that very hour he is entered into covenant, he is translated from death to life, he hath now received the promised seed."[48] And so we have reached the point where regenerate man, by name, must prepare for saving grace.

In Greenham, Rogers, and Hildersam, man's spiritual status in preparation was undefined. In Perkins, and especially in Sibbes, preparatory activity was assigned to "reprobates." Now, however, man in preparation is clearly regenerate, striving to make the seeds of faith fully effectual; for "faith proves ineffectual" says Preston, "for want of preparation and humiliation that should go before it." Because "the heart is . . . not broken yet . . . not emptied of those things that it must be emptied of before a man can take Christ," there must be "a certain work of preparation or humiliation by which these strong lusts are broken in us." Faith is effectual only when "there is a good way made for it"; when "the rubbish and false earth is taken away"; when "the humiliation is sound and good"; when "the preparation is perfect."[49]

Like Sibbes, he thinks of preparation in terms of man's love of God. But first, he insists, we must be baptized with "the baptism of the Holy Ghost." Then God looks for a love that is the mark of a faith "unfeigned" and not "counterfeit." Since faith that is "disjoined from love" is never true, we must be "thus prepared to seek Him and to esteem Him"; for "wheresoever love is not, there is nothing but hypocrisy in such a man's heart." When the heart of man is taken up with the

48. *The New Covenant*, pp. 394, 398.
49. *The Breastplate of Faith and Love*, pp. 14–16.

world, says Preston, "it eats and devours all the thoughts, all
the intentions of the mind . . . and the hidden man of the heart
is left starved and pinned within." Therefore, we must be
"diligent" in preparing for the Lord's coming and do as John
the Baptist came to do, "prepare ye the way of the Lord"
(Luke 3:4). This "diligence of love" is shown by "opening to
the Lord when He knocks"; as it is the nature of true love
that it "enlargeth and wideneth the heart." So we must "keep
our hearts clean" if we would have the Lord "delight to dwell
with us." We must "remove out of His sight whatever He
hateth"; for while "faulty preparation" may bring us to "prize
Christ," it is "not so deep a preparation as to love Christ."[50]

Thus Preston exhorts the covenant "seed" to prepare for
God's entrance into their hearts. And he does this on the basis
of baptismal regeneration. Although it is true "the Lord must
do it," he says, "yet He doth it by yourselves, you are the agents
in the business. . . . To exhort you to be doers, that your faith
may be effectual faith, and that your love be diligent love; that
is the great business which we have to do, and the thing which
for the most part we fail in." But "this you must know," he
cautions, "that still the promise is made to the coming and not
to the preparations." If you are at your "journey's end," it is
"no matter" how you came there. If you find you are "in Christ,"
without previous preparation, and have a "testimony from His
Spirit," know that "the promise is made to that." You must,
without the smallest doubt, have the Spirit "in good earnest";
"but mistake not," he warns, "that turbulent sorrow, that
violent disquiet of mind goes not always before."[51]

This warning, perhaps the first of its kind among Puritan
preparationists, lends a touch of irony to the entire development of the concept; for Preston is saying, along with Zwingli,
Peter Martyr, and other early Reformers, that man may be
saved through the effectual call only; that preparatory activity

50. Ibid., pp. 396, 42, 16–17, 125.
51. Ibid., pp. 203, 80.

need not go before. Furthermore, by recalling to mind this basic tenet of orthodox Reformed theology, he shows a genuine awareness of lurking opposition. By offering an alternative, he clearly indicates that some Puritan divines felt that the preparationists had gone too far. John Cotton, for one, to whom Preston is said to have owed his conversion, would certainly have welcomed these qualifying remarks, at least by the time he had reached Massachusetts. Indeed, Preston's warning, had it been heeded in New England, might well have provided a basis for compromise in the Antinomian Controversy. But by 1637, as we shall see, Massachusetts orthodoxy had committed itself to the preparationist camp. There could be no retreat or compromise in a community where "that turbulent sorrow, that violent disquiet of mind" had always to go before.

✠

Preston had been dead but a few months when in 1628 the first settlers of the Bay Colony embarked for Massachusetts; and the man most responsible for the structure of their quest was William Ames Although Ames was virtually a contemporary of Sibbes and eleven years older than Preston, he must be considered last for several reasons. First, he was not a moderate Puritan of the general type we have considered thus far, with the exception of Hildersam, but a major architect of the Congregational system as it was soon to be established in New England. In addition, he professed a fully developed concept of baptismal regeneration which, together with Preston's views, represents a considerable departure from the mainstream of thought that we have been following. Finally, he outlived Preston by some five years, during which time he published "Cases of Conscience" (1631), giving the concept of preparation a genuinely secure position in Puritan thought.

Born in 1578 of an ancient family in the county of Norfolk, he went up to Christ's College in time to have Perkins as his

tutor. But where Perkins tended to conform in his views on
Church discipline, his student did not. After Perkins' death
in 1602, Ames refused, as a newly ordained divine, to wear a
surplice in the College chapel. By 1609 he had been suspended
by the vice-chancellor from all ecclesiastical functions and from
all degrees "taken or to be taken." Whereupon he left the
University for a life of wandering until appointed to the chair
of theology at Franeker in 1622.[52]

In the meantime, however, he had been chief adviser to the
strict anti-Arminian faction at the Synod of Dort (1618–19) as
well as the author of several works pointing toward a Congregational reformation of the Church. As early as 1610 he had
argued that Church membership should be restricted to the
elect within autonomous congregations and that each congregation should be formed only by the mutual consent of covenanting believers. Unlike the Separatists, who in 1592 had
repudiated the Church of England and had established totally
separate churches under the leadership of Robert Browne,
Ames held that the Church of England was still to be considered
the "true Church" and that each congregation should labor to
make it "pure."[53]

The Congregational ideal of a "pure church" had ordinarily
required that those in external relationship to the covenant
were to become full members only if they walked in a godly way,
gave a clear profession of faith, and showed a reasonable knowledge of doctrine. But so long as men of Congregational persuasion remained in England, where every resident of a parish was
automatically a member of the Church, there was no way by
which the unqualified could be expelled. Nor had Ames or his
followers yet developed a concept of Church membership
whereby each candidate should be tested for signs of saving
grace. This was a practice first ecclesiastically instituted in
Massachusetts, where it was further required that candidates

52. Mullinger, *1*, 355–57.
53. Perry Miller, *Orthodoxy in Massachusetts* (Cambridge, 1933), p. 77.

provide a convincing testimony of God's regenerating work.[54]
Had Ames lived a few years longer, he undoubtedly would
have followed his disciples to America, where he might have
resisted the new requirements, or lent them his support. But
in 1633 he died after prolonged ill health, leaving his family
with barely enough to take themselves and his books on the
long voyage over.

"What ought a man to do," asked Ames, "that he may be
translated out of a state of sin into a state of grace?" If indeed
there is something he can do, how greatly is he constrained by
the Law, and to what extent does he function willingly within
the covenant relationship? First, said Ames, the sinner must
"seriously look into the Law of God, and make an examination
of his life and state." In other words, he must take it upon
himself to evaluate his moral condition in the light of what the
Law demands. Then, once he has compared his condition with
the Law, "conviction of conscience" should lead to "despair
of salvation" and finally to "true humiliation of heart." All
four steps, Ames maintained, are absolutely necessary before
effectual conversion: otherwise there can be no assurance of
faith. But the process itself must take place within a voluntary
frame of mind, as part of man's willing response to the covenant
obligations. For Ames there is virtually no constraint involved.
Because the promises pertain to the baptized covenanter, or to
all those who have the "first seal of the covenant," if they be
"partakers of any grace," said Ames, it is "by virtue of the
covenant of grace." Therefore, they need not have achieved an

54. In *Visible Saints; The History of a Puritan Idea* (New York, 1963),
Edmund S. Morgan traces the emergence of experiential testing as a
qualification for full church membership. On the basis of extensive research
he argues quite conclusively that both separating and nonseparating Puritans at first required merely a godly life, a profession of faith, and knowledge of doctrine before membership could be granted. The practice of
testing candidates for actual inward signs of saving grace began in Massachusetts some time between 1630 and 1640, spread to Plymouth, Connecticut,
and New Haven, then eventually back to England.

immediate sense of salvation or to have suffered vigorous constraint by the Law in order to anticipate God's covenant grace.
If the covenant pertained only to those who had gained absolute
assurance, or "only to the faithful," as Ames expressed it, then
the grace of God would be "more narrow." But repentance and
faith "do no more make the covenant now than in the time of
Abraham." Because the spiritual descendants of Abraham are
born into the covenant relationship, that relationship is efficacious long before they have gained full knowledge of Christ. If,
on the other hand, anyone "opposes himself out of malice," or
rejects the covenant promises (which are "propounded to the
hearts of men, as it were by an inward word"), then that person
has committed a sin "against the Holy Ghost," which is "un-
pardonable" or "unto death."[55]

The baptized, for Ames, are the "sons and heirs of the promises." As such they must turn toward God and acknowledge
their sins. Apart from self-examination under the Law, "it is
further required," said Ames, "that a man do go altogether out
of himself, renouncing his own righteousness." Indeed, no
baptized soul may seek righteousness by faith unless "he do
first acknowledge himself to be destitute of all righteousness
in himself." (And here we are reminded of Bullinger's words,
"for unless we do acknowledge our own corruptions and un-
righteousness, we shall never by true faith lay hold on Christ.")
What is more, unlike ordinary sinners, the baptized do not
begin entirely without faith; for baptism, though not a sign of
saving faith, is nevertheless "the very beginning of regeneration" or the embryo of spiritual thirst.[56]

Ames, perhaps the greatest of Puritan covenant theologians,

55. William Ames, "Conscience with the Power and Cases thereof,"
Bk. II, Cap. 4 "How a sinner ought to prepare himself to conversion";
Works (London, 1643), p. 8; *The Marrow of Sacred Divinity* (London, 1642),
pp. 182–83, 111–12.
56. *The Marrow*, p. 182; "Cases of Conscience," p. 12; Bullinger, p. 572.
For Paul's views on baptismal regeneration, see above, pp. 43 n., 75 n.

was therefore willing and anxious to allow for man's affective nature in the preparatory phase. As the seed of the covenant, man looks to the Law voluntarily to examine his estate. He seizes upon the Law, the Law does not seize him. Far from being "shaken with a great wind," he turns into the wind of his own accord. Thus self-examination under the Law goes hand in hand with a genuine spiritual thirst for saving grace; and both are part of the preparatory experience. Moreover, this thirst is man's as heir to the promises offered; so that before his full "creation" in Christ, he has much he must or "ought" to do. If he "judgeth it possible that his sins should be forgiven," says Ames, he will openly desire "that mercy which God hath promised."[57]

With Ames, who would have been among the first of New England divines had he lived to see these shores, we have come to the end of a germinal period in Puritan thought. Above all, we have come to the end of a time in which two generations of spiritual preachers ceaselessly devoted themselves to describing the interior life. Out of it, without question, has come a sense of the regenerative process rarely if ever equaled in the history of spiritual thought. Apart from the great Medieval mystics few theologians of like mind have ever produced such a formidable body of devotional literature; and they did this, it should be remembered, out of concern for individual salvation alone. As pastors they spoke of man's duty to examine himself privately and made it quite clear that no man should probe into the "heart and conscience" of another. Moreover, they considered the Church to be made up of members who professed to believe as well as of those who had actually received saving faith. Assurance of salvation, in terms of the inner life, had nothing to do with church membership. As Ames himself said, "Those who

57. "Cases of Conscience," p. 9.

are only believers by profession, so long as they remain in that
society are members of that Church, as also of the catholic
church as touching the outward state, not touching the inward
or essential state."[58] But by 1640, as we have noted, a person
wanting to be admitted to full membership in a Massachusetts
church was required to describe his interior struggle for grace
as well as his effectual call.

For Calvin, the test of the elect had been by profession of
faith, an upright life, and participation in the sacraments;
but for the Congregational founders of New England an inward
test of personal experience was now also required. No other
group at this time, with the exception of some Baptists and
perhaps certain remaining Anabaptist groups, demanded so
much.[59] Thus the conversion process, often indiscernible to
the inner man, now urgently required a sense of order, if only
to be intelligible to others. And where the continued life of
the congregation depended upon full regeneration in external
members, the preparatory phase came to have greater significance than Rogers, Sibbes, or Ames himself could ever have
imagined.

Indeed, through his emphasis on the efficacy of baptism, Ames
had introduced concerns with far-reaching consequences for
New England; as external covenanters would be exhorted to
prepare for effectual conversion on the basis of baptismal "abilities." But in no sense did he imply that baptism should be the
sole foundation for preparatory activity. Covenant theologians
could be concerned with those entirely outside the covenant,
seeking entrance, as well as with those in external relationship.
In fact, Ames could qualify his stand with the remark that
baptism is "not so absolutely necessary to salvation that the
absence or mere privation . . . doth bring a privation of this

58. *The Marrow*, p. 140.
59. See C. C. Goen: *Revivalism and Separatism in New England, 1740–
1800: Strict Congregationalists and Separate Baptists in the Great Awakening*
(New Haven, 1962), chap. I.

institution."[60] Just as Preston did not assume the absolute
necessity of preparation, so Ames did not insist that men first
be baptized to achieve saving grace. Most important for Ames
were the covenant promises themselves and our willingness to
acknowledge the promises, whether we be thoroughly reprobate
or given some kind of regenerate status through baptism. In
New England this plea for acknowledgment would shape and
inform the theory and practice of preparation to help make it
what it became: a vital factor in both the nurture and stamp
of the Commonwealths.

60. *The Marrow*, p. 181.

4

The American Preparationists

From 1628, when William Laud was made Bishop of London, moderate nonconformists as well as extremists were refused permission to preach; and Holland offered the only free pulpits. After 1633, when Laud became primate of England, Puritans who had gone to the Netherlands saw little hope for a speedy return home, and those who were still in England had either to flee to America or face unrelieved persecution. And so the time had come to build a "pure church" in which the elect and their seed might renew the covenant without ecclesiastical interference. The day was at hand to cast off the "Assyrian yoke," the "burden of Babylon." ("And it shall come to pass in that day, that his burden shall be taken away from off thy shoulder, and his yoke from off thy neck." Is. 10:27) In New England, more than ever before, the covenant community became a "Holy nation," a "New Israel," a "remnant according to the election of grace" (Rom. 11:5). No longer did they "stay upon him that smote them," but "upon the Lord, the Holy One of Israel, in truth" (Is. 10:20). And the seed of the remnant were admitted to the "outward" covenant in the hope that all might become "Jews inwardly." ("Ye are a chosen generation . . . an holy nation, a peculiar people." I Peter 2:9)

Of the numerous Puritan divines who fled to Massachusetts between 1628 and 1640, Thomas Hooker, Thomas Shepard, and Peter Bulkeley were among the leaders. Each was a duly ordained minister of the Church of England, each had been silenced by Archbishop Laud, and each was to become a leading exponent in America of the concept of preparation. In English Puritanism, as we have seen, preparatory activity had been an individual, or pastoral, concern. Now it became a social concern and a part of the American experience; for when these exiled divines preached preparation in New England, they had a covenant community foremost in mind.

As we turn first to Hooker, then to Shepard, and finally to Bulkeley, several considerations must be taken into account. If Preston and Ames had assumed that those in external covenant possessed the seeds of regeneration, to what extent did this assumption prevail in America? Indeed, if some New England preachers taught that there was a certain connection between baptism and effectual conversion, while others taught that there was only a probable connection, the efficacy of preparation could well depend upon the efficacy of baptism. Moreover, if some New England preachers were anxious to encourage conversions, while others were fearful lest hypocrites gain full church membership, preparation could mean something different in each case. A minister who was eager to accept into full membership as many as earnestly desired might emphasize covenant acknowledgment in terms of baptismal "faith." A minister who was more concerned to keep out hypocrites might emphasize legal constraint and stringent introspection in terms of baptismal "privilege." Therefore, we must first determine to what extent "baptismal regeneration" was accepted, and what effect it had. Then, too, we must consider the degree to which man's affective response to the covenant promises outweighed divine constraint. What part had constraining preparation still to play in America?

What is more, we must determine whether the preparatory steps themselves, as points of introspective meditation, were allowed to blot out the promises. Both Hooker and Shepard

were criticized by their contemporaries, as well as by later
scholars, for making the standards of grace too high. One such
critic, the English theologian John Bickerton Williams (1792–
1855), wrote that each made statements which "by checking
the freeness of salvation, become, though contrary to intention,
stumbling blocks, and the occasion of mental trouble." Instead
of "at once directing sinners . . . to the finished atonement,"
said Williams, "these good men . . . evidently thought a routine
of tedious preparation needful before coming to the Saviour.
Qualifications . . . unknown to the Word of God were prescribed, and rules laid down, which not merely concealed great
and precious promises, but savored of a legal spirit." And so
it remains to be seen whether or not the "rules" of preparation
were allowed to overshadow the "experience."[1]

Hooker was the first of the three to come and the first of the
New England preachers to express himself fully on the preparatory phase in conversion. Born the son of a country squire at
Marfield, Leicestershire, about 1586, he had gone to Queen's
College in 1604, the same year Preston entered King's. Later
he transferred to Emmanuel, where he took the B.A. in 1608,
followed by the M.A. in 1611. At the Emmanuel of Chaderton,
in the Cambridge of the spiritual brotherhood, he was exposed
to the leading Puritan divines of his day. Although Perkins had
died two years before Hooker arrived, Sibbes and Ames were
beginning their careers; and the town was breeding a corps
of men destined to carry the Congregational banner to New
England. Nathaniel Ward, later minister at Ipswich, had taken
his master's degree at Emmanuel in 1603; Peter Bulkeley, afterwards pastor of the Concord Church, took the M.A. at St. John's
in 1605; John Cotton, who would sail with Hooker on the
Griffin, proceeded to the M.A. from Emmanuel in 1606; John
Wilson, later Cotton's associate in the Boston Church, was at

1. John Bickerton Williams, *Letters on Puritans* (London, 1843), p. 170.
Quoted in John A. Albro, *The Life of Thomas Shepard* (Boston, 1870),
pp. 309–10.

Cambridge in 1610 for additional studies under Ames; and Thomas Shepard, later pastor at Newtown, would be admitted to Emmanuel in 1619.[2]

From 1611 to 1618 Hooker was catechist and lecturer at Emmanuel. Between 1618 and 1626 he preached in the parish of Esher, Surrey, under the donative benefice of a Mr. Francis Drake. There he married Mrs. Drake's waiting woman, Susanna, who later accompanied him first to Holland and then to America. There his daughter Joanna was born, later to be the wife of Thomas Shepard. In 1626 Hooker was invited to be lecturer at Chelmsford, Essex, a town about thirty miles east of London. Here he set aside one day a week to discuss cases of conscience privately with his parishioners. And here he began to preach in a "popular way" on preparation for Christ, contrition, and humiliation, a subject his Essex followers would ask him to resume in New England.[3] In 1629 Hooker was deprived by Laud of his lectureship. By 1630 he had fled to Holland, having refused to answer a second summons from the Court of High Commission.

In Holland he went first to Amsterdam, then to Delft, and later to Rotterdam, where William Ames had come to die. In 1632 he wrote "An Advertisement to the Reader" and a "Preface" for Ames' last book, *A Fresh Suit against Human Ceremonies in God's Worship*. According to Cotton Mather, who wrote the fullest early account of Hooker, Ames let it be known before he died that "though he had been acquainted with many scholars of divers nations, yet he never met with Mr. Hooker's equal, either for preaching or for disputing." After Hooker had seen Ames' book through the press, he arranged to go to America. A group known as "Mr. Hooker's Company" had gone from England to Massachusetts in 1632, apparently with the under-

2. George L. Walker, *Thomas Hooker: Preacher, Founder, Democrat* (New York, 1891), pp. 21–23.

3. Cotton Mather, *Magnalia Christi Americana, 1* (Hartford, 1855), III, 346–47.

standing that he would follow. Accordingly, in the spring of
1633 he returned to England, where he joined John Cotton and
the Reverend Samuel Stone on board the *Griffin* for Boston.[4]

The *Griffin* reached port September 4th, after eight weeks
at sea. Cotton remained in Boston while Hooker and Stone
went on to Newtown (later Cambridge) as pastor and teacher.
But by May of 1634 all was not well. Hooker's congregation had
petitioned the General Court for permission to have more land
or to move to another part of the country, for "want of accom-
odation for their cattle." Conferences on the question of
removal took place from October 1635 to March 1636, when
it was finally decided that Hooker and his company should
be allowed to go to Hartford, Connecticut. Meanwhile, in the
autumn of 1635, Thomas Shepard had arrived to organize a
new church alongside Hooker's. During the winter of 1635–36
both congregations lived in Newtown; and in May Hooker left
with thirty-six families on the Indian paths to the West.[5]

Scarcity of land, however, was certainly not his sole motive
for leaving. Indeed, as Antinomianism flared in Massachusetts,
Hooker and Cotton were already at odds on the subject of
preparation. Moreover, there is evidence to suggest that Hooker
disagreed with the strict qualifications for Church membership
then being enforced in Massachusetts. The Reverend Robert
Stansby, a Puritan minister at Suffolk, England, wrote to John
Wilson, April 17, 1637, that he had heard "there is great division of judgment in matters of religion amongst good ministers

4. Walker, pp. 33–63; Mather, *1*, III, 339. In 1633 Hooker wrote from
Holland to John Cotton in England: "The state of these provinces to my
weak eye seems wonderfully ticklish and miserable. For the better part,
heart religion, they content themselves with very forms, though much
blemished. But the power of Godliness, for ought I can see or hear, they
know not; and if it were thoroughly pressed I fear least it will be fiercely
opposed." Mather, *1*, III, 340.

5. John Winthrop, *Journal*, ed. James Hosmer, *1* (New York, 1908), 132;
Charles M. Andrews, *The Colonial Period of American History*, *2* (New
Haven, 1936), 77–81.

and people which moved Mr. Hooker to remove"; that "you
are so strict in admission of members to your church, that more
than half are out of your church in all your congregations";
and that "Mr. Hooker before he went away preached against
it." The historian William Hubbard, writing fifty years later,
commented: "Two such eminent stars, such as were Mr. Cotton
and Mr. Hooker . . . could not well continue in one and the
same orb."[6]

By the autumn of 1636 Hooker and his company had established themselves at the mouth of the "Little River" in Hartford. From there he returned to Boston in August 1637 to
attend the Hutchinsonian Synod, and again in March 1638 to
take part in Mrs. Hutchinson's church trial. There were other
trips back in the next few years, mainly to attend a series of
meetings called to defend Congregationalism against the Presbyterian leanings of the Westminster Assembly (1643–49). Out
of these discussions came Hooker's *Survey of the Sum of Church
Discipline,* in which he presented the case for the Congregational Way. But by the time the book was published (London,
1648), having been lost at sea and rewritten, Hooker had died
in an epidemic. In the summer of 1647, when the disease struck,
he was sixty-one years old.[7]

On the question of baptismal efficacy, Hooker believed that
according to a "right rule from God" persons may have faith
in the "course of charity," and that some children are "thus
fitted" so that faith is "sealed unto them in circumcision." Although "men of years," or the unbaptized, must "embrace the

6. *Massachusetts Historical Society Collections,* Series IV, 5 (Cambridge,
1865), 10–11; Hubbard, *A General History of New England,* Massachusetts
Historical Society (Boston, 1848), p. 173. John Cotton's views on preparation,
together with documents relating to the first preparation controversy in
New England, will be taken up and discussed in Chapter 5.

7. Walker, pp. 134–51.

covenant" and "approve the things of God" upon their first entrance, in children this is not required "if the father had embraced the faith." Moreover, what Hooker called the "spiritual efficacy" of baptism proceeds not from children "immediately" or inherently, but "as they are used by the Holy Ghost." "We find the good Spirit of God going along with this ordinance to see it done," he said. " 'That is circumcision that is of the heart' [Rom. 2:29]. So the Spirit of God must make good God's engagement, so as the heart cannot get away from goodness."[8]

To this extent the "main worker" in baptism is the Spirit. And while its spiritual efficacy has "no saving quality," yet it "establisheth the heart," so that "we work by ourselves and by the help of the Spirit." Baptism is a "seal of our first entrance" by which we have a "gracious principle" put into us. Infants are "capable" in that they have a "portion and provision of grace." As external covenanters in "federal holiness," they have a "relative holiness" which is not "any inherent grace" and may "fall away." But if they should be required to give an experiential account of conversion, they must be judged "according to rational charity"; for one man cannot know the heart of another or "discover it really."[9]

If any "black Moors," people of "other nations," or "men out of the East Indies" will submit to the covenant, they must be baptized. The promises are theirs as well. But those who have been "consecrated to God" from birth have an "inward right to glory." They have received "more helps from the Almighty" than those who have not been God's children and so must "return more." Like the ancient Hebrews, their circumcision, or baptism, implies that they have sworn to be "His people." Until effectual conversion they are like the "stubborn and rebellious" against God "whom the Lord complains of, Isaiah 1:2." ("Hear,

8. Hooker, *The Covenant of Grace Opened* (London, 1649), pp. 36, 11, 13, 15.
9. Ibid., pp. 15–24, 41–44.

O heavens, and hearken, O earth: for the Lord hath said, I have nourished and brought up children, and they have rebelled against me.") Therefore, it is possible to enter the inward covenant only by "coming in and acknowledging your debt," and by "craving pardon, though you cannot pay." "When you are gotten home," Hooker told his congregation, "call to mind . . . this covenant which you have entered into with the Lord, and say, O Lord that I had such an heart; good words are well, but O a heart, a heart Lord is that which thou requireth, and I would have."[10]

The baptized, then, have a heavy obligation to acknowledge the covenant by virtue of their external relationship. As a community analogous to the circumcised of the Old Testament, they must first acknowledge their sins and then the promise of a "new heart."[11] What is more, the degree to which conversion resembles a forceful seizure or, conversely, a turning toward God, may depend upon their very awareness of this covenant obligation. And Hooker's own conversion provides a vivid illustration of the principle involved.

According to Cotton Mather, Hooker was converted some time between 1611 and 1618, when he was catechist and lecturer at Emmanuel. At first "It pleased the Spirit of God very powerfully to break into the soul of this person with such a sense of his being exposed unto the just wrath of Heaven, as filled him with most unusual degrees of horror and anguish, which broke not only his rest, but his heart also, and caused him to cry out, 'While I suffer thy terrors, O Lord, I am distracted!' " In the

10. Ibid., pp. 20–23, 30, 41; The Faithful Covenanter (London, 1644), pp. 16–19, 33–34, 25.
11. The commentary on Isaiah in the Geneva Bible indicates how far the prophetic tradition had influenced Puritan thought by 1595. The Prophets "expounded to the covenant of grace and reconciliation," runs the commentary; and they "applied the promises particularly for the comfort of the Church and the members thereof." In this "Isaiah did excell all the prophets," applying the doctrine "as he saw that the disease of the people required."

"time of his agonies," Mather goes on, "he could reason himself to the rule, and conclude that there was no way but submission to God." Yet "when he came to apply this rule unto
himself in his own condition, his reasoning would fail him, he
was able to do nothing." Tormented by the "Spirit of bondage"
to no avail, he began to consider his "interest in the new
covenant." It became his manner, "at his lying down for sleep,"
to "single out some certain promise of God, which he would
repeat and ponder, and keep his heart close unto it." And afterwards he counseled others "to take the same course," telling
them that "the promise was the boat which was to carry a
perishing sinner over unto the Lord Jesus Christ."[12]

In Mather's account the agonies of divine constraint are
clearly moderated by the covenant promises, for "horror and
anguish" cease with open acknowledgment of the "promise of
God." Hooker, to be sure, was violently constrained by the Law:
but his willingness to enter the covenant voluntarily was also
of the utmost importance. Therefore, he did not uphold the
initial violence of his own conversion as normative. Like
Hildersam, he allowed for an alternative to seizure. The
promises of "largest extent" in Scripture, said Hooker, belong
to those who "take up their own hearts." If a man be a "scandalous liver," God "lays a heavy blow upon the heart . . . as He
broke Paul's heart." But the Word "saith not" that it must be
done in an "extraordinary and fearful manner."[13]

Paul was not willing to take up his own heart, for that
was mad against the Lord. . . . If a man have been an out-

12. Mather, 1, III, 333–34. While much that Mather says in the Magnalia
may be attributed to his own imagination, we may assume that this account
is fairly accurate. Although written fifty years after Hooker's death, Mather
cites for sources "The Life of Mr. Angier, lately published" and "some
observations of that Reverend and excellent man, Mr. Whitfield," who had
known Hooker.

13. The Souls Preparation for Christ (London, 1632), pp. 172–80. See
above, pp. 58–59, for Hildersam's views on this point.

rageous, rebellious wretch, alas it is not a little matter
will do the deed, it is not now and then a gracious promise
that will break his heart; but the Lord must come down
from heaven and break open the door by strong hands, by
awakening his conscience, that all the country rings of
him.[14]

Lydia was a "sinful woman," Hooker observes, but because
she looked to the promises, God "opened her eyes and melted
her heart kindly" and brought her to a "taste of His goodness
here and glory hereafter." Therefore, "Lay your hands upon
your hearts" and say, "Good Lord, this is my portion, the
Lord knows I have confessed my sins." Except a man be utterly
broken, as was Paul, legal terror brings only "a little hellish
sorrow." Man is not "cut off altogether" but "only unjointed"
and so may return to his old corruptions again. Let it never be
said of you, Hooker warns, as it was said of them in Hosea:
"They have not cried unto me with their hearts" (7:14). When
God stirs, "do you stir your hearts too . . . get up thy hearts higher in the very apprehension of sin. . . . Begin you where the Holy
Spirit begins that you may find his presence with you, and his
effectual power and blessing to accompany your endeavors in
that way"; for where there is "little saving sorrow," there is
"little saving grace"; where there is "no preparation for Christ,"
there can be "no true evidence of grace."[15]

Thus Hooker conceives of preparation in terms of man's
willingness to stir up himself with the "assistance of the Spirit."
As a baptized creature of God, "something on man's part must

14. *The Unbelievers Preparing for Christ* (London, 1638), II, p. 70; *The
Souls Preparation*, pp. 180–81.

15. *The Souls Preparation*, pp. 180, 190–98, 202–03; *The Application of
Redemption*, p. 114. Heinrich Heppe, in discussing man's response to the
Holy Spirit, says that the Spirit "so works upon a man as to esteem him
a personal creature and so does not regard him as a clod or a stone, but
acts so that . . . man receives in conversion the will to convert to God and
so his conversion takes the form of spontaneity." Heppe, *Reformed Dogmatics*, ed. Ernst Bizer, trans. G. T. Thomson (London, 1950), p. 521.

be considered," while "something on God's part must be observed." If God through the promise of love and mercy cannot
draw the sinner, only then will He "lay hooks upon him" to
"rend the heart . . . and pluck it to pieces." In short, man's will to
come to God, or "disposition of heart," stands at the center of
preparatory activity.[16]

> A heart in Scripture, besides that which it signifieth nat-
> urally, is applied to the will of man, or to that ability . . .
> whereby he willeth or rejecteth a thing . . . together with
> love, delight, joy, hatred, and grief, which are attendants
> upon this will. . . . So that now a fleshy heart is nothing else
> but a heart lovingly teachable and . . . willing to entertain
> any impression that it shall please the Lord to stamp upon
> it.[17]

The preparatory process itself, however, may be "harsh and
tedious and long." What is more, there can be no certainty of
success. While Hooker is always eager to judge a Christian by
the rules of charity, he is still afraid lest effectual faith seem too
easy. Where Preston had said that anxiety need not go before,
that the promise was made to the "coming" and not to the
"preparation,"[18] Hooker holds to the absolute necessity of
preparatory activity. "Nay, there is no faith can be infused into
the soul before the heart be prepared," he says. "No preparation, no perfection. Never humbled, never exalted." And the
result is that each stage becomes, in fact, a point of elaborate
introspection along the way.[19]

In the first stage, says Hooker, "contrition" loosens a man
from his sin and makes him see "an absolute necessity to be
another man." In the second stage "humiliation" loosens a
man from himself and makes him see "an utter unsufficiency

16. *The Unbelievers*, II, pp. 2, 40.
17. Ibid., I, pp. 127–30.
18. See above, p. 78, for Preston's statement on this issue.
19. *The Souls Humiliation* (London, 1638), p. 145.

in what he hath or doth." Contrition is essentially the work of the Law, by which the soul is brought to "sight of sin" and "sound sorrow." Humiliation is an "emptying" of the soul from "whatsoever it hath that makes it swell." Once both are achieved, they bring "contentedness of heart," so that man is willing to be at God's "disposing." But neither can be attained without strenuous self-examination.[20]

In the stage of contrition we must examine our "resistance and opposition against God" and see it as "the greatest evil of all others." This clear and "convicting" sight of sin severs and "unlocks the heart" from its "noisome corruptions." To achieve contrition we must enter a period of prolonged meditation. We must look back to the "lineage and pedigree of our lusts" and track the "abominations of our lives," step by step, until we come to "the very nest where they were hatched and bred." Such meditation "pries into every particular" and "keeps the conscience under an arrest," so that we cannot escape the "evidence and authority of truth." And here, it could be said, man's sense of sin takes precedence over his hope for salvation. But "desperate discouragements," Hooker insists, should be avoided at all costs. No matter how overwhelming our sins, we can rise above them by "grappling with the heart." If we remember that the contrite heart (while helpless against God's truth) can be supreme over its own corruptions, we will not despair. Although the sinner may be "at odds with his own heart," still he can struggle. Moreover, if he truly sorrows for his "departure from God," he may come "nearer to God." While hardhearted sinners are "locked within the iron gate of a hard and stupid heart" and have not "the least preparation or expectation of good," for those who truly sorrow, "Sound contrition and brokenness of heart brings a strange and sudden alteration into the world. . . . Such judge not by outward appearance as it is the guise of men of corrupt minds, but upon

20. *The Application of Redemption*, pp. 15–16; *The Souls Humiliation*, p. 134.

experience, that which they have found and felt in their own hearts." There is a "secret hope," says Hooker, by which the Lord supports "such as be soundly contrite"; so that if preparative contrition never guarantees saving grace, this hope upholds the heart against despair.[21]

In the stage of humiliation Hooker is again concerned with avoiding despair, or "discontentedness." First, he says, we must examine the "measure" of our humiliation; then we must look to our "discouragements." In examining the measure of humiliation, all the "difficulty" of a man's course "lies here"; for no matter how deep this humiliation may be, there remains a "perverse darkness" in the heart which may lead to "desperate distraction." Indeed, Hooker realizes how difficult it is under such conditions to prevent despair. "I confess it is true," he says, "that the heart truly humbled judgeth itself unworthy." But there is a great difference, he insists, between a truly humbled and a discouraged heart. True humiliation leaves the soul "calm" and better able to undergo a "light blow," whereas the discouraged soul is unable to bear "any trouble." It is one thing for a man to be discontented with his corruptions, and another to be discontented with his condition. While his heart may be "frothy" and "frantic," despair will only put him "farthest off" from the "beginning of grace."[22]

Seen in this light, the preparatory process is meant to guard against undue laxity or easy optimism. Yet if the process itself is long and tedious, it must nevertheless be centered on mercy or the promise of divine love. "We speak not in wrath and anger, as you imagine," says Hooker, "but in mercy." Without preparation man keeps off the "light of God's love in Christ." With preparation there is never any "want of love" on "His part." Thus the Spirit of bondage in preparation fits the soul for the Spirit of love in vocation. We must prepare not out of

21. *The Application of Redemption,* pp. 102, 111, 215–16, 265, 406, 401, 411, 413, 432, 557, 596.
22. *The Souls Humiliation,* pp. 170–95.

fear but in anticipation of divine love. If the Spirit constrains us, it also "lets in some intimation of God's love into the soul . . . and conveys some relish of the love of God into the heart." And when the soul has "tasted" how good the Lord is "in any measure," it "covets union." This taste is the "ground" of love which "stirreth up hope" and "quickens up desire." Divine love, having settled upon the heart, "breeds a love to God again"; for "the greatness of the freeness of this mercy of God, being settled upon the heart, enflames it. This sweetness warms the heart, this freeness kindles the fire; and when the greatness of the freeness comes to be valued, this sets the heart all upon a fire."[23]

Here, as in Sibbes, man's sensory response to the "sweetness" of the Spirit fits him to receive God's love.[24] Moreover, in Hooker's thought this sense of taste makes way "for the promise to come and meet with the soul." The passage itself, as an example of Puritan poetics, is eminently distinguished. Few writers of the spiritual brotherhood, other than Sibbes, ever achieved such strength of imagery or intensity of feeling. Like Sibbes, Hooker is not primarily concerned with metaphors denoting coercion but with that which "warms the heart" and "kindles the fire." Like Sibbes, he stresses the spark of love, or our need to "value" grace before effectual conversion. But where Sibbes exhorted to natural love as well, Hooker insists that "God cares not for this." What love man has for God is but a reflection of God's love for him. We must have "spiritual love" to welcome a "spiritual father"; and this we have through the "spiritual efficacy" of baptism.[25]

The baptized may have only a "glimpse of hope," but it is sufficient. What is more, they may appeal to their minister to

23. Ibid., pp. 205, 216, 213; *The Souls Implantation* (London, 1637), pp. 162, 171, 203, 172, 175, 178.
24. See above, p. 72, for Sibbes on "taste."
25. *The Souls Implantation*, pp. 233, 253; *The Souls Vocation or Effectual Calling* (London, 1638), pp. 238–39.

"cover" and "maintain" it. Through the preaching of the Word
the minister may "bring on" and encourage doubters to a
"sensible experience" of Christ. A "powerful ministry," says
Hooker, is the only "ordinary means" God has appointed to
the work of preparation. As John the Baptist came "to make
ready a people prepared for the Lord" (Luke 1:17), so the
minister must "set fire on the hearts of men to melt their souls."
Through a "spiritual heat" in his own heart he must "speak
home to the hearts of the people." If he speaks from the "head
only," he speaks to the "ear only"; but if he comes "for hearts,"
he will "have hearts" before he goes.[26]

In spite of rigorous and demanding introspection, there can
be little doubt that Hooker was essentially concerned with
hopeful anticipation. In actual practice, if a man could give
"a reason of his hope towards God," said Hooker, "this casts
the cause, with judicious charity, to hope and believe there is
something of God and grace in the soul," making it "fit for
Church society." While at Hartford, Hooker maintained that
this hope, together with the "causal power" of baptism, "doth
make a member of the visible Church." Moreover, when baptized covenanters applied for full membership, he asked only
those who were "willing to do it" to relate "the manner of
their conversion to God." Usually such candidates merely
"answered unto certain probatory questions which were tendered them"; and then "they were admitted to church communion."[27] Indeed, if the founder of Connecticut had left
Massachusetts partly because he thought church admissions
too "strict," we may assume that candidates in the Bay were
not being judged with such "judicious charity."

Still, the preparatory phase was by far the most important
single activity in Hooker's conception of conversion. Rarely
did he preach to his covenant community without exhorting

26. *The Souls Implantation*, pp. 38, 58–75.
27. *A Survey of the Sum of Church Discipline* (London, 1648), III, I,
p. 5; I, VI, p. 61; Mather, *1*, III, 349.

the unconverted to prepare for grace. Seldom did he turn to
the regenerative process without initial concern for the "heart
prepared." Hooker, it is safe to say, wrote more on preparation
than any other pastor in New England. What is more, he applied himself to the needs of the unregenerate with extraordinary vigor. In one sense, he relied upon a common expectation
of grace to hold the community together. In another, he de-
liberately fostered an attitude of doubt so that no man could
claim to be regenerate without close self-examination. Yet
when all was said and done, he did not demand that candidates
recount the preparatory phase for admission to his church. He
refused, in other words, to search into "the heart of another"
which "no man can know." And this respect for the sanctity
of the human heart allowed him to judge with charity. He
insisted, to be sure, that all in "federal holiness" prepare for
salvation; but by the time they came forth with a "hope towards God," he assumed the work had been done.

✠

Thomas Shepard, on the other hand, not only enforced strict
admissions but exhorted to preparation in order to safeguard
the purity of gathered churches. In March 1636, two months
before Hooker left Newtown, Shepard was asked to help organize a second church at Dorchester, the first having gone to
Connecticut. But when pastor Richard Mather presented his
candidates, they were refused as "not meet, at present, to be
the foundation of a church." Several weeks later Shepard wrote
to Mather: "O let not a little waiting be sad or grievous to you,
while your people are preparing themselves. . . . This might
make them more humble, and make them search themselves
more narrowly, and make them cast away all their blurred
evidences . . . to satisfy the consciences of other men." And
Mather wrote back: "They pressed me into it . . . till I was
ashamed to deny any longer . . . because there would be, said
they, no church at all in this place, and so a tribe, as it were,

should perish out of Israel. . . . In this, sir, you lay your finger
upon our sore directly; neither can we here put in any other
plea but guilty. The good Lord pardon, saith Hezekiah, every
one that prepareth his heart to seek God."[28]

Nehemiah Adams, the nineteenth-century editor of Shepard's
Autobiography, tells us that Shepard disdained the "indiscrim-
inating judgment of charity" as a "mistaken and ruinous
principle"; for "if those individuals to whose admission he
demurred were really Christians, their rejection could not prej-
udice their final acceptance by Christ." According to Adams,
Shepard "chose to err, if at all, on the side of the general good
rather than of individual feeling."[29] In fact, six months after
the first attempt the Dorchester church was actually gathered,
and Mather continued as pastor until he died in 1669. But
whether the "general good" had really been advanced at the
expense of "individual feeling" was a question still to be debated. And when the time came, the conscience of the country
would have to decide.

Shepard was born the son of a grocer at Towcester, Northamptonshire, November 5, 1604. Orphaned at the age of ten,
he was adopted by his older brother John, educated by a local
schoolmaster, and "conceived to be ripe for the University"
at fifteen. In 1619 he was admitted to Emmanuel as a pen-
sioner, where he took the B.A. in 1623 and the M.A. in 1627.
Six months before proceeding to the M.A. he went to live with
Thomas Weld (later minister at Roxbury, Massachusetts) in
the parish at Tarling, Essex. Here he enjoyed the "blessings of
. . . Mr. Hooker's ministry" at nearby Chelmsford, and Hooker
began to play a part in his life. When Weld suggested that
Shepard take a lectureship at Cogshall, Hooker thought him
"young and unexperienced"; whereupon Shepard went to
Earles-Colne, where he preached until suspended by Laud in
1630.

28. Albro, *Life of Thomas Shepard*, pp. 213–22.
29. Shepard, *Autobiography* (Boston, 1832), pp. 127–28.

By 1632 he was chaplain at the Yorkshire manor house of Sir Richard Darley, whose kinswoman Margaret Tauteville he married the same year. But when Laud alerted the Bishop of York, Shepard was forced to go to Heddon, Northumberland, where in 1633 he lived "privately in Mr. Fenwick's house." And there he stayed until Hooker and Cotton had gone to America. "I saw the Lord departed from England," wrote Shepard, "when Mr. Hooker and Mr. Cotton were gone . . . and I did think I should feel many miseries if I stayed behind."

In October 1634 he sailed with his wife and child from Harwich, a port in Essex, accompanied by John Norton (later teacher at Ipswich and Boston). But a storm drove them back upon the sands, and the child died of a "sickness." Through the winter of 1634–35 he lived at Bastwick, Norfolk, where he wrote *Certain Select Cases Resolved*, first published in 1648. His second son, named Thomas after the first, was born in April; but Shepard withheld baptism until a church could be gathered in New England. In August 1635 he again embarked with his family, this time on the ship *Defence*, and "after many sad storms and wearisome days and many longings to see the shore, the Lord brought us to the sight of it upon Oct. 2, Anno 1635."[30]

By October 5th Shepard had taken his followers to Newtown, where Hooker's group was "willing to sell," and where his own brethren "did desire to sit still" and "not to remove farther." In February 1636 he organized the first permanent church, where his son was finally baptized and his wife taken in, two weeks before her death. But when the church had been gathered only a short time, Antinomianism "exercised" the whole country; and so he began *The Parable of the Ten Virgins* in order to refute the heresy. In August 1637 he organized the Hutchinsonian Synod; and in 1638 he took part in Mrs. Hutchinson's church trial. Meanwhile, partly because he had preserved his own congregation from antinomian opinions, New-

30. Ibid., pp. 17–43, 46–58.

town was chosen in 1636 as the site of Harvard College; and
Shepard, one of the founders, set about raising funds for
scholarships.

But as time went by his loyalty to the colony waned. In 1640,
three years after his marriage to Joanna Hooker, he thought
of moving to Matabeseck (later Middletown) on the Connecticut River. His father-in-law advised him by letter, "if you can
sell, you should remove"; for by now the Bay was in financial
straits, and Shepard was deeply in debt. What is more, he was
depressed by "the sad state of the Church." He saw "all men's
souls and estates out of order," and "many evils in men's hearts."
His own heart, he said, began to "withdraw itself" from "his
brethren and others." Yet he stayed on, and in 1644 he wrote
A Defense of the Answer, in which he defended the New England Way against charges from abroad.

Shepard's *Defense,* along with Hooker's *Survey of Church
Discipline,* paved the way for the Cambridge Platform of 1648,
in which the Congregational position was fully defined for the
Commonwealth. But by the time the Platform had been drafted,
his career was rapidly drawing to a close. Joanna had died in
childbirth in 1646, and in 1647 he had remarried for the last
time. During the summer of 1649 he came down with a fever,
and on August 25th he died at the age of forty-five.[31]

✠

In turning to Shepard's thought, we must remember that
he was a man of considerable stature. In Massachusetts, at
least, he left a mark on the orthodox mind that should not be

31. Albro, pp. 224–95. In 1636 a group of Puritan ministers in England,
having been told that the New England churches had developed a new
discipline, addressed "Nine Questions" to the New England ministers.
These questions were sent back with an *Answer,* which in turn was answered
by John Ball, a minister of Staffordshire. Ball's *A Trial of the New Church
Way* (1644) was sufficiently critical to evoke Shepard's *A Defense of the
Answer made unto the Nine Questions,* which Shepard hoped would satisfy
the English brethren.

underestimated. Although his life was cut short, he survived to see the Commonwealth fall closely in line with many of his most cherished views. If at times he was discouraged by "the sad state of the Church," he held a firm grip on discipline and policy. Moreover, on the subject of preparation he expressed an attitude of mind that can only be described as one of high complexity. More than any other preparationist, either in England or in America, he was caught in the dilemma of covenant theology: that God alone can bend the heart to grace; and that man must enter the covenant of his own free will. As a figure of immeasurable influence, he deserves our closest scrutiny.

To get at the root of his thought, we must begin, as in Hooker, with baptism; for here we are faced with significant differences. Unlike Hooker, Shepard never suggested that the baptized are "capable." Nor did he speak of the "spiritual efficacy" of baptism. Rather, his emphasis fell on what he called baptismal "privilege." Baptized covenanters, he said, should be given an "outward dispensation" only. They enter "federal holiness" through God's promise to "work faith"; but baptism itself is no more than a "special help" to turn them toward God. "When they see how God calls them to return," said Shepard, their baptismal bond acts as a "high privilege" and "great favor" to draw them and works "to encourage their hearts to return again." But they have no "gracious principle" put into them, no "inward right to glory." The baptized, he maintained, are "the children of the promise and covenant"; but they "be not children . . . by effectual . . . communication."[32]

"After we came to New England shore," he once wrote to his son, "God gave thee the ordinance of baptism . . . and this is a most high and happy privilege." But "torments" and "anguish," he insisted, must first "affect Reprobates" (meaning baptized covenanters) before the seeds of grace are planted. What is

32. *The Church Membership of Children and their right to Baptism* (London, 1662), pp. 2–35.

more, the first signs of grace are no indication that the new life
has begun: "Do not judge of general and common workings of
the Spirit . . . to be the beginnings of effectual conversion."[33]
And this meant, in effect, that the baptized could not be judged
by the rules of charity until further evidence of grace had been
discerned. As we have seen, William Perkins held that man must
be terrified by the Law before the Spirit plants the first seed
of grace. But once man had the seed he was "even at that
instant the very child of God."[34] For Shepard, however, there
could be little evidence of faith even after a violent shaking by
the Law; and we have only to look at his own conversion to
find the experiential origins of his thought.

During his first year at Emmanuel, Shepard tells us, "I heard
old Doctor Chaderton, the master of the College when I came.
. . . My heart was much affected, but I did break loose from
the Lord again." Then, in 1622, "the Lord . . . sent Doctor
Preston to be master of the College, and . . . I began to listen to
what he said." According to Shepard's account, Preston preached
his first sermon on "the change of heart in a Christian," from
Romans 12:2, "be ye transformed"; and the young student
thought him "the most searching preacher in the world." After
taking the B.A., Shepard began "daily meditations, sometimes
every morning, but constantly every evening before supper,"
on the "evil of sin," the "terror of God's wrath," and the "deceit-
fulness of the heart." But conversion seemed unattainable, and
in time he began to question whether "that glorious estate
of perfection might not be the truth," and whether "old
Mr. Rogers' Treatises . . . the book which did first work upon
my heart," might not be "Legal."[35]

Rogers, in his *Seven Treatises,* had clearly emphasized the
use of the Law as the "First Work" of the Spirit.[36] From initial

33. *Autobiography,* p. 11; *The Sound Believer* (London, 1645), pp. 56, 91.
34. See above, p. 63.
35. *Autobiography,* pp. 17–24.
36. See above, p. 52.

constraint, however meager, man moved toward perfection in Christ. But Shepard, unable to progress from "terror" of conscience to the slightest evidence of faith, now rejected the work of the Law as "Legal." In desperation he looked for "that glorious estate of perfection," or direct and immediate salvation by the Spirit alone, as an easier path to "assurance." And this, ironically enough, was the antinomian heresy he would one day denounce.

Curiously enough, the new master of Emmanuel had unknowingly set him off, this time in a sermon from I Corinthians 1:30, "Christ . . . is made unto us wisdom and righteousness and sanctification and redemption." When Preston had opened "how all the good I had, all the redemption I had, it was from Jesus Christ," said Shepard, "I found therefore the Lord revealing free mercy," and so began to question: "Why did the Lord Jesus keep the Law? He had no guile in his heart . . . but holiness there. Was it not for them that did want it?" But these doubts about the Law did not last long, for shortly thereafter "the terrors of the Lord began to break in like floods of fire." In a fit of torment, he was tempted to run his head "against walls," to "brain and kill" himself. He saw God "like a consuming fire, an everlasting burning," and thoughts of "eternal reprobation" flashed across his mind. After this his heart became "humbled and cast down," the terrors of the Law began to "assuage sweetly," and he felt that God had given him "a heart to receive Christ with a naked hand."[37]

Shepard's conversion, like Hooker's, was long and painful. But where Hooker, in his own conversion, had emphasized personal acknowledgment of the promises as an alternative to excessive constraint, Shepard put the efficacy of the Law at the center of his experience. In fact, once he had corrected his antinomian "error," he ended with far greater emphasis on legal constraint than "old Mr. Rogers" ever allowed. This is

37. *Autobiography*, pp. 24–28.

not to say, however, that a man could be saved by the Law
alone. No Reformed theologian would hold to that. What needs
to be pointed out is that Shepard, more than Hooker, held to
the efficacy of legal constraint. Hooker, to be sure, was greatly
concerned with the use of the Law, but he tended, like Sibbes,
to be more concerned with the drawing activities of the Spirit.
Moreover, baptized covenanters, for Hooker, had the seeds of
grace prior to the working of the Law, which was not true for
Shepard.

With Shepard's low conception of baptism in mind, together
with his commitment to legal constraint, we may now explore
his theory of preparation. Here we must determine whether or
not the qualifications prescribed "conceal" the promises, as
John Bickerton Williams claimed, or whether in a larger sense
acknowledgment of the promises prevails. Here, within the
complex structure of Shepard's thought, we must discover
whether the restrictive or expansive attitude of mind gained
ascendancy, and what the consequences were for the early history of New England.

What Hooker called "contrition," Shepard broke down into
"conviction of sin" and "compunction for sin," which are
followed by "humiliation." In conviction the Law jolts a man
into an awareness of his sins, although his heart may remain
unaffected with "true remorsefulness"; for a man may have
"sight of sin" without any "sorrow" and "sense" of it. In compunction the "affections and will" are aroused in such a way
that the heart is made to "stir toward Christ" and does not
"remain hard." These stages then bring on humiliation, in
which the sinner is cut off from all self-confidence. "Lie down
under Him," said Shepard, that God may "tread upon thee"
and "exalt Himself" as well as "lift thee up and exalt thee."[38]

Unlike Hooker, Shepard does not elaborately describe each

38. *The Sound Believer*, pp. 4–48, 129, 147.

stage. Nor does he give extensive instructions for self-examination. Yet the procedural difficulties are formidable in another way. Where Hooker maintained that "sound contrition" should derive from the "experience" which men have "found and felt in their own hearts," Shepard insisted that the "rules" of preparation come first. "Crook not God's rules to the experience of men," he said, "but bring men unto rules, and try men's estates by that. . . . We are not in this or any other point to be guided by the experience of men only." We must "attend the rule," let the rule stand, and let men "stand or fall according to the rule." Many are "miserably deceived," he insisted, by "crooking and wresting God's rule to Christian experience." What is more, they deceive themselves by following scriptural examples. "Do not make the examples of converted persons in Scripture patterns in all things of persons unconverted. Do not make God's work upon the one run parallel with God's work upon another. . . . To say that God opened Lydia's heart to believe in Christ, and yet opened not her heart to lament her sin and misery in her estate . . . is more than can be proved from the text."[39]

In earlier Puritanism, as we have seen, the stages were essentially guideposts for the individual conscience, while biblical prescription was invoked to support felt experience. For Shepard, however, it would appear that man must be limited in his range of preconversion experience, with preparatory "rules" imposed "to satisfy the conscience of other men." And on this account we may well conclude that he has erected a genuine barrier to grace. But we must also remember that Shepard, both in England and America, was haunted by the specter of antinomianism. When Christian experience was allowed a free rein leading to direct revelation by the Spirit (so that some may say God "melted their hearts" and that

39. Ibid., pp. 52–54.

"experience proves this"), it then became necessary to reassert the Word, to preach the Law, and to "bring the heart to acknowledge freely that it deserves death."[40]

On the other hand, Shepard was fully aware that every man is not a Heman who suffers "distracting fears and terrors." ("While I suffer thy terrors I am distracted" Psalm 88:15.) Like Hooker, he allowed that some men are educated "more civilly" than others and so have contracted less "guilt" and "stoutness of heart." No matter what he had to say about the virtues of "rules" and the evils of "experience," he was ultimately concerned with those who must acknowledge their covenant obligations. And the baptized, although farther removed from grace in Shepard's eyes than in Hooker's, are still the children of the promises. Moreover, the promises themselves are sufficiently important for Shepard so that he extends them not only to the baptized but to those who are "out of covenant indeed" yet "making towards it."[41] Like Hooker, he takes into consideration those who may be ripe for the Church without having been reared in it. But unlike Hooker, he cannot reconcile personal acknowledgment of the covenant with divine constraint. Having emphasized terrors and the working of the Law to an extreme, he is hard put to fit them into the covenant relationship; and he ends, as we shall see, with a duality of experience reminiscent of Greenham.[42]

In fact, if he dismisses experientialism and biblical prescription where they overshadow the Law, as a covenant theologian he is more than anxious to retain them. On reading Hosea 14:4, "I will heal their rebellion, I will love them freely, for mine anger is turned away," Shepard wrote: "Because of His promise . . . I considered when I could not bring Christ's will to mine, I was to bring mine to His." If there be "any hope" for the

40. *Certain Select Cases Resolved* (London, 1648), p. 53.
41. Ibid., p. 99.
42. See above, pp. 50–51, for a summary of Greenham's inability to reconcile acknowledgment with constraint.

unconverted, he thought, the Lord "pitieth," for it may be "they will return." And this, he confessed, "made me . . . to pour out my heart in true and plain confession of my vileness . . . with groans for grace. . . . I gave up myself to the Lord thus: I acknowledged all I had, or was, was His own. . . . I saw that the Lord desired and commanded me to give Him my heart. . . . O, the command which saith yet return and seek and come is exceedingly sweet love. . . . I saw this was not only by a command, though firstly, but nextly by His promise. . . . Return, and I'll return to you! [2 Chr. 30.]"[43]

Thus Shepard concludes that baptized covenanters must take "special notice" of God's "readiness and willingness" to receive them. Through sense experience they must "feel the evil" of their "hard hearts" and through biblical knowledge of the covenant "come out of their bondage"; for a people who might have "everlasting mercy" and still will not "submit to the Lord" have broken the "everlasting covenant."[44]

Within the covenant framework, then, man's desire for faith, which is the condition of the covenant, has greater significance than constraint by Law. And here Shepard draws a clear distinction between the "absolute" and "conditional" promises. Since God has undertaken to fulfill the covenant "absolutely," He does not actually depend upon us to fulfill the "condition." But our very knowledge that God will do this for us makes us desire faith. "The absolute promise," says Shepard, "works hope of relief from Christ"; and as it works hope, so it works a "coming to Christ by desire." Were it not for the absolute promise, "no soul would desire," as there would be "no hope to be saved." Therefore, if the baptized covenanter can find "the condition or qualification within himself," he may conclude that the absolute promise is "his own"; for he is then

43. *Meditations and Spiritual Experiences* (London, 1749), pp. 25–28, 30–31, 37.

44. *The Sincere Convert* (London, 1646), p. 230; *Subjection to Christ* (London, 1657), pp. 9–10, 33.

"midway" between the "eternal purpose" and the "decree of love."[45]

To "seek for the good" of the absolute promise, he must first acknowledge his sins, or be "contented gladly" to have "God his God." The sick man, "being utterly unable to cure, or to know how to cure himself," must say to his physician: "I am content you should begin and perfect the cure." Indeed, if the feverish patient is able to understand what is promised, he will stir himself up to say, "Lord, give of that water to drink." The sick in soul, no matter how despondent, must always look to the "fullness" of the promise, as the promise itself will "draw his heart" to long for it. He must, in effect, overcome his "secret unwillingness" to seek help, as in no other way can he prepare himself for conversion. "Make it sure on your part," says Shepard, "else how can you be in readiness to meet the Lord Jesus." The baptized children of God, desiring from a "son-like disposition," must find "a need of the Lord to draw them"; for none shall have Christ "hereafter" but those who are "prepared here." "If unready now, you will be more unready the next day . . . you will be more unfit the longer you delay . . . thy heart will be harder every day than other. . . . Hath the Lord come to thee in the Temple, and manifested His love by His own promise . . . and wilt thou not yet own Him? . . . Oh therefore know the worst of your own heart now . . . thou shalt see the gate shut upon thee hereafter."[46]

From this we may conclude that in spite of qualifications prescribed and "rules laid down," the "great and precious promises" are not, in the end, concealed. Yet at the same time it is hard for Shepard to reconcile his demand that man respond voluntarily to the promises with his equally firm insistence on divine constraint and preparatory rules. Richard Greenham, of course, had long since discovered the need for "voluntary sub-

45. *Certain Select Cases,* pp. 39–103.
46. Ibid., pp. 103–24; *The Parable of the Ten Virgins* (London, 1660), pp. 45, 76, 148, 152, 162.

mission" to the covenant as opposed to "violent subjection" by the Law; but he had made no attempt, theologically, to account for the voluntary motions required. Richard Rogers, in turn, had tried to provide for these motions by treating man's inner responses to the preliminary workings of the Spirit. He had retained the efficacy of legal constraint but had argued as well that man could be said to submit voluntarily upon the slightest "prick" of the Law.[47] And this formula, to a large extent, was followed by Hooker. But Shepard, in reaction to his own antinomianism, felt compelled to reassert the preeminence of the Law. Although he had once thought Rogers "legal" for retaining a minimal concern with constraint, he now exalted this constraint; and the result was that he found himself in a predicament similar to Greenham's. Indeed, when he coupled his renewed commitment to the efficacy of the Law with an equally strong commitment to voluntary acceptance of the covenant, he was left with two opposing theories of preparatory activity —one stemming from Calvin's concern with fearful constraint, and the other from Bullinger's concern with personal acknowledgment of divine love—and all he could do, under the circumstances, was occasionally to strike an awkward compromise. "Though Christ doth threaten, or terrify His people sometimes," wrote Shepard, "let a man accept the offer of Christ, not violently only by terror, but by stronger cords, even the cords of love."[48]

When he preached preparation to safeguard the purity of churches, he emphasized, to be sure, the difficulties of the process: he insisted upon legal constraint and upon the need to follow prescribed rules.[49] But in circumstances other than those surrounding the Dorchester gathering, his attitude may have been entirely different. The criticism of John Bickerton Williams, that the "rules laid down" concealed "great and

47. See above, pp. 52–54.
48. *The Parable of the Ten Virgins,* p. 184.
49. See above, Shepard's letter to Richard Mather, p. 101.

precious promises," applies, as we have seen, to only one side of Shepard's thought.[50] Moreover, it applies with even less validity to Hooker, who seldom exalted rules and always upheld the promises. Shepard, then, must have at times felt free to abandon his loyalty to rules and to call for spontaneous response. Only rarely, it would seem, could he have sustained such a strained compromise between the threats of Christ and the "cords of love." In fact, both Shepard and Hooker, as we shall see, could be accused of lowering the standards of grace as well as of raising them.

✠

Finally, with Peter Bulkeley, covenant theology came to its full flowering in early New England, with the result that the "heart prepared" was at last set free from the confines of divine constraint. Bulkeley, although three years older than Hooker and twenty-one years older than Shepard, must be considered last for this reason. More than either one, whom he outlived by some ten years, he preached the covenant. In his attitude toward conversion the conditional promises set the tone for the entire range of preparatory activity, so that the heart had only to acknowledge them to cement the bond. Bulkeley, it might be said, was a covenant theologian in the purest sense of the term.

These views he vividly put down in his only book, *The Gospel Covenant,* a collection of sermons delivered at Concord in the first ten years of settlement. The first edition, published in 1646, contained a preface by Thomas Shepard. The second edition, expanded and first published in 1653, retained the preface, although it postdates Shepard's death by several years. Both editions, as documents in themselves, are a monument to New England theology. In the words of Cotton Mather, they are to be "reckoned among the first born of New England"; for

50. See above, p. 88, for Williams' original statement.

Bulkeley addressed himself, first and foremost, to the American experience. "New England," he cried, "the Lord looks for more from thee than from other people; more zeal for God, more love to His truth . . . Thou shouldst be a special people, an only people, none like thee in all the earth."[51]

Bulkeley came from a branch of an old Cheshire family. His mother, like Hildersam's, was of noble birth, a daughter of the house of Irby in Lincoln. His father, the Reverend Edward Bulkeley, was pastor at Odell in Bedfordshire, where the son was born in 1583. At sixteen he went to St. John's College, Cambridge, where he was chosen fellow as a "junior bachelor" and took the M.A. in 1608. In 1620, on the death of his father, he succeeded to the living of Odell and inherited the family estate. There, under the liberal rule of the Bishop of Lincoln, he remained unmolested for fifteen years. But in 1635 he was at last suspended by Laud.[52]

Having sold the estate, Bulkeley sent his wife and smaller children ahead, to deceive the government spies, and sailed for New England with three of his sons. After a brief stay at Newtown, he took his family and followers west of Boston, where in 1636 he settled the town of Concord and founded the twelfth church in the colony. There he was not only pastor but landlord and guardian of the community as well. He had "many and godly servants," according to Mather, "whom, after they had lived with him a fit number of years, he dismissed with bestowing farms upon them, and so took others after the like manner." Moreover, during these early years he was closely associated with Hooker and Shepard. Along with Hooker he was appointed moderator of the Hutchinsonian Synod in 1637, and he later attended Mrs. Hutchinson's church trial. But unlike Shepard, whom he frequently questioned "concerning the Church's power in matters of discipline," he was thoroughly

51. Mather, *1*, III, 402; Bulkeley, *The Gospel Covenant, or the Covenant of Grace opened* (London, 1646), pp. 14–15.
52. Gordon Goodwin, *Dictionary of National Biography, 3*, 235–36.

liberal in his views on church membership. Indeed, shortly after
the Concord church had been founded, he disagreed with the
"will of the ruling elder" on a matter of "charity," and the result
was an "unhappy discord" which ended with the elder's "ab-
dication."

Above all, his sense of the covenant community and personal devotion to his own Concord, which he named, were
outstanding characteristics of his life and thought. Yet he felt
"shut up" in the small town and more than once begged
Shepard to "write me what you know." While he loved New
England and endowed the Harvard library with "no small part
of his own," he thought of England as "my dear native country
whose womb bare me, whose breath nourished me, and in whose
arms I should desire to die." But when the time came, in March
of 1659, he was still in Concord preaching at the age of seventy-
six.[53]

Shepard, to be sure, admired Bulkeley; but at the same time
he never fully trusted his theology. In fact, Shepard's preface to
The Gospel Covenant could hardly be considered a full endorse-
ment of the author's views, for he was obviously concerned lest
the older man carry covenant concepts too far. God "reveals
His covenant," Shepard assured the reader, only "to them that
fear Him"—a point rarely mentioned in the text. Moreover,
he went out of his way to draw a sharp distinction between
external and internal covenanters, a distinction that cannot be
found in the sermons themselves. He allowed, however, that
"this aged, experienced, and precious servant . . . hath taken
much pains to discover . . . the great mystery of godliness wrapt
up in the covenant, and hath now fully opened many questions
concerning the same, which . . . have not been brought to light
until now." This much he would concede. But the "efficacy of
the covenant," which for Bulkeley was all-important, he thought
it better not to mention.

53. Mather, *1*, III, 400–02; Albro, pp. 231–32; *The Gospel Covenant*, p. 13.

The "efficacy of the covenant," said Bulkeley, shall never be "disanulled" but shall "go on to you and your children forever." "By your covenant, you have such hold of God, that you may be assured he will be a God not to you only but to a thousand generations after you. . . . Some of your seed shall stand before the Lord, to serve him forever. . . . They may go to God and plead the covenant of their fathers." As in the time of Abraham, "the oil that is poured out upon the head will run down to the rest of the members." All "spiritual salvation" is communicated by the covenant, through which the baptized have saving grace. "We have made a covenant with Him in our baptism," Bulkeley maintained, and on this ground we may "plead the promise of His grace." We are "sons by faith," and being sons, we are "also heirs." From God we have the "habit of faith" in baptism, and then He requires "acts of faith" by which we lay hold of the promises to "receive the grace offered in the covenant."[54]

In Bulkeley the efficacy of baptism is brought to its highest point; for the "habit of faith," given in the external call, becomes, in fact, "our effectual calling." As such, it allows for "acts of faith," or "that which is required on our part." After the sacrament of baptism has been administered, the Lord "withdraws Himself." Then, if we wish to be taken into the inner covenant, we must "seek after Him." "For though the Lord hath withdrawn Himself, yet He hath left such a touch of His Spirit upon the heart as makes the soul affectionate towards Him, so as now it cannot rest, but feeling its own woe, being without God and without covenant, and having heard of the Lord's willingness to enter into a covenant . . . it now begins to seek after the Lord." In short, the baptized, while not effectually converted, are effectually called through baptismal grace. They must acknowledge the covenant through baptismal faith, which is the beginning of the "new creation."

54. *The Gospel Covenant*, pp. 13, 21–22, 26, 44, 46, 296–99.

Bulkeley assumes that the heart in preparation is a part of the "new creature"; and upon this assumption the "judgment of charity" is brought to bear.[55]

If the new creation is taken to mean "imputation" only, said Bulkeley, then "Charity wants rules to judge by"; for if Christ is imputed to us without a preparatory "working of faith in us," the new creation "standing only in imputation" makes "only such an invisible creature of which charity cannot judge." In effect, the judgment of charity can be brought to bear only where faith may be gauged in terms of weakness and strength. It cannot be brought to bear where faith is an abstraction, lacking preparatory evidences. "I would then know whether the

55. Ibid., pp. 22, 26, 47, 299–300, 370–71. According to J. G. Davies:

The meaning of baptism may be defined in different but complementary ways, depending upon the particular image of the Church that was consciously or subconsciously influencing the thought of any one writer. Thus if the Church is considered to be the Messianic Community, baptism is the means of initiation into it and is analogous with the rite of circumcision, whereby a proselyte became a member of the Israel of God and an heir to the promises. 'Ye,' wrote Paul to the Colossians, 'were also circumcised with a circumcision not made with hands, in the putting off of the body of the flesh, in the circumcision of Christ; having been buried with him in baptism.' (Col. 2:11, 12) Christians are therefore those who have been 'sealed' (II Cor. 1:22)—'sealed' being a Jewish term for circumcision. . . . If the Church is regarded as the Temple of the divine presence, then baptism is the means of bringing the individual into immediate contact with the Holy Spirit. 'Know ye not that ye are a temple of God, and that the Spirit of God dwelleth in you?' (I Cor. 3:16) Consequently Christians are those who 'were once enlightened and tasted of the heavenly gift, and, were made partakers of the Holy Ghost.' (Heb. 4:4) When the Church is viewed as the Body of Christ, baptism is the means of incorporating the individual into that living organism: 'in one Spirit were we all baptized into one body.' (I Cor. 12:13) As the Bride of Christ, the Church is the mother of believers and so baptism is the means of adopting and regenerating the individual. [Davies, *The Early Christian Church* (London, 1965), pp. 59–60]

Bulkeley, it would appear, held closely to both these views, as he frequently mentions the efficacy of the Spirit in baptism as well the belief that the baptized are heirs to the promises.

act of imputation alone, considered abstractly . . . be this new creation," Bulkeley asked, "or whether . . . we are his workmanship created? . . . This former seemeth not to be the meaning, because . . . Christ is imputed to one without faith, and thereby it comes, that man (though without faith) is counted a new creature. . . . But this is a strange kind of charity, to judge of the tree contrary to the fruit." Therefore, preparatory faith must precede imputation, as there is a "preparation thereto by faith" which gives charity its "rules to judge by."[56]

✠

All men, according to Bulkeley, must "come and seek reconciliation" as did the children of Israel; for "this is that which Hezekiah exhorted to." Though there be an "infinite disparity" between God and man, if man will "seek to Him," He will not "turn His face." "You are not aliens from the covenant or commonwealth of Israel," he told the baptized, "all the good which God hath promised to His Israel belongs to you." Therefore "return unto the Lord," for in the covenant of grace "God looks at the repentance of His people, and accepts of humiliation."[57]

> Arise therefore out of thy sin by repentance. . . . Learn hereby to acknowledge God. . . . This is one reason why the Lord promiseth these things to us in His covenant, that we might learn thereby to acknowledge that they come not unto us by chance . . . but look at them as blessings coming from the Lord Himself. . . . Let us in our heart acknowledge that it is not our own hand, but the Lord which hath given us all.[58]

This is covenant theology in its purest form. Indeed, it need hardly be said that we have come round again to Bullinger.

56. *The Gospel Covenant,* 2d ed. pp. 370–71.
57. *The Gospel Covenant,* pp. 45–46; 2d ed. pp. 389, 76.
58. Ibid., 2d ed. pp. 271–72.

Through the oil poured upon Abraham's head, through baptism as the antetype of circumcision, the seed of the covenant
have the will and ability to turn toward God if only they will
"acknowledge" Him in their hearts. And in no sense, it should
be observed, is there a hint of contractual bargaining.[59] When
you come to make a covenant, said Bulkeley, you must not
"give laws unto God" but "take laws from God." You must
not impose laws upon Him, that "He shall save you so and so,"
but "leave God free to make the conditions of the covenant
after His own mind and will." In fact, "Faith doth not pre-
scribe unto God, it will not presume to appoint the conditions
of the covenant; it only answers and applies itself to God's
offer, taking conditions of peace, but giving none. It doth not
seek to wind about the promise of grace to our own mind and
will. Faith . . . offers nothing to stand in exchange for the mercy
offered; it receives a gift, but giveth no price."[60]

In all of this the "first grace," or the will to turn to God, is
an "absolute promise" that is given "without condition on our
part." Then the promise of eternal salvation is given on the
condition that we manifest our "faith and obedience." First
the Lord disposes us to a "walking in covenant with Him" by
putting into us "His own Spirit." Then He requires "an actual
performance of covenant on our part." First He takes away the
"heart of stone" and then gives us a "Spirit of faith," so that
man in preparation has the "new heart" promised in Ezekiel
36:26. ("A new heart also will I give you, and . . . I will take
away the stony heart . . . and I will give you an heart of flesh.")

For Richard Rogers, the "heart of flesh" came last in a series

---

59. Perry Miller has advanced the theory that the covenant relationship
put man in a bargaining position with God, and that Puritan divines
conceived of preparation as a term to be fulfilled in a contract: if man does
his part God must do His (*The New England Mind*, 2, 55). Bulkeley's views,
however, clearly do not support this theory. For a full discussion of Miller's
thesis, see Epilogue, pp. 219–20.

60. *The Gospel Covenant*, pp. 45, 300–02.

of preparatory stages;[61] and this held true for Shepard as well. But with Bulkeley man begins, in baptism, with the new heart, which he must then bend toward God. He must examine himself in preparation not to discover whether he has faith but to discover whether, by the first grace, he is fulfilling the conditions of the covenant. "Examine thine own heart," said Bulkeley, to see whether it "maintains the breach between God and thee"; for our "way of trial" is by the "conditional promises," and we must examine ourselves "by the graces expressed in them."[62]

The expression of faith as a condition does not, however, exclude the freeness of grace; "nor doth the expressing of freeness of grace exclude the condition." In preparation we know of the "things promised," and this stirs the heart to a "deep and serious consideration" of the "blessed state" to be achieved. Our "high esteem" of grace begets a "longing desire of it." Although weak in faith we "hunger and thirst" for effectual conversion, "as we see in Lydia." In the process itself we have fears, doubts, and discouragements, as our faith is "young and faint." But here we must "sustain the heart" so that it "sink not down in discouragement." If we "acknowledge Him to be our God," we will not despair; for He has "vouchsafed" to make us His people. "Though you can see nothing in yourselves," wrote Bulkeley, "grace is never the further off." The promises themselves are a "ground of encouragement" not only to the baptized but to those who are "afar off," "aliens to God," and "strangers to His covenant."[63]

For Bulkeley, as for Bullinger, preparation is not a pattern of prescribed stages but a state of mind. Desire, acknowledgment, repentance, and humiliation are all spontaneously felt. And all lead toward a moment in time when "fire kindles," the heart "waxeth bold," and man "entertaineth the promise." In

61. See above, p. 53.
62. *The Gospel Covenant*, pp. 285, 44, 290.
63. Ibid., pp. 291, 299, 302, 304; 2d ed. pp. 392, 404.

this the Law may be brought to bear or not, but it is neither an integral nor effectual part of the process. The Law may work an "outward reformation," Bulkeley observes, and by this "work of restraint" the unclean spirit may "seem to be cast out." But such is "far from true." No matter how terrified the conscience may be, the "frame and disposition of the heart" is still "the same as it was before." We must never look for constraint, but "seek after truth of heart," and strive for "that grace which will last and hold out." We must "call" and "cry" for it, "dig deep" and search for it, as this is our covenant obligation. If faith were only an "assurance," says Bulkeley, a knowing that Christ is ours, then "that little faith so often spoken of in Scripture were no faith"; and "those little believers whose faith is but a grain of mustard seed, or like a little spark of fire in smoking flax, should be reported as no believers." But "men of little faith" may be true believers, "wanting assurance," who must prepare themselves for saving grace.[64]

Thus "faith" itself no longer implies a clear "sign" of election, an immediate "assurance" of salvation, as it did for Zwingli, Martyr, and Calvin. Yet the "true believer" may be counted among the elect on the basis of "that little faith so often spoken of in Scripture." He need not have felt the pangs of constraint, however sudden or gradual. Nor need he have known a moment in time when he could say that Christ is his. If his love for God is but a "spark of fire," he must be given the benefit of the doubt. ("Know therefore that the Lord . . . keepeth covenant and mercy with them that love him." Deut. 7:9) The elect, to be sure, are the children of God "even before they believe"; but since no man can know the heart of another, or discover what is known to God alone, those who proclaim themselves "believers" must be numbered amongst the chosen.

✟

64. Ibid., pp. 306, 309, 227, 258; 2d ed. p. 364.

In Hooker, Shepard, and Bulkeley we have followed a line of tension between acknowledgment and constraint, a line on which the image of the "heart prepared" is consistently fixed. Moreover, for all three theologians the part man has to play depends, to a large extent, on his baptismal beginnings. For Hooker the baptized are "capable" and prepare for saving grace through the "spiritual efficacy" of baptism. Although the process is long and tedious, the promises "sustain" the heart, and covenant acknowledgment stands as an alternative to excessive constraint. With Shepard the baptized are "privileged," in that God, through His covenant, has promised to "work faith." But as "reprobates" under the Law, they are subject to rigid constraint and preparatory "rules." The covenant relationship stands, but is not fully realized; for Shepard, as for Calvin, God restrains while He invites, and man's affective response does not significantly alter the divine pattern. Then, for Bulkeley, the "efficacy of the covenant" prevails, and the baptized may achieve salvation through preparatory acknowledgment alone. Where covenant faith is the ground for covenant acknowledgment, constraint can only be superfluous—and preparation for grace but an opening of the heart to God.

Indeed, as Puritan divines relied more and more upon the Old Testament exhortations to return to God's covenant and upon the analogy between external covenanters and Israel, they had necessarily to attribute a high degree of efficacy to the sacrament of baptism; for the purer their covenant notions became, the more "abilities" the "circumcised" required. As they developed a covenant theology with its roots in Hebraic prescription, they had also to allow for the best in Reformed tradition. They had somehow to comply with the Augustinian stand which said that man is genuinely free only insofar as he is imbued with prevenient grace. Augustine had said that man after the Fall is utterly depraved, that Adam's sin has deprived his descendants of free will, and that prevenient grace is necessary for the first turning back; but no similar assumption sur-

rounds the biblical covenant. Therefore, in order to supply
man with the will to return, Puritan divines had somehow to
provide for this grace; and this they did through the efficacy
of baptism.[65]

With these distinctions in mind, we may turn to the issues
of the time and to the criticism preparation evoked. Reformed
theology, as we have seen, was never entirely at ease with the
concept. In New England, from the time of the first settlements
to the period of the Great Awakening, preparation was argued
out and its validity questioned. The extent to which it was
synergistic, a hindrance to faith, or both, became a matter of
frequent dispute. The degree to which it should be required
became a major question of church policy and a matter of large
social and practical import. By examining these controversies
we may determine the practical as well as ideological significance of the concept. We may determine the effect it had on
the political and social history of the time, as well as on the
course of New England theology.

65. For a thorough discussion of the differences between the Hebraic and
Augustinian conceptions of the will, see Wolfson, *Religious Philosophy*,
pp. 159–75.

5

Early Criticism
and the Antinomian Controversy

The concept of preparation, as it had developed in England, first came under extensive critical examination at the Synod of Dort (1618–19). There Bishop Joseph Hall (1574–1656), a delegate of the English Church, argued the question with Continental Calvinists, who refused to be persuaded. Dort had been called as a general council of Calvinist churches to sit in judgment on the views of Jacobus Arminius (1560–1609), a native of Holland and professor of theology at Leiden. Arminius, in his various writings, had rejected the doctrine of unconditional election and had asserted that man, by his own natural will, may assist in the work of salvation. From 1603 his followers had multiplied, and in 1610 they drew up their creed into a Remonstrance, addressed to the Estates of Holland and West Freisland. In it they affirmed conditional election on the basis of foreseen faith, universal atonement, and man's ability to resist the Holy Spirit. Most important of all, they held that the call of God could not be sincere if it eliminated man's affective response, a point on which their views, while openly synergistic, resembled those of the English divines. But as the Synod was dominated by high Calvinists, determined to discredit the Arminian arguments, the Canons of Dort maintained the inability of man to influence his salvation in any way, with the result that two hundred Arminian preachers were deposed.[1]

Bishop Hall, who identified himself with most of the Synod's findings, did not give in on the subject of preparation. Although he confirmed that there is no power in man's natural will to achieve his own conversion, he nevertheless maintained that "there are yet certain foregoing acts that are pre-required to the conversion of a man . . . as the knowledge of God's will, the feeling of our sin, the fear of hell, the thought of deliverance, some hope of pardon." The grace of God, he said, "doth not use to work upon a man immediately by sudden ruptures, but by meet preparations." Moreover, "these inward acts tending towards conversion are by the power of the Word and the Spirit of God wrought in the heart of a man not yet justified." If our hearts are truly "excited and prepared," said Hall, God by His "secret and wonderful" work "doth regenerate and renew them."[2]

Thus a major spokesman for the English Church, sent to the Synod of Dort by James I, upheld the concept of preparation. At the same time, however, he eagerly condemned the characteristic tenets of Arminian theology. In Arminian doctrine as in orthodox Reformed theology, man cannot, strictly speaking, achieve saving grace by his own will. But for Arminius, if saving grace is received, it must be received in terms of a decision on man's part—a decision totally unrelated to the efficacy of the grace itself. Therefore, the Arminian Remonstrants at Dort insisted on "free assent," holding that "The Operation of grace in the beginning of conversion is indifferent and might be resisted, so that man can be converted by it or not: and the conversion does not necessarily follow unless man

1. George Park Fisher, *History of the Christian Church* (New York, 1888), pp. 428–29. See also Rosalie L. Colie, *Light and Enlightenment* (Cambridge, England, 1957), chap. I.
2. Joseph Hall, *Works* (London, 1863), 9, 493–94.

has by his free consent decided for it, and wants to be converted."[3]

There is a significant, if subtle, distinction between the
Arminian conception of conversion and that maintained by the
English preparationists. For the latter, grace is never "indifferent." Indeed, the concept of preparation as conceived by the
English divines was rooted in the belief that God cares for "His
People" and so gives man the will to convert. But the Canons
of Dort, as drawn up by Orthodox Continental Reformed theologians, refused to allow for this distinction and declared man's
unwillingness to turn to God until the moment of effectual
conversion: "All men are conceived in sin . . . incapable of any
saving goodness. . . . They neither want to nor can return to
God, correct their perverted nature, or bring themselves to its
correction except through regeneration."[4]

Joseph Hall, who tried to mediate between the Orthodox and
the Remonstrants, held to the conception that conversion is by
grace alone, but at the same time he allowed for cooperation
on man's part. "God fetches the act of our believing and turning to Him," said Hall. "God gives that power which the will
exercises; so that it is at once both ours and God's: ours in that
we do work, God's in that He works in us."[5] From the first implantation of the spiritual life, man is no longer passive but
willing to turn to God. In this way Hall distinguished his position from the Orthodox on the one hand and from the Arminians on the other. In this way he defended the preparationists
against accusations of Pelagian error. According to the Dutch
Reformed theologian Herman Wits (1636–1708), the English
divines at Dort differed from the "favors of Pelagianism" in

3. Quoted in Charles Hodge, *Systematic Theology* (3 vols. London, 1880),
2, 681.
4. Ibid.
5. Hall, *Works, 9,* 495. See above, pp. 68–69, for Sibbes' views on man's
cooperation in conversion.

that they were "not for having these things proceed from nature" but professed them to be "the effects of the spirit of bondage, preparing a way to himself for their actual regeneration."[6]

The preparationists, however, continued to be attacked in the years following the Synod. "High Calvinists" in England, as well as abroad, took an increasingly dim view of what they considered to be "lax principles." Among them was William Pemble, reader and tutor at Magdalen Hall, Oxford, from 1614 until his death in 1623. In his *Vindiciae Gratiae,* first published in 1627, he not only defended the Continental faction at Dort but called for a strenuous reassertion in English divinity of Calvin's original convictions. The "antecedent preparations to bring men unto conversion," said Pemble, are not "those affections which our adversaries place in man unregenerate." Only "fear and horror of God's punishing vengeance," he held, can bring a man to Christ. Pemble, who was famous as a preacher and well known as an "able exponent of Calvinism," criticized the Arminians "in the late Synod" for holding that "conversion itself remains . . . free in our power." He also condemned all others, "however branded," who did not hold that God "in His manner of working . . . is without the help of anything in man." "I am fully persuaded," he said, "that whatsoever any man may conceive in abstract speculation . . . he will acknowledge that it is impossible there should be . . . such preparations and forward dispositions."[7]

In America, the preparationists were always careful to insist that man by his natural will could not achieve salvation. However, their concept of preparation could be interpreted as Arminian if the affective nature of the will, functioning under

6. Herman Wits, *The Economy of the Covenants between God and Man* (3 vols. New York, 1798), 2, 58.

7. William Pemble, *Works* (Oxford, 1659), pp. 81, 78, 71, 28–29; Gordon, *Dictionary of National Biography,* *15,* 728.

preventing grace, were denied. At the Synod of Dort Bishop Hall had not denied man's affective response, which for him followed the convicting work of the Law. But in New England, seventeen years after the delegates to Dort had disbanded, the subtlety of this distinction led to controversy and strife; for John Cotton, in the tradition of Pemble, began his ministry in the Bay by denying that man could respond affectively to the external call. In reasserting the doctrine of human helplessness, Cotton refused to allow for preparation in the sense of a personal turning toward God. Man is brought to salvation, he insisted, only by divine constraint. "If the Lord mean to save you," said Cotton, "He will rend, as it were, the caul from the heart . . . as a man would rend the entrails of a beast from him. . . . This is true brokeness of heart . . . when the heart and will is broken."[8]

Sibbes, it should be recalled, had said that "It is not enough to have the heart broken"; for as "a pot may be broken in pieces, and yet be good for nothing; so may a heart be, through terrors and a sense of judgment, and yet be not like wax, pliable." For Sibbes the "spirit of love," as preached in the Gospel, had always to be prized above the "spirit of bondage." "True tenderness of heart," he held, is first wrought by an expectation of God's love.[9] But for Cotton, "true brokeness of heart" mattered more. Indeed, this alone is what he meant by "preparation." For "our first union," said Cotton, "there are no steps to the Altar."[10] Unlike Hooker, Shepard, or Bulkeley, he made no provision whatever for man's affective nature before the effectual call: so that when circumstances brought him into conflict with these men, the issue boiled down to whether the process of conversion for New England would be patterned

8. John Cotton, *A Treatise of the Covenant of Grace* (London, 1671), pp. 128–29.
9. See above, pp. 69–70.
10. Cotton, *A Treatise*, p. 54.

after Cotton's interpretation of Reformed dogmatics or more
closely aligned with the prevailing preparationist point of view.

✛

Cotton was born in the market town of Derby, December 4,
1585, the son of Roland Cotton, a lawyer of strong religious
conviction. At thirteen the boy was sent to Trinity College,
Cambridge, where he took the B.A. in 1602 and the M.A. in
1606. During his university years he read Calvin with great
interest. His grandson, Cotton Mather, tells us that he "preferred one Calvin" above all others. "Even such a Calvinist
was our Cotton!" In his later years, according to Mather, he
loved to "sweeten his mouth with a piece of Calvin" before
going to sleep.[11]

As an undergraduate, Cotton heard Perkins preach on the
efficacy of the Law and on the need for threats and terrors to
bring a man to Christ. It was this side of Perkins' preaching,
more than any other, which struck him as significant. But so
little could he respond to any sense of terror in his own heart
that he breathed a sigh of relief when the bells of Cambridge
announced the famous preacher's death. It was not until 1612,
while a fellow of Emmanuel College, that Cotton began to feel
the first stirrings of grace. Until then he had despaired of his
condition and was sure he would die in eternal reprobation.
But now, at the age of twenty-seven, he could count himself
amongst the elect; and the man he had to thank was none
other than Richard Sibbes.

From 1609 Cotton had gone frequently to hear Sibbes preach.
Having despaired of righteousness through legal constraint, and
having heard that the lecturer at Holy Trinity preached the
Gospel above the Law, he eagerly sought out this great "phy-
sician of the soul." In time his anxieties and doubts diminished.
He felt the Holy Spirit illuminating his heart. Soon he began

11. Mather, *Magnalia*, *1*, III, 274.

to imitate Sibbes in his own sermons. On one of these occasions he converted John Preston, then a fellow of Queen's. Cotton, in fact, quickly gained a wide reputation as a preacher of the Spirit. At Emmanuel he became head lecturer, dean, and catechist. At St. Mary's, where he lectured, he acquired a large following. In 1612, the year of his conversion, he was chosen pastor at the parish of St. Botolphs, in the Lincolnshire seaport of Boston. There he continued to preach in the tradition of Sibbes. There, in 1613, he brought his bride, Elizabeth Horrocks, who died childless in 1630. Two years later he married Sarah Hankridge, who, after his death, became the wife of Richard Mather.

While at St. Botolphs Cotton argued that sinners, although utterly depraved, could still be held accountable for their failure to achieve salvation. By "voluntarily falling . . . from the knowledge of God in nature," he said, or by "abusing other talents and helps," they shall find that God "rejecteth or reprobateth them."[12] Reprobation, then, according to Cotton's doctrine at the time, was clearly conditional; and for this he was taken to task by William Twisse, who questioned his consistency. How could reprobation be conditional, asked Twisse, if the elect are predestined for salvation from the beginning of time? Cotton, however, chose to ignore the rebuke. From 1612 to 1632, when he held to this doctrine, the growth of Arminianism in Lincolnshire had led him to believe that it was better to tone down the rigors of God's eternal decrees. Otherwise his flock might be attracted to those who would deny predestination altogether.

To the extent that Cotton preached conditional reprobation, he had, in a sense, developed a concept of preparation. Natural

12. William Twisse, *A Treatise of Mr. Cottons Clearing Certain Doubts Concerning Predestination, Together with an Examination Thereof* (London, 1646), pp. 54, 43. For a detailed account of the influence of Sibbes on Cotton, see Larzer Ziff, *The Career of John Cotton, Puritanism and the American Experience* (Princeton, 1962), pp. 30–33, 41.

men, he said, might "walk according to the knowledge and helps
which they had received."[13] But the influence of Sibbes never
went so far as to rid his mind of the need for fearful constraint;
and herein lies the essential difficulty of Cotton's theology. Had
he fully accepted Sibbes' views, had he entirely discarded
Perkins' teachings on the need for an acute sense of sin, he
would have been left with little choice but to reject the efficacy
of the Law. He would have claimed instead that man's natural
response to the drawing activities of the Spirit is in itself
efficacious. But this he did not do. In fact, the more he read
Calvin, the more he began to insist upon the uses of the Law.
While preaching at Lincolnshire, he gradually departed from
his earlier concern with the gifts of the Spirit, or the notion that
man should be drawn to Christ, and turned his attention to
conviction of conscience and fear of divine punishment—an
extraordinary fact in the light of his own conversion. Most
important of all, it was this rigorous side of his theology that he
eventually carried to New England.

Until 1632 Cotton had enjoyed a peaceful ministry at the
English Boston. But when process was begun against him in
the Court of High Commission, he, like Hooker, refused to
answer the summons and fled to the nearest port. The watch
set upon the ports made it difficult to escape, but he and his
wife managed to slip onto the *Griffin* and, with Hooker and
Stone, got away. His first son, Seaborn, was born on shipboard;
but Cotton, like Shepard, refused to allow baptism until a
congregation could be gathered. On September 8, 1633, four
days after landing, he was admitted to the Boston Church in
the Bay, where the child was baptized. On October 10 Cotton
was elected teacher; and John Wilson, who was pastor, laid his
hands upon his head.[14]

During his first year in the wilderness, Cotton left the memory

13. Twisse, p. 230.
14. Williston Walker, *Ten New England Leaders* (New York, 1901),
pp. 54–70.

of Sibbes behind and began to preach according to his own interpretation of Calvin—an ominous turn of events for the early history of the Commonwealth. In contradiction to his previous position, he now held that man cannot trust the first gifts of the Spirit and so remains totally passive in conversion. "Rest in none of these," he said, "for these you may have and yet want Christ and life in him; common graces may and will deceive you." What is more, he now discarded conditional reprobation on the grounds that "it is not all the promises in Scripture that have at any time wrought any gracious changes in any soul, or are able to beget the faith of God's Elect." From the day Cotton delivered his first sermon in Boston, the differences between his own doctrine and that generally held by his fellow ministers became increasingly apparent. According to John Winthrop, who as governor had welcomed Cotton to the Bay, John Wilson feared a schism in the Boston church. Such a schism, he believed, would eventually dislodge his church from its normal relationship with the other churches of the Bay and so disrupt the Holy Commonwealth.[15]

It was not long, in fact, before controversy ensued; for Cotton's shipmate on the *Griffin,* Thomas Hooker, was now at Newtown preaching an entirely different doctrine of conversion. To Cotton's mind, the doctrine Hooker preached could be criticized from two sides: it both lowered and raised the standards of grace at the same time. It lowered the standards in that preparatory "evidences" of grace put sanctification too far down the scale in the *ordo salutis*. It raised the standards in that preparatory anxiety put off "assurance," so that man could never really know whether or not he was saved. For Cotton, however, the greater danger was that of bringing the standards down. Hooker was admitting external covenanters to full church membership on the basis of preparatory "motions," or a chari-

---

15. John Cotton, *Christ the Fountain of Life* (London, 1651), p. 27; *A Treatise,* pp. 199–200; John Winthrop, *The History of New England from 1630 to 1649,* ed. James Savage (Boston, 1853), *1,* 249–50.

table "hope." Such evidences, Cotton believed, were not con-
clusive proof of visible sainthood. Moreover, baptized covenanters, said Cotton, should have no more claim to "charity"
than anyone else. Not all the covenant seed shall have the
promises. Indeed, some are "choked with the cares of this
world," and the "best seed" that was sown in them may be
"unfruitful." Although the Prophet exhorts Israel to "return
unto the Lord" (Hosea 14:1), Israel cannot return, said Cotton,
"unless the Lord take away their iniquity"; for "this is the way
of the covenant of grace; whatsoever duties the Lord requireth
to be done on our part, let us look unto Him . . . Do not think
you shall be saved because you are the children of Christian
parents."[16]

Baptized children, he stated, are "born in sin, and children
of wrath." None of them is "born in grace." To speak of "holiness since the fall in children" is "strange language in Christian
ears"; for "we do not teach that all within the covenant are
saved. We do not say that children of believers are holy . . .
though we say they were born under the covenant of grace."[17]
Therefore, those who sit in judgment on candidates for church
membership must be "satisfied in the sincerity of the regeneration of such who are to be received (especially in the first gathering and plantation of a church)." New members, whether in
covenant or not, cannot be admitted "till we be convinced in
our consciences of the certain and infallible signs of their
regeneration." These precautions, said Cotton, are necessary
to maintain "the purity of the church," particularly with respect to "such as are born and baptized members of the church."
Candidates who cannot claim "spiritual communion with
Christ," or assurance of faith, "should not be received as members of the church whereof Christ is head"; and "those that have
the keys to the Church should not open the doors." It follows,

16. Cotton, *A Treatise,* pp. 204, 208.
17. John Cotton, *The Grounds and Ends of the Baptism of the Children
of the Faithful* (London, 1647), pp. 20, 115, 125, 126.

then, that "we receive none as members into the church but such as may be conceived to be received of God. . . . This practice is a pillar of purity and piety. . . . We receive none but such as may be conceived to be regenerate . . . such as we conceive to be in a visible state of salvation."[18]

Peter Bulkeley in *The Gospel Covenant* had brought the efficacy of infant baptism to its highest point—even to the point where the Law is no longer required to bring a mature man to effectual conversion.[19] In Cotton the efficacy of baptism is brought to its lowest point, where the judgment of "charity" is based not upon the ability of candidates to point to interior motions of the Spirit, stirring the affections, but upon "whether the Law has convinced them of sin." And if the elders, "in strictness and exactness of judgment," are not "fully satisfied in the truth and sincerity of their sanctification," such candidates are to be refused admission. Terror of the Law, or the fear worked by the Law, is the ultimate test: "Though the Lord giveth himself freely to the soul, without respect unto any work of the Law," said Cotton, "yet the Law is of special and notable use, working fear in the heart." We may be sure, he maintained, that "the Law of God is of marvelous use in the days of the Gospel . . . to break their hearts and drive them to Jesus Christ." In conversion, God brings them to salvation not by stirring up the embers of faith, but through the "spirit of bondage" joined with the "spirit of burning." ("For behold, the day cometh that shall burn as an oven; and all the proud . . . shall be stubble. And the day that cometh shall burn them up . . . and shall leave them neither root nor branch." Mal. 4:1) Together, these constraining activities provide all the preparation God will allow.[20]

18. John Cotton, *Of the Holiness of Church Members* (London, 1650), pp. 2, 19, 26, 18, 39, 41, 43, 53, 54.
19. See above, p. 117, for Bulkeley's views on the efficacy of baptism.
20. John Cotton, *A Copy of a Letter* (1641), p. 5; *Holiness of Church Members*, p. 43; *A Treatise*, pp. 68–69.

Seldom in Cotton's thought are the baptized encouraged to anticipate the promises as rightful heirs of the covenant seed. Although at times he could assert that the covenant is "sure and everlasting," that it "decays not at all," and is "a certain ground for our eternal inheritance," through his insistence on divine constraint he then diminishes the efficacy of baptism to the point where the external relationship is virtually destroyed. First, he says, the spirit of bondage "worketh trembling and fear" and "presseth men down to the nethermost hell." Then, with the spirit of burning, "all confidence that they had in Abraham's convenant . . . is burned up, and so they have no root left them to stand upon." The Lord "layeth them low that they see no hope of mercy, no likelihood that God should show them any hope. Thus doth the Lord burn up the root of Abraham's covenant wherein men trust." Moreover, the baptized covenanter, under the Law, "can do nothing but wait for faith"; and in this condition he remains until "the Lord cometh indeed to engraft him into Jesus Christ." Even then, however, there can be no guarantee of salvation; for "this a Spirit of burning may do, and yet leave the soul in a damnable condition, for all I know; such as many a soul . . . never come to enjoy saving fellowship with Jesus Christ."[21]

This helpless condition Cotton calls "prostration of the heart." In it "a man is so cast down he cannot tell what to make of himself; but there he lieth, to see what the Lord will do with him, whether He will reach forth the hand of salvation unto him." Man is left "utterly void." He has "neither root nor

21. John Cotton, *The Covenant of God's Free Grace* (London, 1645), pp. 18, 25; *A Treatise*, pp. 115–20. By the time Cotton reached America the Christophany at Damascus had assumed such a central position in his theology of conversion that he was forced more than ever to ignore Paul's teachings on the efficacy of baptism. Not content with this, however, he then went on to emphasize the fact that seizure, although essential, may not in itself be a certain sign of saving grace. Shepard, in his more rigid moods, also held to this view; but Cotton's descriptions of man under the Law, devoid of mercy, are perhaps the most severe in Puritan thought.

branch," nor can he tell "whether Jesus Christ be his portion." But if salvation is to come, it comes immediately; so that "prostration of the heart" is the surest sign of saving grace. Therefore, says Cotton, "We must teach ministers not to be afraid of driving nails to the head . . . to the hearts of sinners. There are a generation of preachers that would now have no Law preached, but only draw men unto Christ. But unless the proud, wanton, and stubborn heart be pierced and wounded to death, there is no hope of salvation."[22]

For Cotton, then, the external covenant, and with it the conditional promises, is overshadowed by the rigors of legal constraint. On the one hand, he can assure the unconverted that "God's covenant is sure and unchangeable." On the other hand, he allows them literally no security in their external relationship to God. Nor will he permit them to build upon the promises. There is no condition before effectual conversion, said Cotton, as "Christ is offered in a promise of free grace without any previous gracious qualification mentioned." The promises "were never given to bring us to Christ," as "faith uniting us to Christ is ever upon an absolute promise." Therefore, he who looks to the conditional promises "hath built upon an unsafe foundation . . . hay and stubble," or a doctrine of "works."[23]

> Take heed you do not close with promises before you have Jesus Christ. Especially take heed you make not use of promises to a qualification to give you your part in Jesus Christ. . . . Do not turn them upside down beyond the scope and intentment of the covenant of grace. . . . Trust not unto every leaning of your souls upon conditional promises; for so you may build upon a covenant made upon works, and

22. Cotton, *A Treatise*, pp. 121–23; Cotton, *The Way of Life* (London, 1641), pp. 133–34.
23. Cotton, *A Treatise*, pp. 37, 40, 61, 63.

in the end you and your covenant will fail together. . . .
If you know that you are in Christ, you may then know
that the promises are yours.[24]

In the light of Cotton's theology it is no wonder that he came
into conflict first with Hooker, then with Shepard, and finally
with Bulkeley. Hooker and Shepard, to be sure, allowed for
legal constraint; but Cotton carried the concept to an extreme
position, far beyond the point to which they were willing to go.
What is more, his views were utterly opposed to everything
Bulkeley valued in the covenant tradition. Cotton, in fact,
spoke for that side of Reformed thought which cannot be
reconciled with covenant concepts, which virtually denies
the Old Testament relationship between man and God—the
relationship on which Abraham's covenant was founded. Man
cannot turn to God, as did Abraham, but must be seized. Man
cannot willingly acknowledge God until he is wrenched, turned
about, forced to believe in a new relationship which until that
moment has played no part in his life. And Cotton, in order to
impose such a process of conversion upon covenant theology,
had first to destroy the external bond. The baptized covenanter,
not being so much as "privileged," can have no "evidences"
whatever of sanctifying faith before the moment of effectual
conversion.

In Hosea it is written: "I will meet them as a bear that is
robbed of her whelps, and will break the caul of their heart, and
there will I devour them like a lion: the wild beast shall tear
them" (13:8). But it is also written: "I will love them freely,
for mine anger is turned away from him. I will be as the dew
unto Israel; he shall grow as the lily. . . . They that dwell under
his shadow shall return; they shall revive as the corn, and
flourish as the vine" (14:5, 6, 8). In Hosea, as in other Prophets,
the divine threat is invariably followed by an offer of reconciliation: "O Israel, return unto the Lord thy God" (14:2). The

24. Ibid., pp. 65–66.

opportunity for choice is never excluded. For Cotton, however, there is no such opportunity. Indeed, there can be no return until the threat has been actually carried out. Therefore, he told his congregation: "If the Lord mean to save you, He will rend, as it were, the caul from the heart . . . as a man would rend the entrails of a beast from him." Until then, said Cotton, we have no "gifts" of the Spirit to provide us with choice; for "Christ is one thing, the soul is another," and "the spirit of God that uniteth them is different from both." Before total reconciliation with God, we are "utterly unable to help ourselves."[25]

Thus "conversion," as Cotton describes it, is synonymous with assurance of salvation. In keeping with Zwingli, Martyr, and other Reformed theologians of the strictest school, the experience itself is reduced to a preordained "sign" of election. It is, in this sense, narrow and limited rather than broad and expansive, for the efficacy of the external call is clearly excluded from the *ordo salutis*. Unlike Calvin, Cotton carried his doctrine to such an extreme that he was unable even to accept the divine exhortations to preparation as "useful." Therefore, he could not comply with those for whom the "heart prepared" had become an essential part of the interior life. "Reserving due honor to such gracious and precious Saints as may be otherwise minded," he once remarked, "I confess I do not discern that the Lord worketh and giveth any saving preparations in the heart till He give union with Christ. For if the Lord do give any saving qualifications before Christ, then the soul may be in the state of salvation before Christ; and that seemeth to be prejudicial unto the grace and truth of Jesus Christ. . . . It seemeth to me that whatsoever saving work there be in the soul, it is not there before Christ be there."[26]

✛

25. Cotton, *A Treatise of Faith,* no date, pp. 14, 6.
26. Cotton, *A Treatise,* p. 35.

In the new Boston, to a far greater extent than in the old, Cotton preached a doctrine of divine omnipotence and human depravity with relentless rigor. Once he had established himself in Massachusetts, he was ever careful to remind his following that nothing done on their part could bring them closer to Christ. But the preaching of a state of depravity from which man may be saved only by seizure could lead (and often had in the sixteenth and seventeenth centuries) to antinomian opinions. Etymologically, the word "antinomianism" means antagonism or opposition to the Law. By usage it meant without the help of the moral Law, independence of it, and elevation above it. In Europe the group known as antinomians were followers of Johannes Agricola, a tailor born at Eisleben in 1494 who later became a university scholar and preacher. As a disciple and later an opponent of Luther, Agricola had carried to an extreme the doctrine of justification by faith in opposition to works. Anxious to defend the Protestant view more distinctly from the Catholic doctrine of salvation by faith and merit, he argued that repentance is the direct work of gospel love alone and not the work of the moral Law. Although he later renounced his error, all who held to immediate revelation were thereafter called "antinomians."[27]

Those who were infected by the heresy, as Shepard had been at Emmanuel, trusted to an inner assurance of being brought into a right relation with God by direct revelation of His Spirit.[28] They claimed to have "individual revealings" from God. But delusion, enthusiasm, and libertinism were held to be the perils of the doctrine. As Cotton himself later realized, an extreme emphasis on the freeness of grace, no matter how

27. George E. Ellis, *The Puritan Age and Rule in the Colony of the Massachusetts Bay, 1629–1685* (Boston, 1888), pp. 303–04, 322–23. The antinomians, as Ellis points out, were the predecessors of the Quakers, who, because they claimed direct revelation without the "word," were also persecuted by the New England Puritans.

28. See above, pp. 106–07, for Shepard's brief exposure to antinomianism.

strenuously one held to the Law, could easily lead to antinomian opinions. "If any shall accuse the doctrine of the covenant of free grace of antinomianism," he wrote, "and say it teacheth men freedom from the Law, we see how false such an aspersion would be."[29] But "false" or not, this is what happened; and herein lies the irony of the Antinomian Controversy in Massachusetts. As Perry Miller has said, out of Cotton's "radical disjunction between nature and grace," the Boston antinomians derived their conclusion that "no works could have anything to do with justification."[30] Therefore, nothing, not even "legal terrors," could be offered as "evidence" before absolute assurance. In other words, they denied preparation on grounds that were clearly an offshoot from Cotton's views, although they were significantly different and more extreme. But it was not until the controversy was well under way that the teacher of the Boston church began to realize the full significance of this.

✛

In the autumn of 1634, on September 18, a boatload of immigrants arrived at Boston. Among them was Anne Hutchinson, a woman of mature years, who had been under Cotton's ministry in Lincolnshire. She had come to New England, she said, "but for Mr. Cotton's sake." As for Mr. Hooker, she "liked not his spirit." Soon she began holding meetings to discuss Cotton's sermons with the women of the Boston church. Later the men joined in. At the same time she advanced the theory that anything short of a conscious feeling of union with God was a covenant of works; while being under a covenant of grace meant undoubted assurance of salvation. At first Cotton gave large support to her and her followers, for he regarded her views as a valuable means by which "many of the women (and by them their husbands) were convinced they had gone on in a covenant of works." But in time matters began to get out of hand.

29. Cotton, *A Treatise,* p. 65.
30. *The New England Mind,* 2, 59.

In October 1635 Henry Vane, the youthful son of an influential
royal counselor, landed at Boston; and the colony, which had
tired of John Winthrop as governor and had tried both Thomas
Dudley and John Haynes in the job, elected Vane. It was
not long before Vane declared himself an active supporter of
Mrs. Hutchinson; and through their combined influence the
Boston church came over to the antinomian persuasion.[31]

Only the pastor, John Wilson, and ex-Governor Winthrop,
a leading member of the church, opposed the movement inside
the church itself. But the ministers of the other towns, among
them Thomas Hooker and Thomas Shepard at Newtown,
strongly supported their opposition.[32] Then in May 1636,
as Hooker was leaving for Connecticut, the opposition was
thwarted by the arrival of another Hutchinsonian supporter,
Anne's brother-in-law, the Reverend John Wheelwright. The
antinomians wanted to install Wheelwright as a second teacher
at the Boston church. Winthrop and Wilson managed to block

31. Charles Francis Adams, ed. *Antinomianism in the Colony of Massachusetts Bay, 1636–1638* (Boston, 1894), p. 272; Williston Walker, *A History
of the Congregational Churches in the United States* (New York, 1897),
p. 139; John Cotton, *The Way of Congregational Churches Cleared* (London,
1648), p. 51.

32. The historian Charles M. Andrews believes that Robert Stansby's
letter to John Wilson, which contains the remark, "There is great division
of judgment in matters of religion . . . which moved Mr. Hooker to remove" (see above, pp. 90–91, for Stansby's full statement), refers not only to
the controversy in general but to a personal dispute between Hooker and
Cotton on the subject of faith and works (Andrews, *The Colonial Period*, 2,
84–86). Andrews cites as further evidence a letter received at the Colonial
Office, London, dated January 3, 1637, from a Mr. Law, minister in
Barbados Island. Law submits certain "grievances of the clergy" for consideration by church authorities and asks "whether there be any saving
preparation in a Christian soul before his union with Christ." This, says
Law, is "Hooker's opinion," whereas Cotton is "against him and his party
in all" (Great Britain, *Public Record Office, Colonial Record*, Class 1, Vol. 9,
No. 72, Library of Congress Microfilm Ac. 10, 741, Reel 4). The eighteenth-
century historian Thomas Hutchinson (1711–80) tells us that "the great
influence which Mr. Cotton had in the colony inclined Mr. Hooker to
remove to some place more remote from Boston than Newtown . . . some

their efforts and to arrange that Wheelwright be given the
church at Mount Wollaston, outside Boston. But the Bostonians
now accused their own pastor, John Wilson, of teaching a
covenant of works.[33]

In recalling these events, Winthrop wrote down that on
December 10, 1636, "Mr. Wilson made a very sad speech of the
condition of our churches, and the inevitable danger of separation, if these differences and alienations among brethren were
not speedily remedied; and laid the blame upon these new
opinions risen up amongst us, which all the magistrates, except
the governor and two others, did confirm, and all the ministers
but two."[34] Wilson's speech, however, was "taken very ill by
Mr. Cotton and others of the same church," so that Cotton and
"divers of them," according to Winthrop, "went to admonish
him."[35] Soon Governor Vane took up the cry, with the result
that Wilson, now confronted by a hostile congregation, was put
to the task of defending himself:

> The governor pressed it violently against him, and all the
> congregation, except the deputy and one or two more, and
> many of them with much bitterness and reproaches; but
> he answered them all with words of truth and soberness,
> and with marvelous wisdom. It was strange to see how the
> common people were led by example to condemn him in

---

of the principle persons were strongly attached to one of them, and some to
the other" (Hutchinson, *The History of the Colony of Massachusetts* [2 vols.
London, 1765], *1*, 43). And finally, Perry Miller, in his essay "Thomas Hooker
and Connecticut Democracy" (*Errand into the Wilderness* [Cambridge,
1956], pp. 16–47), argues that Hooker and Cotton were also divided on
several political issues related to Congregational polity, such as the power
of magistrates in civil affairs and the degree to which political rights should
be extended beyond visible believers. Hooker held that the power of
magistrates should be limited and that nonbelievers should have some say
in the government. Cotton held the opposite view.

33. Walker, pp. 139–40.
34. Winthrop, *1*, 249–50.
35. Ibid., p. 250.

that which (it was very probable) divers of them did not
understand, nor the rule which he was supposed to have
broken.[36]

Winthrop himself was acutely aware of the theological difficulties involved, for during the preceding autumn he had tried
to work out his own defense of the orthodox position and had
actually written a document listing his arguments against the
Hutchinsonians. Before submitting it to his opponents, however, he had sent it to Shepard for approval; and while the text
has since been lost, Shepard's criticism shows how sensitive the
preparationists had now become to the vulnerability of their
doctrine. On December 15, 1636, five days after Wilson had
been admonished, Shepard wrote to Winthrop:

> In your five arguments your words are out of the parable of
> the sower; a man must have an honest and good heart
> before the Word can have any saving effect. That is as I
> expand, briefly; before the Word work faith to believe to
> Justification, the heart must be made honest and good, in
> preparation; which though it be a truth which for the
> substance of I have ever held and would not deny, yet an
> adversary will or may take much advantage upon the start-
> ing of so deep and doubtful a question, and may keep you
> off from the pursuit of his errors by pursuing you for this,
> wherein he knows many of your friends that would stand
> by you in other controversies will be against you in this;
> and so while you are about to convince them of errors, they
> will proclaim yourself to hold forth worse.[37]

We may assume, on the basis of this letter, that Winthrop
preferred to destroy his document rather than open himself

---

36. Ibid., pp. 250–51.
37. *Winthrop Papers,* 1631–37, Massachusetts Historical Society (Boston,
1943), *3,* 328.

to charges of Arminianism.[38] Like the "common people" who had attacked Wilson, he was not, after all, a professional theologian.

That same December of 1636 the ministers of the colony gathered in Boston to debate with Mrs. Hutchinson, who now openly proclaimed that only Cotton and Wheelwright preached the covenant of grace, while the rest of the clergy were under a covenant of works. On the last day of the year Cotton publicly rebuked John Wilson for teaching "sanctifying methods severely exacting," while he himself taught "heart piety . . . self-assuring."[39] Twice during the autumn and winter of 1636–37 Cotton was asked by his fellow ministers to answer in writing their questions on the disputed points. When asked whether there are any conditions in the soul before receiving the promises, Cotton answered, "Before regeneration we are not active at all in any spiritual Christian action"; for "Works of creation . . . needeth no preparation." All a man can expect, said Cotton, is "restraining grace to keep him from known sins" and "constraining grace to provoke him to duty." When hard pressed on this point, Cotton cried, "Let Calvin answer for me!"[40]

The ministers, in questioning Cotton, hoped to convince him that in order to "lay hold" on Christ we must first have the rudiments of faith, by which we prepare ourselves for effectual conversion. But Cotton maintained that we are effectually converted "before our faith doth put forth itself to lay hold on him." Otherwise, said the Boston minister, we fall prey to the Thomistic conception of habitual grace, which "some of the Schoolmen" and some others, "even judicious Protestants," erroneously uphold. Either Christ is there, "permanent in us . . . before the act of Faith," said Cotton, or "no spiritual act can be done by us." His examiners, however, were quick to

38. See Edmund S. Morgan, *The Puritan Dilemma* (Boston, 1958), p. 142.
39. Ellis, p. 308.
40. John Cotton, *Sixteen Questions of Serious and Necessary Consequences* (London, 1644), pp. 9, 13.

point out that in no sense should their doctrine be confused with Scholastic teachings. Thomas had made a clear distinction between a first and second grace, the first of which requires the other to complete it. Since both, by their very nature, are intrinsically different, the first is essentially inefficacious.[41] In New England, on the other hand, the seeds of grace were considered to be neither inefficacious in themselves nor different in kind from sanctifying grace. They merely required additional fertilization to bring about full union with Christ. The Spirit of God increases His gift to man, but the nature of the gift remains the same. Therefore, man may act in a spiritual way before effectual conversion.

In the wake of all this the magistrates called a general fast, hoping that a day of meditation might mend the discord. But on the day proclaimed, January 20, 1637, John Wheelwright came to the Boston church, stood before the congregation, and delivered a sermon on direct revelation by the Holy Spirit in which he bitterly attacked the concept of preparation. Significantly enough, he preached on I Corinthians 1:30, "Christ . . . is made unto us wisdom and righteousness and sanctification and redemption," the same passage that had launched Shepard on his brief flirtation with antinomianism. Christ must do all, said Wheelwright; and for our part we are unable "before our conversion . . . to put forth one act of true saving spiritual wisdom." There must be nothing revealed to man but Christ, he told them, as "none other doctrine is able to justify any but merely revelation of the Lord Jesus Christ." Therefore, "when the Lord is pleased to convert any soul to him, he revealeth not to him some work, and from that work carrieth him to Christ, but there is nothing revealed but Christ. If men think to be saved because they see some work of sanctification in them, as hungering and thirsting and the like, if they be saved they are saved without the Gospel. No, no, this is a covenant of works,

41. Cotton, *The Way Cleared*, pp. 41–42. See above, pp. 24–27, for the Thomistic position on conversion.

for in the covenant of grace nothing is revealed but Christ for our righteousness."[42]

When the General Court met in March 1637, Wheelwright (in spite of protests from Vane and the Boston Church members) was censured for his sermon. The proceedings of the meeting tell us that Wheelwright "seemed to scare men not only from legal righteousness but even from faith and repentance, as that also were a covenant of works," and "the ministers present declared their grief to see such opinions risen in the country of so dangerous consequences."[43] Cotton, who had been a close friend of Wheelwright's in England, stood up for him. This may be the reason why sentence was withheld until the next meeting, which the Court appointed to be held at Newtown, as Boston was so much in sympathy with Wheelwright. That same spring, Vane, Cotton, Wheelwright, and the rest of the Boston church refused to attend Peter Bulkeley's ordination on the grounds that Bulkeley was a "legal" preacher (meaning that he taught salvation by legal "merit," not legal constraint).[44]

By this time the whole colony was against the Boston group, which nevertheless had now become the largest single congregation in Massachusetts. In the election of May 1637 Vane was dropped from office, and Winthrop was again made governor. A law was passed which forbade the sale of land to any stranger without permission of the magistrates. This law, said Winthrop, was to keep out persons "who might be dangerous to the Commonwealth"; for in England the Reverend Roger Brierly of Grindleton had been preaching doctrines similar to the Hutchinsonians', and Winthrop suspected that Brierly's followers, called "Grindletonians," might soon be coming to the Bay.

42. John Wheelwright, "Fast-day Sermon," in *John Wheelwright, his writings*, ed. Charles H. Bell (Boston, 1876), pp. 163–64. See above, p. 107, for Shepard's response to Preston's sermon on I Corinthians 1:30.
43. "A Brief Apology in defence of the general proceedings of the Court . . . against Mr. J. Wheelwright," in Adams, p. 199.
44. Ellis, p. 323.

The magistrates, in effect, were now able to restrict settlement to those whose opinions were acceptable to the established orthodoxy. This meant that any prospective settler who openly denied preparation, no matter what his status as a Christian, could be excluded from the colony. Winthrop, in fact, wrote to Vane that "A man that is a true Christian may be denied residence among us, in some cases," implying that a great deal depended upon his theological point of view. Thus potential candidates for church membership were to be screened by the magistrates before they could even consider presenting themselves to the elders of a congregation.[45]

When Cotton was told of the law, he and sixty of his congregation threatened to move south to a place called "Quinipyatk." His friend John Davenport, who had landed at Boston in June with a small body of disciples, suggested a joint expedition. But events which occurred throughout the summer and autumn of 1637 led Cotton to change his mind, and Davenport waited until the following spring before leaving to found the colony of New Haven.[46]

The Synod held in the late summer of 1637, now called the Hutchinsonian Synod, had been suggested by Thomas Shepard as the only way to deal with the controversy. Cotton, in spite of the threat it presented to his doctrine, hoped that the meeting would clear up the prevailing confusion. As yet he could not be convinced that his theology had anything to do with the current wave of enthusiasm. Therefore, he would take the opportunity to present his case fully. How could he, of all preachers, be held responsible for the rise of antinomianism? Did he not, after all, preach the efficacy of the Law more vigorously than most? Hooker, interestingly enough, had originally opposed the

45. Winthrop, *1*, 267; "A Defence of an Order of Court Made in the Year 1637,"*Publications of the Prince Society* (Boston, 1865), *1*, 82; Morgan, p. 146; Ziff, pp. 128–30.

46. Davenport's attitude toward preparation, together with his views on the efficacy of baptism, is discussed in Chap. 6.

calling of a Synod, as he believed such a gathering would "make things more and worse than they are." In April 1637 he had written to Shepard from Hartford, "Your general Synod, I cannot see either how reasonable or how salutary it will be for your turn, for the settling and establishing the truth."[47] But Shepard, who had never run from Cotton, was determined to have the matter settled. His reply to Hooker, since lost, apparently convinced the Connecticut pastor to come back to Massachusetts and stand his ground. Accordingly, on August 5th, two days after Vane had sailed back to England in disgrace, Hooker arrived in Boston; and the Synod's opening date was fixed for August 30, 1637, at Newtown.[48]

Here, in the rude meetinghouse with "a bell upon it," the leading New England divines gathered for the first Congregational synod in America. With Thomas Hooker and Peter Bulkeley as moderators, the Synod held its sessions twenty-four days, during which time eighty-two "erroneous errors" were confuted and condemned. The majority of these, all of which were said to be held by the Hutchinsonians, either directly or indirectly denied the concept of preparation. The "errors," collected by John Winthrop, were published by Thomas Weld in *A Short Story* (1644).[49] They contain the following representations:

> Error: There can be no true closing with Christ in a promise that hath a qualification or condition expressed.
> Confutation: This opinion we conceive erroneous, con-

47. In Albro, *Life of Shepard*, pp. 205–06. For a vivid description of Cotton's feelings about the Synod, see Ziff, pp. 131–34.

48. Walker, pp. 141–42.

49. Thomas Weld (1590–1662) was pastor at Tarling, Essex, when Thomas Shepard first went there in 1626 (see above, p. 102). He came to New England in 1632, was made preacher at Roxbury that same year, and later took an active part in all the proceedings against the antinomians. In 1641 he was sent to England as an agent of the colony. While in London, in 1644, he came upon an account of the Hutchinsonian affair called "A Catalogue of Erroneous Opinions condemned in New England," to which

trary to Isaiah 55:1, "Ho, every one that thirsteth come ye
to the waters."

Error: The Spirit acts most in the Saints when they
endeavor least.

Confutation: The more we endeavor, the more assistance
and help we have from Him. . . . Ask, seek, knock.[50]

Weld, in his preface to *A Short Story*, lists some of the other
errors discussed at the Synod: "That a man is united to Christ
only by the work of the Spirit upon him, without any act of his;
that a man is never effectually Christ's till he hath assurance;
that this assurance is only from the witness of the Spirit." One
of the "unsavory speeches" confuted by the Synod (delivered
either by Anne Hutchinson or Wheelwright) clearly states the
antinomians' position: "Here is great stir about graces and looking to hearts, but give me Christ. I seek not for graces but for
Christ. I seek not for promises but for Christ. . . . Tell me not
of meditations and duties, but tell me of Christ."[51]

Cotton refused to sign the official document listing the errors,
as he would not condemn them all. But by now he had begun
to fear for his own well-being. He realized at last that the doctrine he preached lay behind virtually all the errors cited. He
was, indeed, in greater danger than ever before. "There was a
dark day at the Synod," wrote Cotton Mather, when his grandfather denied that the first motions of faith are preparatory
to effectual conversion. "But after sorrowful discourses . . .
Mr. Cotton the next morning made an excellent speech unto
the assembly tending toward an accommodation of the controversy . . . an happy conclusion of the whole matter."[52]

---

he added a *Preface* and issued as *A Short Story*. It is generally believed that
John Winthrop had drawn up the main account. In 1646 Weld was re-
called to New England but chose to remain in London the rest of his life.
(Gordon, 20, 1071).

50. John Winthrop, *A Short Story* (London, 1644), in Adams, pp. 107–14.
51. Ibid., p.128.
52. Mather, *Magnalia*, 2, VII, 514–15.

The "matter," however, had not as yet been brought to the "happy conclusion" Mather would have us believe. Although Cotton, as the Synod progressed, now willingly condemned additional errors, still he would not entirely disassociate himself from the opinions his followers expressed. What is remarkable about his behavior is not that he began to alter his position, but that he remained in the opposition so long; for the critical charge against the antinomians was not that they denied preparation as such, but that they denied it on the basis of immediate revelations. This meant that they scorned not only the necessity of the Word—the basis of Christianity, the foundation of the Christian community—but the necessity of the Law, by which man is made conscious of his sins. Another "error" Weld lists is that "the Law and the preaching of it is no use at all to drive a man to Christ." Yet Cotton would not sign the document that condemned this error! How, then, can we explain his support of the Hutchinsonians beyond the point that he, intellectually, was willing to go?

Even during the Synod, Cotton believed that he still had control over the Boston group. If certain wayward enthusiasts had gone to extremes, he was sure he could bring them round to his own convictions. In fact, he had identified himself with the Bostonians to such an extent that he fully believed their cause to be his own. It was not until he realized that the efficacy of the Law had clearly been challenged that he turned his back on the antinomians once and for all. Only when members of his church attending the Synod began to contest errors he himself had condemned, did he alter his course. From that moment on he shifted his emphasis from the degree to which his doctrine supported their views to the degree to which it fell in line with the opinions of his fellow preachers. And when the Boston laymen left the Synod in disgust, he pronounced "some of the opinions to be blasphemous, some of them heretical, many of them erroneous, and all of them incommodiously expressed."[53]

53. Cotton, *The Way Cleared*, p. 48.

The Synod adjourned September 22, but the Hutchinsonians remained defiant of its conclusions; and so the General Court took matters into its own hands. At the November session Anne Hutchinson and John Wheelwright were put on trial; and in these proceedings we gain additional insight into Cotton's continuing dilemma. Although he knew by now that Mrs. Hutchinson had departed from his doctrine far more than at first he had suspected, still he could not believe that she had committed the crime of heresy:

> Then the court laid to her charge the reproach she had cast upon the ministers, and ministry of this country, saying that none of them did preach the covenant of free grace but master Cotton . . . because they pressed much for faith and love without holding forth such an immediate witness of the Spirit as she pretended. . . . Then she appealed to Mr. Cotton, who being called and desired to declare what he remembered of her speeches, said that he remembered only that which took impression on him, for he was much grieved that she should make such comparison between him and his brethren; but yet he took her meaning to be only of a gradual difference, when she said that they did not hold forth a covenant of free grace as he did. . . . Upon this the Court wished her to consider that Mr. Cotton did in a manner agree with the testimony of the rest of the elders.[54]

But Cotton, although he had satisfied the ministers to some extent, still would not condemn Mrs. Hutchinson on her revelations. For all he had to say about the necessity of legal constraint, he was strangely ambivalent on the subject of revelations. We may even suspect that he, like Shepard, had at one time been drawn to the antinomian persuasion, for he wrote: "You have heard of many that have attended to revelations,

54. Winthrop, *A Short Story*, pp. 169–72.

that have been deceived. . . . But yet on the other side, let not men be afraid, and say that we have no revelation but the Word."[55] The remark itself, to be sure, in no way defends the notion of direct revelation. Here Cotton may simply be saying that, apart from the efficacy of the Word, it is also necessary to have the internal testimony of the Spirit. But if the statement is not extreme, still it may shed some light on what now took place at the trial, as Cotton at first hesitated on the question of revelations. Indeed, if we again ask ourselves why he was so reluctant to abandon the cause of his parishioners, we may find a partial explanation here. Thomas Dudley, the new deputy governor, cross-examined him:

> Dep. Gov.: I desire Mr. Cotton to tell us whether you do approve of Mrs. Hutchinson's revelations as she hath laid them down.
> Mr. Cotton: I know not whether I do understand her . . .
> Dep. Gov.: Do you believe that her revelations are true?
> Mr. Cotton: That she may have some special providence of God to help her is a thing I cannot bear witness against . . .
> Dep. Gov.: Sir, you weary me and do not satisfy me.[56]

Before the trial was over, however, Cotton had changed his ground. When he realized that her denial of preparation was based entirely on divine illumination, he drew the line and turned against her. He came to see the danger of her stand not only for his position in the colony but for his own conception of conversion. As much as he may have sympathized with her views on revelations, he more greatly prized the finality of Scripture and the efficacy of the Law. He had backed her initially because she had denied preparation; but her insistence on divine illumination threatened the supremacy of biblical au-

55. Cotton, *A Treatise,* pp. 177–78.
56. "The Examination of Mrs. Anne Hutchinson at the Court at New-town, November 1637," in Adams, pp. 274, 276.

thority and with it the very foundations of the state and church. Her opinions and practices, as Winthrop later recalled, had been the "cause of all our disturbances" in that "such bottomless revelations as either came without any word or without the sense of the word . . . if they be allowed in one thing, must be admitted a rule in all things; for they being above . . . Scripture, they are not subject to control."[57] And so, after she and Wheelwright had been sentenced to banishment by the Court, a trial for excommunication was held before the Boston church. At this trial, in March 1638, Cotton became her chief prosecutor.

If at first he thought he might finally correct her errors, and so save her from banishment and excommunication, his hopes were soon quashed; for as the ministers of the Bay again gathered, they heard Anne Hutchinson proclaim: "I do not acknowledge any graces in us accompanying salvation before conversion. . . . We are dull to act in spiritual things savingly." Had Cotton been able to avoid the subject of preparation, had he simply persuaded her to deny her revelations outright, he might have saved her. But to the mind of Mrs. Hutchinson, Cotton's own rejection of a preparatory phase was still the chief source for her doctrine of sudden conversion. Just the year before Cotton had told these same ministers: "Before regeneration we are not active at all in any spiritual Christian action . . . passive to receive help from God to do it." Now Thomas Weld spoke to the ministers: "She told me that Mr. Cotton and she were both of one mind, and she held no more than Mr. Cotton did in these things." Whereupon Cotton turned to Mrs. Hutchinson and said: "I confess I did not know you held any of these things . . . but it may be it was my sleepiness and want of watchful care over you."[58] And with these words he not only cut himself off from her for good but denied what had been

57. Winthrop, *A Short Story*, p. 177.
58. "A Report of the Trial of Mrs. Anne Hutchinson before the Church in Boston, March, 1638," in Adams, pp. 315–27; Cotton, *Sixteen Questions*, p. 13.

a basic tenet of his public theology. Indeed, in no other way could he escape from the dilemma which enclosed him.[59]

As the church trial came to an end, Thomas Shepard admonished Mrs. Hutchinson for having slighted the ministers of the colony. Had she not accused them of preaching a covenant of works? To which she replied: "It was never in my heart to slight any man, but only that man should be kept in his own place and not set in the room of God." Then Cotton, whom she claimed as the source of her opinions, pronounced the sentence of excommunication. We are told that "first he remembered her of the good way she was in her first coming, in helping to discover to divers the false bottom they stood upon in trusting to legal works without Christ. Then he showed her how by falling into these gross and fundamental errors she had lost the honor of her former service." "I confess," said Cotton, "I have not been ready to believe reports, and have been slow of proceeding against any of our members for want of sufficient testimony to prove that which hath been laid to their charge. But now they have proceeded in a way of God and do bring such testimony as doth evince the truth of what is affirmed, it would be our sin if we should not join in the same, which we are willing to do."[60] And when she left the church, the concept of preparation, in which man is assigned a part to play of his own, had triumphed over seizure, whether by legal constraint or direct revelation.

✠

With the trial over, Cotton again considered moving to New Haven, as it was hard for him to remain in a situation

59. Anne Hutchinson's revelational views were her undoing in that she was, in a way, a proto-Quaker. Quaker theologians are not unjustified in claiming her. To do so, however, reveals an aspect of Quakerism that is often forgot or suppressed: that it was an extension of Puritan enthusiastic radicalism and not of medieval mysticism. See Geoffrey Nuttall, *The Holy Spirit*.

60. "A Report of the Trial," pp. 321, 309; Winthrop, *A Short Story*, p. 224.

where respect for his doctrine had been considerably diminished. Shepard, for one, was convinced that "Mr. Cotton repents not, but is hid only"; and others saw him as "the Trojan Horse, out of which all the erroneous opinions and differences of the country did issue forth."[61] Winthrop, on the other hand, was determined that the teacher at the Boston Church should stay; for his leaving would indicate to the mother country that the colonists in New England were far from united in their theology. And Cotton finally agreed that this was by far the most important consideration. If it was necessary to compromise on doctrine, he would do so for the sake of the Holy Commonwealth.

In his preaching after the controversy Cotton stressed the efficacy of the Law as he had done before. But he realized, at last, that it was also necessary to stress the drawing activities of the Spirit—if only to avoid another antinomian reaction. This is not to say that he altered his doctrine in a radical way. Quite to the contrary. He neither discarded his low conception of baptism nor considered the conditional promises to be efficacious. As he now viewed the process of conversion, he insisted that we must, in a sense, respond to the gifts of the Spirit. But more than likely, he asserted, it may "be our death that we come not off in duties with spiritual life."[62] It was not until the mid-1640s, when the need to defend the Congregational Way became his chief concern, that he began to attribute the least degree of efficacy to federal grace. Even then, however, he refused to concede any direct correlation between "common graces" and effectual conversion.

After her excommunication Anne Hutchinson went to Portsmouth, Rhode Island, where she lived until 1642. The following year she moved to Westchester county, where she was murdered by the Indians near the Hutchinson River. Wheelwright went to Exeter, New Hampshire, which he helped to

61. Shepard, *Autobiography*, p. 386; Cotton, *The Way Cleared*, p. 53.
62. John Cotton, *The Churches Resurrection* (London, 1642), pp. 29-30.

settle. Later he repudiated his stand and returned to Massachusetts, where in 1679 he died peacefully as minister of the Salisbury church.[63] But the issue of preparation was far from resolved by the banishment; for the Puritan churches soon after the Antinomian Controversy began their debates on the extent of church membership and the right to baptism. In these debates, which were determined to a large extent by the changing state of affairs in England as well as America, preparation remained an important and lively issue.

63. Walker, p. 145.

6

Later Criticism:
to the Halfway Covenant and Beyond

By the early 1640s the development of Congregationalism in New England had aroused the concern of Puritans at home. The English Puritans, through the initial influence of Cartwright and other Reformed thinkers, were now greatly affected by Presbyterian attitudes. Therefore, their polity on church membership did not differ significantly from that of the established church. Under such a polity little distinction was made between external and internal covenanters. The baptized, on coming "of age," had only to declare themselves professing Christians. Since no relation of the inner workings of grace was required, external members were virtually assured of full standing in the church.

So different was this practice from what had been established in the Bay that, when word reached England of exclusiveness in Massachusetts, pressure was brought to bear on the colony. As early as 1637 the English Puritans had begun sending queries to America in which they asked about the constitution of the church, qualifications for membership, and the whole range of ecclesiastical polity. Thomas Shepard's *A Defence of the Answer* was a reply to one of these.[1] Others were Thomas Hooker's

1. See above, p. 104 n.

Survey of Church Discipline, John Cotton's *Way of the Congregational Churches Cleared,* John Davenport's *An Answer of the Elders,* Richard Mather's *Church Government and Church Covenant Discussed,* and John Norton's *The Answer.*[2] Although none of the authors precisely agreed with the others, either on the efficacy of baptism or on qualifications for church membership, all were united in their common effort to defend the New England Way. All, moreover, were fully aware of the extent to which they had gone beyond accepted practices at home. Cotton and Norton, for example, were far more concerned with concealing the strictness of their policy than with developing arguments in its favor.

Most of these pamphlets were written during 1643 and 1644; and the majority were composed with parliamentary opposition in mind. In 1642 Parliament, in its military struggle with Charles I, had been forced into union with the Scots. This union signified the adoption of the Scottish type of church polity already in favor with the majority of English Puritans. It signified, in short, the gathering of the Westminster Assembly, made up of the leading British divines of Reformed persuasion. The Assembly, with its predominance of Presbyterian sympathizers, began its sessions in July 1643. By 1645 it had prepared a full scheme of Presbyterian church government. Meanwhile, in November 1643, Parliament had established a board called "The Commissioners for Plantations," with power "to provide for,

2. In 1644 the Presbyterian divines at the Westminster Assembly had asked the Dutch Reformed theologian William Appolonius (1603–57) to write a book which would set forth the practices of the churches in Holland, and which they hoped would hinder the progress of Independency in England. Instead, Appolonius sent the dissenting brethren a set of questions; and it was decided by the Independents at the Assembly that the answer should come from New England, which could speak from experience. The New England ministers asked John Norton to draw up the *Answer,* which he finished in 1645 and published in 1648. (Douglas Horton, "Translator's Preface,' John Norton, *The Answer to the whole set of questions of Mr. William Appolonius,* Cambridge, 1958.)

order, and dispose all things" in the realm beyond the seas; and there was fear in New England lest Parliament enforce uniformity in the colonies. It was not until 1648, when the course of events in England had put the Presbyterians out of power, that New England was more or less free to go its own ecclesiastical way.[3]

From the late 1630s to the late 1640s, then, the American divines were obliged to define the Congregational Way for a predominantly Presbyterian brethren at home. In short, they were forced to defend their innovations in ecclesiastical polity. By 1642 it was generally known in England that candidates abroad were required to give a detailed account of the conversion experience. One visitor to the colonies had reported that the timid often "choose rather to go without the communion than undergo such public confessions and trials"; and this same observer had questioned "whether . . . these public confessions be not extremes, and whether some private pastoral or Presbyterial collation . . . as in the Church of England is approved, be not better than those extremes."[4]

3. Williston Walker, *A History of Congregational Churches*, pp. 153–57. At the Westminster Assembly the Independents were not prepared to present a scheme of church government that could deal with the political realities of the time. While in exile they had ignored these problems, having been concerned only with "the dark part, the evil of those superstitions adjoined to the worship of God, which have been the common stumbling block and offense of many a thousand tender consciences" (*Apologetical Narration Humbly Submitted to the Honourable Houses of Parliament*, 1646, 2). Because they had not been engaged in the struggle of politics and warfare, they had little understanding of the difficulties Parliament now faced: "We had no new Commonwealths to rear, to frame Church-government unto, whereof any one piece might stand in the others light, to cause the least variation by us from the Primitive Pattern; we had no State-ends or Political interests to comply with; no Kingdoms in our eye to subdue unto our mould. . . . We had nothing else to do but simply and singly to consider how to worship God acceptably, and so most according to his word" (*Apologetical Narration*, 3f.). For a detailed discussion of this issue, see Robert S. Paul, *The Lord Protector; Religion and Politics in the Life of Oliver Cromwell* (London, Lutterworth Press, 1955), pp. 53–55, 62.

4. Thomas Lechford, *Plain Dealing* (London, 1642), p. 7.

In Massachusetts there were Presbyterian sympathizers as well. By 1643 Thomas Parker and James Noyes, pastor and teacher at Newbury, had openly supported the Presbyterian system. At Hingham the Reverend Peter Hobart shared their views; and the colony began to stir. That September a convention of ministers was held at Cambridge, with Cotton and Hooker as moderators. Hooker had come up from Connecticut in fear of Presbyterian subversion. He therefore argued with the Newbury ministers in an effort to bring them round to the Congregational Way. The "judgment of charity," he maintained, need not be so rigorously exclusive as they imagined. Cotton, however, took the opposite point of view. With Presbyterians in the colony, it was time to tighten up the system, not tone down its rigors. He therefore led Massachusetts on the offensive and eventually won the day. No matter what Hooker may have said or felt, candidates were now subjected to increasing strictness and greater restraints than ever before.

Cotton, in 1637, had lost on the issue of preparation. But he held, as we have seen, a stricter view on church admissions than Hooker. Candidates, he maintained, must submit to a searching examination of their "experience in the ways of grace." This did not mean, in Cotton's eyes, that they should relate preparatory experiences of their own doing, but rather of God's constraining preparation in their passive souls. Hooker still held to his original views on the judgment of charity, and in Hartford candidates were admitted accordingly. But Cotton, now back in favor in Massachusetts, made his influence felt; and his strictness, combined with the accepted principle of preparation, resulted in a policy of admissions similar to what Shepard had imposed on the Dorchester church in 1636.[5] This is not to say that Cotton himself complied with Shepard's concept of preparation. In the privacy of his study he still wrote against it. But once he had publicly given in to the concept, it

5. See above, pp. 101–02, for Shepard's part in the first gathering of the Dorchester church.

became a part of the New England Way; and when the ministers demanded preparatory experiences of an extensive nature while at the same time holding to Cotton's strict admissions policy, they erected a formidable barrier to the communion table.

By 1644 Cotton had been attacked by several vigorous spokesmen for the English Presbyterians. One of these, Robert Baillie, was incensed that Massachusetts should hold to a policy that excluded from the sacraments those who ordinarily would be considered members of the Church of England. "Of all the bypaths wherein the wanderers of our time are pleased to walk," said Baillie, "this is the most considerable"; and his views were echoed in the colonies.[6] By 1645 William Vassall of Plymouth and Dr. Robert Child of the Bay had led a movement in opposition to the established policy. They had gained their support from a group of followers who objected strenuously to the barriers erected between the unregenerate and the communion table.[7] Vassall and Child, to be sure, may have cared less about the Lord's Supper than the limitation of full political rights to church members, but their petition to the General Court, signed by many, indicates that all were not satisfied with the present state of affairs. When their wishes were not granted, they threatened to appeal to Parliament for redress. Had they not been frustrated by the great political upheaval of 1647, which put Cromwell and the Army Independents into power, the New England Way might well have been altered by Parliament within a year.

Vassall and Child had wanted the strict qualifications for full church membership thrown out. They had also wanted baptism for the children of those who had never been able to give a convincing relation of the conversion experience. Partly be-

6. Robert Baillie, *A Dissuasive from the Errors of our Time* (London, 1645), p. 53. Other attacks written at this time were Samuel Rutherford's *The Due Right of Presbyteries* (London, 1644) and Thomas Edward's *Antapologia* (London, 1644).

7. Walker, *A History*, p. 157.

cause of the high level of piety demanded in Massachusetts, there were many adult baptized covenanters still unconverted; and these people were now demanding baptism for their off-spring. Accordingly, in May 1646 the General Court called for a Synod to be held at Cambridge the following September, "there to discuss, and clear up, by the Word of God, such questions of church government and discipline . . . as they shall think needful and meet."[8] Child's petition, although it eventually failed, had nevertheless provoked the clergy to make a united stand; for as yet the churches had no authoritative statement of their position.

When the Synod finally opened in November (after all the delegates from Plymouth, Connecticut, and New Haven had arrived), the General Court issued a "Declaration," stating that admission to the church was open to all who were "fit" while the right to baptism was under discussion.[9] As to the petitioners, said the Declaration:

> These remonstrants are now come to the Church door. . . . They tell us that divers sober, righteous, and godly men are detained from the seals. . . . The petitioners are sure mistaken or misrepresent the matter; for the true reasons why many persons in the country are not admitted to the seals are these: Many are fraudulous in their conversions or notoriously corrupt in their opinions. . . . It is not for want of respect or good will towards them, but only for distinction's sake, to put a difference between those that do communicate together at the Lord's table, and those who do not.[10]

Shortly thereafter the Court fined Dr. Child fifty pounds. When he tried to sail for England, petition in hand, he was arrested.

8. Quoted in Walker, p. 158.
9. Williston Walker, *The Creeds and Platforms of Congregationalism* (New York, 1893), pp. 176–77.
10. "Declaration, November, 1646," in Walker, *Creeds*, p. 177 n.

By the time he finally got there, in October 1647, the Army
Independents had taken over.

The Independents, who were essentially Congregationalists
in their views on church government, were sympathetic to New
England. Thus it was clear, by the autumn of 1647, that New
England's institutions were not to be disturbed; and this guarantee caused a decisive change in the Synod's attitude. Any
thought of compromise on the questions of church membership
and baptism (questions that had been forced into the open by
the petitioners) was shoved aside. New England no longer had
to think of concealing its rigidity to please the English Presbyterians; and the colonies now were perfectly willing, for the
sake of unity, to subscribe to the main doctrinal articles of the
Westminster Confession of Faith.

The Confession, however, contained several statements contrary to the New Englanders' views on preparation. Therefore
their adherence had to be qualified. Chapter IX of the Confession maintained that man before effectual conversion has "lost
all ability of will to any spiritual good accompanying salvation"
and therefore "is not able . . . to prepare himself thereunto."
Chapter X stated that vocation is "of God's free and special
grace alone, not from any thing at all foreseen in man, who is
altogether passive therein."[11] Consequently, when the Cambridge Synod went into its final session, August 15, 1648, it
prefaced its *Platform of Church Discipline* with the remark:
"We may not conceal that the doctrine of vocation expressed
in Chap. 10 . . . passed not without some debate. Yet considering
that the term of vocation, and others by which it is described,
are capable of a large or more strict sense and use . . . there
hath been a general condescendency thereto."[12]

The Cambridge Platform of 1648, which the Synod unani-
mously approved, was the colonies' first authoritative statement on church discipline. It was also their final answer to

11. Schaff, *Creeds, 3*, 623–25.
12. Walker, *Creeds,* p. 195.

Dr. Child. Specifically, it affirmed in writing what had generally come to be accepted as common practice. It justified the principle of strict admissions to full church membership, yet it recognized at the same time the need for a "calling and winning of souls" to "some hope of a godly conversion." It upheld the notion of exclusiveness, yet it insisted that the main function of a covenant community was to convert the "contrary minded." Because of its close attention to details, it has come to be called "the most important monument of early New England Congregationalism" and "the closest reflection of the system as it lay in the minds of the first generation on our soil after nearly twenty years of experience."[13] In time it was endorsed "for the substance of it" by the Reforming Synod of 1679, and it continued to be one of the legally recognized standards of ecclesiastical practice until 1780. Although it would not, in actual practice, continue to be legally binding, it stood for an attitude of mind which later generations would often be asked to recall, especially when their own times cried for modifications and changes. On the subject of church admissions it cautioned against all easy solutions and went on to explain the virtues of preliminary care.

> We are not ignorant that . . . exceptions are taken at our way of church government . . . as admitting none into the fellowship of our church but Saints by calling. . . . But peace of conscience is more desirable than the peace of the outward man; and freedom from scruples of conscience is more comfortable to a sincere heart than freedom from persecution. . . . To the exception [charge] that we take no course for the gaining and healing and calling in of ignorant and erroneous and scandalous persons, whom we refuse to receive into our churches . . . we conceive the

13. Ibid., pp. 200–01; 185, 188. In its overall structure, the Cambridge Platform of 1648 anticipates the Savoy Declaration of 1658, which defined Congregational polity in England. See Walker, *Creeds,* pp. 340–402.

> receiving of them . . . would rather loose and corrupt our
> churches than gain and heal them. . . . We therefore find
> it safer to square rough and uneven stones, before they be
> laid into the building, rather than to hammer and hew
> them when they lie unevenly in the building.[14]

Candidates for membership, said the Platform, should comply with certain "things which are requisite" before admission. They must then "profess and hold forth in such sort
as may satisfy rational charity that the things are there indeed."
Referring to the manner in which converts were admitted to
the apostolic churches, the document recalls that "Those three
thousand, Acts 2:37, 41, before they were admitted by the
Apostles, did manifest that they were pricked in their hearts
at Peter's sermon, together with earnest desire to be delivered
from their sins"; so that now, in keeping with Scripture, it
may be argued that "a personal and public confession and
declaring of God's manner of working upon the soul is both
lawful, expedient, and useful." Citing I Peter 3:15 as an additional proof text ("Sanctify the Lord God in your hearts, and
be ready always to give an answer to every man that asketh you
a reason of the hope that is in you"), the Platform adds: "We
must be able and ready upon any occasion to declare and show
our repentance for sin, faith unfeigned, and effectual calling."
Finally, because the officers of the church are charged with "the
keeping of the doors of the church," it is they who must
"make trial of the fitness of such who enter"; and this trial of
candidates is to be required of all those who "were never in
church society before," as well as of those who "were baptized
in their infancy, or minority, by virtue of the covenant of their
parents."[15]

On the efficacy of baptism the Platform appears to be more
liberal than Cotton, although not so liberal as Hooker or

14. Walker, *Creeds*, pp. 196–200.
15. Ibid., pp. 222–23.

Bulkeley. The baptized, says the Platform, "have many privileges which others (not church members) have not." They are "in covenant with God, have the seal thereof upon them, viz. baptism," and so "if not regenerated, yet they are in a more hopeful way of attaining regenerating grace, and all the spiritual blessings both of the covenant and seal." In keeping with Shepard's views, the concept of "privilege" is clearly stressed. Moreover, the phrase "if not regenerated" suggests that those in federal holiness may anticipate spiritual gifts, while nowhere is it openly stated that the baptized may rely upon baptismal grace for effectual beginnings. In the words of the Platform, they must look to their hearts for "the weakest measure of faith." If they are able to respond accordingly, then that "weakest measure of faith is to be accepted." But the baptized, as well as all others, must satisfy the examiners. They must remember that "the doors of the Churches of Christ upon earth do not by God's appointment stand so wide open that all sorts of people, good or bad, may freely enter therein at their pleasure," and that "such as are admitted thereto as members ought to be examined and tried first, whether they be fit and meet to be received into church society or not."16

The Cambridge Platform thus fully instituted spiritual tests as requisite to full church membership and, by implication, to full political rights in Massachusetts. Furthermore, the wording of the text would imply that the "personal and public confession," the "declaring of God's manner of working upon the soul," should not exclude the preparatory stages. Since those who were admitted to the primitive church spoke freely of their "wounded consciences" and their "ready receiving of the word of promise and exhortation," the Platform concludes, "We are to be ready to render a reason for the hope that is in us to every one that asketh us."17

16. Ibid., pp. 221–24.
17. Ibid., p. 223. It has recently been argued that the Cambridge Platform tended to ease admissions requirements, mainly because it provided that

Other colonies at the time were similarly involved in working out their own requirements. By 1648, according to William Bradford, the Plymouth church had become "more strict and rigid in some proceedings about admission of members and things of such nature." By 1669, according to a later account, the practice at Plymouth was "for men orally to make confession of faith and a declaration of their experiences of a work of grace in the presence of the whole congregation, having been examined and heard before the Elders in private."[18] In Connecticut, which followed Hooker's policy, the requirements for full church membership were never so strict. (Nor were external covenanters, or even those outside "church society" altogether, ever legally denied an equal voice in the civil government.) But in New Haven, where John Davenport had founded his community of Saints, not only was the electorate restricted to full church members but the barriers to the communion table were higher, perhaps, than in any other colony. As early as 1639, when the New Haven church was first gathered, Davenport had laid down his policy: "We count it our duty," he said, "to use all lawful and convenient means whereby God may help us to discern whether those that offer themselves for Church members be persons so qualified or no." Later he explained that "because the Church cannot see the heart immediately . . . it will

---

"the weakest Christian, if sincere, may not be excluded nor discouraged" (see R. P. Stearns and D. H. Brawner, "New England Church 'Relations' and Continuity in Early Congregational History," *Proceedings of the American Antiquarian Society*, 75 [1965], 13–45). However, it should be observed that the qualifying phrase "if sincere" clearly implies that candidates must satisfy the examiners according to the rules prescribed. In the majority of cases, the most that could be hoped for was the "weakest measure of faith."

18. Colonial Society of Massachusetts, *Publications*, 22 (Boston, 1920) 116, 145. For a close examination of Plymouth's position, see Morgan, *Visible Saints*, pp. 58–63, where the above quotations are cited.

be necessary that the Church be satisfied as by sufficient testimony of the gift of faith, how it was wrought and how it works in them." In fact, nine years before the Cambridge Platform the father of New Haven had made it quite clear that in all cases he must "hear them speak concerning the gift of grace . . . and the manner of God's dealing with them in working it in their hearts." And if the brethren, in examining candidates, should "see just cause to doubt of that," they must "suspend their acceptance till better satisfaction be given."[19]

Like Hooker, Davenport was willing to judge "by rightly ordered charity"; but candidates, he declared, must prove beyond all doubt that "the root of the matter is in them." During nearly thirty years in New Haven he never wavered from his conviction that the experience of grace must be described in minute detail. Since "more is required to qualify for membership of a visible Church than passive vocation," he said, the judgment of charity must be withheld until every response to the "indwelling lively spiritual gifts" has been evaluated: "As Mr. Rogers in his *Treatise of Faith* saith it may be known of men by those trials," so "the confession of faith made to men must hold forth the gift of faith as well as the doctrine of faith. . . . 'Sanctify the Lord God in your heart, and be ready always to give an answer to every man that asketh a reason of the hope that is in you.' I Peter 3:15." Rogers, of course, had been concerned with a private experience of grace never intended for the ears of others; and Hooker, who died while the Cambridge Synod was still in progress, tended to respect this privacy in his own pastoral duties. But Davenport, who probed to the very core of the heart, gave his full support to the Synod's recom-

---

19. John Davenport, *An Answer of the Elders of the Several Churches in New England* (London, 1643), p. 23; *The Power of Congregational Churches* (London, 1672), pp. 17, 21. Although the first work was not published until 1643, it was written in 1639 as an answer to "two and thirty questions sent over . . . by divers ministers in England."

mendations; and this, among other things, set New Haven off from Connecticut.[20]

With Davenport the many threads of Puritan spirituality are woven into a unique pattern. In matters of church discipline he was as strict as Cotton, while in matters of doctrine he was a confirmed preparationist. As a result, he combined the heritage of the "spiritual brotherhood" with an unrelenting quest for purity. Like Cotton, he held to a low degree of efficacy in baptism; but he did not attribute a high degree of efficacy to the Law. Therefore, candidates in New Haven were obliged to relate a complex pattern of responses. Because his rigid discipline was supported by an intricate notion of conversion, he asked for more than Shepard had required. Unlike Hooker or Bulkeley, who went their own independent ways, he followed a path which by 1648 had found its clearest expression in the Cambridge Platform.

Davenport was one of the few New England divines with an Oxford education. Born in 1597 at Coventry, Warwickshire, he went to Merton College in 1613, and later to Magdalen. It was not until 1619, while pastor at the Church of St. Lawrence Jewry, London, that he became acquainted with men of Puritan persuasion. Among them were Richard Sibbes and John Preston, who taught him the rudiments of nonconformity. As late as 1625, however, he still denied any Puritan leanings. Having returned to Oxford for the M.A. and B.D. degrees, he was by then fully entrenched in London as pastor of St. Stephen's Church, where he subscribed to the Prayer Book and wore the surplice. Only in 1632, when he received a visitor who played on his conscience, did he discard this outward show of

20. Davenport, *The Power of Churches*, pp. 14, 17, 21. For an account of Hooker's leniency with candidates, see above, p. 100. According to Cotton Mather, Hooker made allowances for those who were too shy or reserved to offer a full relation: "Some, that could unto edification do it, he put upon . . . relating the manner of their conversion to God; but usually they only answered unto certain probatory questions which were tendered them." Mather, *1*, III, 349.

conformity. John Cotton, on his way to America, convinced
him to change his mind and enlisted his aid in securing a
patent for Massachusetts. On Cotton's departure, Davenport
took off the surplice, worked to obtain the patent, and became
a vigorous nonconformist in open defiance of Laud.[21]

By 1633 he had escaped to Holland, where he became copastor
of the English church at Amsterdam. But soon he discovered
that his colleague, John Paget, was a staunch Presbyterian who
baptized children indiscriminately. When Davenport objected
that only the children of professed believers should be admitted
to the sacrament, a controversy arose which split the congregation. (Later he would tell his friends that God had carried him
to Holland "to bear witness against that promiscuous baptism.")
Meanwhile, Cotton had written to say that the order of the
churches in New England was now settled by common consent,
and that Davenport should come to the Bay. Accordingly, in
1635, he resigned his post in Holland, returned to England,
and with a lifelong friend, Theophilus Eaton, collected a group
of colonists. Two years later, in June 1637, they arrived at
Boston on the *Hector*. On stepping ashore they found the colony
infested with antinomianism; and Cotton, in sincere humiliation, welcomed Davenport "as Moses did Jethro, hoping that
he would be 'as eyes unto them in the wilderness.' "[22]

No sooner had Davenport landed than he began to pull the
colony together. Fresh from controversy in the old world, he
sought to establish harmony in the new. On August 17, at
Boston, he delivered a sermon from the text: "Now I beseech
you, brethren, by the name of our Lord Jesus Christ, that ye all
speak the same thing, and that there be no division among you;
but that ye be perfectly joined together in the same mind and
the same judgment" (I Cor. 1:10). At the close of the Hutchinsonian Synod, which he attended, he was again asked to preach
a sermon; and this time he chose Philippians 3:16: "Neverthe-

21. Alexander Wood Renton, *Dictionary of National Biography, 5,* 560–61.
22. Mather, *Magnalia, 1,* III, 325.

less, whereunto we have attained, let us walk by the same rule, let us mind the same thing." Later on, the people of the Bay were eager to have him settle there. The General Court begged him to accept any region that had not yet been granted. But Davenport, who by now had already visited Quinnipiac, decided not to stay in Massachusetts. He was much taken by the beauty and fertility of the southern tract. Moreover, he was attracted by the idea of settling in an unsubdued part of the wilderness where erroneous opinions could be kept out. Such a withdrawal, he believed, would allow him to further the cause of reformation in the church—away from the "mixed multitude" of the Bay. "As easily might the ark have been removed from the mountains of Ararat, where it first grounded," he remarked, "as a people get any ground in reformation after and beyond the first remove of the reformers."[23] Therefore, he collected his followers, and on April 14, 1638, arrived at the spot which he had chosen for his community.

During the Antinomian Controversy, and while a guest at Cotton's house, Davenport had invited his host to join the expedition. "The truth is," Cotton later confessed, "I did intend to remove . . . because I saw we should receive no more members into our Church but such as must profess themselves of a contrary judgment to what I believed." But in weighing the invitation "to remove to Quinipyatk, whereto at that time a door was opened," Cotton proceeded with caution. Before making up his mind, he tells us, "I took advice of some friends here, especially Mr. Davenport," and then "resolved to see if my continuance here would certainly or probably breed any further offensive agitation." Having discussed the matter with Davenport, he then went to the magistrates for their final opinion on his doctrine of conversion; and they now "declared to me their minds touching such points of Union, or evidencing of Union, which I had taught, that they did not look at them to

23. A. W. M'Clure, *The Lives of John Wilson, John Norton, and John Davenport* (Boston, 1846), pp. 271, 275.

be of such fundamental concernment either to civil or Church peace, as needed to occasion any distance in heart (much less in place) amongst godly brethren."[24]

From this we may surmise that Davenport, in proffering the invitation, wanted first to make sure that Cotton had genuinely modified his views. If the doctrine Cotton had preached could lead to "further offensive agitation" in Massachusetts, would it not shake the very foundations of New Haven? Davenport was determined to restore calm in the Bay; and this could be done either by removing Cotton or by encouraging him to conform where he was. In any event, the founder of New Haven needed some assurance, for the sake of order in the colonies, that his colleague would not renege: and Cotton, for his part, firmly denied "any thoughts of separation from . . . the Churches of New England; for the Churches in Quinipyatk are in New England."[25]

Had Cotton gone to Quinnipiac, he would have approved of the policy on church admissions there. In August 1639, when the church was gathered, Davenport took only those who could pass a "most careful" examination—"on which duty he laid the greatest stress."[26] Like Cotton, he maintained that external covenanters were utterly depraved in that their baptism should not be taken as a first sign of regeneration. "To be baptized," he said, "will nothing advantage any to Church fellowship . . . because though God searcheth and knoweth the heart, yet the Church doth not." Therefore, he declared, "Let them that are to be admitted into membership, by their personal right, show how faith was wrought." Unlike Cotton, however, he held that faith works "not by constraint" but "through the operation of God working faith in their hearts by the Spirit." Let them show "how it works in them in the lowest degree," he maintained, "then the Church will have some ground for their

24. Cotton, *The Way Cleared,* pp. 52–54.
25. Ibid., p. 54.
26. M'Clure, p. 280.

charitable judgment concerning their fitness for regular Church membership and communion." The church, said Davenport, "should awaken their circumspection in looking narrowly to their fitness for personal membership"; and they in turn should declare their "heart-fitness," as "things are not manifested to the Church otherwise than by congruous actings."[27]

On this point, in the privacy of his study, Cotton would have brooded over their differences; for when the Spirit descends, Davenport proclaimed, we are not forced into submission. Rather, we are stirred by a "convincing light" to which we respond as it draws us to Christ. It is an "undeniable" light "like the light of the sun," which "shows the evil of sin . . . and draws the will answerably." Under its spiritual rays we move toward effectual conversion and are "so prepared" that "it quieteth and settleth the heart in peace proportionately to the measure of our trusting and hoping in God." Although we cannot respond through our "natural abilities," we must nevertheless respond; otherwise we cannot describe how faith is wrought. "We act," Davenport maintained, "but instrumentally, insubordinately under the Spirit, who is the principle efficient agent in all spiritual good." "We act," he said, "not in our strength . . . but from the quickening, strengthening influence of the Spirit." What is more, these acts are "effectual to salvation" so long as we "obey from the heart."[28]

"There is an outward calling," he acknowledged, which is "ineffectual unto spiritual conversion, of itself, without the quickening efficacies of the Spirit." But when the work of the Spirit is "added" to the outward call, then "God speaketh to the heart" and the heart must "answer with the voice of the whole soul unto God." We need not be constrained, Davenport

27. John Davenport, *Another Essay for the Investigation of the Truth* (Cambridge, 1663), pp. 49, 28, 6, 17.

28. John Davenport, *The Saints Anchor-Hold* (London, 1682), pp. 51–53, 69–70, 88; *The Knowledge of Christ* (London, 1653), "To the Christian Reader."

argued, so long as the external call is effectual. Indeed, the very efficacy of the Spirit requires that we act in our first awakening —"when all the faculties and affections of the soul do open themselves to give entertainment unto God . . . when the eye of the soul is turned upward to look unto God, inward to reflect upon the inward actings of the soul." Natural man, to be sure, "cannot give life to himself, being dead"; for "the heart of unbelievers is like a standing pool, where that which is cast into it rests." But when the "wind" of the Spirit "bloweth where it listeth," the waters must stir "to make way for true faith and hope."[29]

For Cotton, the affections of the soul in the external call were not the least bit efficacious. Until the will had been turned by force, man remained passive in his spiritual nature. Moreover, man's response to this force was precisely what Cotton had required in experiential relations. Davenport, on the other hand, sought an active "hope," which he said must be "bottomed upon the Word and promises of God . . . as conducing unto preparatory purposes and uses." Like Hooker, he believed that hope evolved from "moderate sorrow" rather than from excessive fear of the Law. But where Hooker saw hope as a veritable sign of faith, requiring little or no proof, Davenport demanded evidence. "He that hath this hope," he said, "purgeth himself"; for unless the church has elaborate visible evidence of self-purgation, it cannot discern a first "principle of life." Furthermore, where Hooker had said that hope in God has its initial source in the "spiritual efficacy" of baptism, Davenport maintained that "the New Testament nowhere alloweth that latitude of speech." To the argument that "some children of the covenant have the beginnings of grace," and that "being in covenant and baptized they have faith sealed in baptism," Davenport replied that "visible want of ability to examine themselves . . . argues a visible want of that faith which is to be

29. Davenport, *The Saints Anchor-Hold*, pp. 12, 36–37, 40–41, 58, 73.

examined and exercised, and a just bar to the admittance of such to immediate and personal Church membership, as well as to the Lord's Supper."[30]

The founder of New Haven, like the founder of Connecticut, taught a theory of conversion which encouraged activity and response; but in New Haven these responses were ultimately confined by rigid procedure. Davenport, like Cotton at Boston, could not be content with anything less than the clearest possible assurance. Nor could he accept the full implications of covenant theology. Although he looked to the promises as a basis for "hope," he could not accept the efficacy of the "seed"; and so, unlike Hooker or Bulkeley, he demanded visible evidence which left "no cause to doubt." Like Shepard, he held that baptism itself is no more than a "privilege" and that "heart-fitness" should take precedence over spiritual desires. In short, he spoke for a consensus of orthodox opinion which by 1648 had clearly left its mark on New England theology.

Underneath this façade of unanimity, however, other forces were at work which would eventually bring about a change. In 1646, when the ministers had first met at Cambridge, they had been mainly concerned with the threat of Presbyterianism. As a result, they had agreed to stress the principle that candidates for communion give a convincing relation of the conversion experience. Furthermore, they seem also to have agreed that the preparatory stages were in themselves efficacious. But by the early 1650s synergistic opinions had begun to take hold in the colonies. New immigrants from England had brought Arminian errors with them; and the line that divided gracious preparatory activities from natural abilities was beginning to

30. Ibid., pp. 98, 116, 231; *Another Essay*, pp. 28–30. In his discussion of baptism, Davenport never comes directly to terms with Pauline teachings on the efficacy of the rite. Nevertheless, he is obviously aware of the passages that could be used against him. Unlike Cotton, he does not uphold the Christophany at Damascus as normative, yet he consistently maintains that any emphasis on baptismal efficacy diminishes the work of faith.

break down. At the same time, antinomianism had spread to various parts of England, and in the guise of "Quakerism" it threatened to invade America again. Therefore, when the ministers found themselves challenged once more by doctrinal antagonists, this time from two sides, they began to reexamine their position. If they had left themselves open to these heresies, in spite of all they had done theologically to guard against them, then surely something was wrong.

In their search for a solution to this problem they had not far to go, as they were soon guided by John Norton, the pastor at Ipswich. Norton, who had sailed with Shepard on the abortive journey of 1634, published his *Orthodox Evangelist* in 1657; and in it he called for a thorough reexamination of New England theology. If the heresies had gained a foothold, he said, the established position on conversion had opened the way. More specifically, if the heresies were to be stamped out, the accepted notion of the preparatory phase had to be revised. Accordingly, he not only altered preparation to fit the needs of the time but offered a critical analysis of the concept as it stood in the Cambridge Platform.

Born of "honorable ancestors" at Bishop's Stortford, Hertfordshire, in 1606, Norton had entered Peter House, Cambridge, at fourteen. He took the B.A. in 1627; but shortly thereafter, on the ruin of his father's estate, he was forced to leave the university. While a tutor at Stortford grammar school, "God gave him a discovery of his own manifold sinfulness and wretchedness in an unregenerate state, and awakened him unto such a self-examination as drove him to a sorrow little short of despair." From then on he devoted himself to the "higher studies of divinity" and became an outspoken nonconformist preacher. His "antipathy to Arminianism" and "dislike of ceremonies" prevented his taking a "considerable benefice" offered him by an uncle. Then Richard Sibbes, as master of Catherine Hall, offered him a fellowship; "but his conscience being now satisfied of the unlawfulness of some things then required in order thereto, would not permit him to do it." In 1634 he married a gentlewoman of good estate and, after his first attempt to sail for New England, finally arrived at Plymouth in 1635. That year he was called as teacher at Ipswich, under Nathaniel Ward, whom he succeeded as pastor in 1639. In 1652, when John Cotton died, Norton became teacher at the Boston church, and there he remained until his death in 1663.[31]

While still at Ipswich Norton wrote *The Orthodox Evange-list,* for which Cotton wrote a preface, dated "Boston, 20. Sept. 1652"—three months before his death. Said Cotton, "The most judicious and Orthodox of our best writers, Calvin, Martyr, Bucer, and the rest," have been "slighted" in New England. "How well therefore doth it become this our Reverend brother, the teacher of an intelligent people (the church at Ipswich) to launch forth into the deep . . . concerning the concourse of grace, and free will therein."[32]

Norton, in fear of Quaker antinomianism, wanted to retain preparatory activity and the idea of a complex, many-staged *ordo salutis* as barriers to "enthusiasm," against the idea of conversion as a completely unmeditated and unprepared inva-sion by the Spirit. Yet at the same time he was against synergistic subversion and determined to assert the high Calvinist principle that man's actions prior to conversion are ineffectual. There-fore, he took both the introspective and affective preconversion activities, which Hooker, Shepard, and Davenport had assigned to man, and insisted that in most cases they must precede saving grace. But at the same time he followed Cotton's pattern for conversion, and so intentionally deprived these activities of

31. Mather, *Magnalia, 1,* III, 287, 288; Charlotte Fell-Smith, *Dictionary of National Biography, 14,* 659–60.
32. Cotton, "To the Judicious Christian Reader," in John Norton, *The Orthodox Evangelist* (London, 1657).

their efficacy. That is, he saw conversion as entirely a matter of divine initiative.

"The term preparatory," said Norton, "is to be considered either in respect of God . . . or in respect of us." Preparation "in respect of God's intention" occurs when the heart is broken by "the tyrannical dominion of the Law in respect of its rigors." To this constraint we respond in six stages of "conviction," leading from conviction of sin to conviction of guilt. But it is not our response that determines God's intention. He may bring us under conviction and leave us there for eternal damnation. "Preparatory repentance worketh not any change of the heart," Norton insisted, so long as we are still under constraint. In this condition men are "totally but not finally lost; totally in respect of their sins . . . but not finally in respect of God's gracious purpose to them." Indeed, "the sovereignty of God in this particular is His absolute free power to show, or not to show, mercy unto man, according to His own good pleasure."[33]

These stages of conviction are then followed by six more stages of preparatory repentance, which are wrought not only by the Law but by the Gospel Spirit. Here man's affective nature, his desire for Christ, is taken into account. But because preparation is ineffectual, even under the first drawing motions of the Spirit, "in this soul-thirsty disposition after Christ, whilst we so restlessly desire, as yet we find we cannot sincerely desire." Our seeking "before faith," said Norton, is the ineffectual "common work of the Spirit." Our seeking "after faith" is something else again—"the effect of the saving work of the Spirit."

Question: Is a distinct experience of the several heads of preparatory work necessary to God's ordinary dispensation?
Answer: No, yet the more distinctness the better.
Question: What measure of preparatory work is necessary to conversion?

33. Norton, *Orthodox Evangelist*, pp. 129–58.

Answer: As the greatest measure hath no necessary connection with salvation, so the least measure puts the soul in a preparatory capacity.

Although these preparatory works are "by some called saving," he added, "we are to know that a saving work falleth not under the compass of this question."[34]

On the conditional promises Norton moved with caution but with firm determination. The "enthusiasts," he said, err by not giving the promises their due—"by denying any preparatory use of them." The Arminians, on the other hand, make too much of them, and teach that "man not regenerate" may meet certain conditions "which ought to be acceptable to God." Between the two extremes are "others with whom the forementioned are not to be named, reverend, learned, judicious, and pious." These men, said Norton of his colleagues, "seem to teach that there are some qualifications before faith that are saving, whereunto faith and salvation may be ascertained." But if their intentions are well meant, they nevertheless open the way for synergistic error. Therefore, the time has come, he proclaimed, "to examine and also to propound the following consideration for the negative: to promise salvation before faith, and consequently before Christ, holds not correspondency with the rest of God's dispensation of His acts of grace."[35]

Before effectual conversion, said Norton, man's best actions are but "painted sins," because "his person, not being accepted, his actions cannot be accepted." If it be held that such actions, or qualifications, are from grace, he went on, "I answer that it is not enough to acknowledge such qualifications to be from God or grace, except it be in such a way, namely, of his peculiar grace, viz., from God according to election . . . from His special grace"; for "no effect of election is before effectual vocation." In other words, Norton was determined to deny the efficacy

34. Ibid., pp. 159–65.
35. Ibid., pp. 165–67.

of man's initial response to the gifts of the Spirit and, like Cotton, to limit conversion itself to the moment of election. Until that time, he said, all men are "children of wrath." In preparation they are still thoroughly reprobate, still "under the Law notwithstanding any Gospel work."[36]

To the objection that "salvation is promised unto hungering, thirsting, poverty of spirit, which are qualifications preceding faith, therefore salvation may be promised to some qualifications before faith"; Norton replied: "All objections raised from these and like promises . . . may receive a full answer by the right answer of the distinction of qualifications into preparatory, or legal, which go before faith, and saving, or evangelical, which follow faith." Furthermore, in order to support his stand, he turned without specific citation to a quotation from Peter Martyr: "Vocation, conversion, or regeneration is wrought in an instant. God in saying live, makes us alive." He then drew from Calvin: "For faith in respect of justification is a mere passive thing" (*Institutes,* Bk. III, chap. 14). Next, in order to drive the lesson home and to show that preparation should once again be relegated to the "reprobate" condition, he referred to William Perkins: "In the beginning of conversion . . . the inclinations of the mind, will, and affections of the heart are merely passive" (*God's Free Grace and Man's Free Will,* p. 737). William Pemble, said Norton, insists that "there cannot be a life act before life"; and finally, "the promise (saith Dr. Preston) is made to the coming and not to the preparations."[37]

Yet in spite of these authorities, Norton still maintained that preparatory activity, however inefficacious, should and must precede the moment of conversion. Unlike Cotton, he followed Calvin's rule that the biblical exhortations to prepare are clearly "useful." They could best be used, he believed, as a nominal check on "enthusiasm." Reprobates, he claimed, should be

36. Ibid., pp. 168, 170.
37. Ibid., pp. 184, 282, 269, 264, 178. For Perkins' full statement, see above, p. 62 ff. For Preston's original statement, see above, p. 78.

reminded at every turn that without the Word the Spirit cannot work, and that direct revelation is contrary to Scrpiture.
They should be exhorted to examine their innermost sins in
fear and terror of the Law. In addition, they should hunger,
thirst, and long for grace according to biblical prescription.
This period of "looking to hearts," he allowed, might eventually bring them to Christ. But having looked to their hearts,
they should never forget that "every essential change is in a
moment." Although "generation is taken improperly for the
way and preparation," actually it "cannot be effected divisibly
and successively, or gradually." "In the moment of conversion,"
said Norton, "God works that blessed work in an instant."[38]

In Norton, as in none other, we find a new and significantly
different attitude toward the function and purpose of preparatory motions. In the tradition of Rogers and Sibbes, he
was determined to uphold an elaborately constructed interior
life. This much is true. But for the earlier preparationists this
life had originally evolved from the conviction that conversion
is gradual, that the soul in effectual stages responds to gracious
activity; while Norton now declared that "the soul itself in this
work is no way active from any principle of activity . . . no more
than in the dead man to produce life." In returning to Peter
Martyr and to the strict Reformed school, he discarded the notion of spiritual "gifts" or "works." As a result, he firmly
maintained that "in vocation (notwithstanding all preparatory
work) life is wrought by the quickening active Spirit of Christ
in the dead passive soul." Because "vocation is a miracle," he
said, "men are always passive in receiving such miraculous
effects or impressions."[39] His essential criticism of preparation,
as taught in New England theology, was that it cheapened
grace and brought God down to man's level. Thus, in his
writings as a whole, we find a vigorous continuation of the
stricter side of Puritan spirituality, closely resembling that of

38. Ibid., pp. 282–83.
39. Ibid., pp. 258–59, 269.

his predecessor at the Boston church. Cotton's position, while clearly reformulated, is nevertheless maintained.

Having rendered preparation ineffectual, Norton then advanced the concept as requisite to full church membership. Without the requirement, he reasoned, faith might seem too easy. Therefore candidates must be exhorted to examine their hearts and confess their faith in the light of God's revealed Word. "This we hold," he said, that "people ought not to be received into the Church . . . except after they have made confession of their faith and their penitence." In addition, he staunchly affirmed that "a certain preparation on the part of candidates besides the mere asking to unite is prerequisite to admission."[40] Because "a certain preparation" did not, however, mean effectual preparation, candidates were to be reminded that they themselves had taken no active role in the process. On the other hand, those who might claim direct "revealings" from God were to be told that "a certain preparation" was essential before the slightest assurance of salvation. In this way, Norton could maintain the highest kind of doctrinal bulwarks against Arminianism, while at the same time he had clearly established a safeguard against the perils of antinomian enthusiasm. In short, he had found an elaborate solution to Cotton's dilemma.

By his return to a more strictly Reformed theology, Norton had reduced the regenerative process to one effectual moment in time. Like Martyr and Calvin, he was not so much concerned with the process per se as with the attributes of sainthood, or piety itself. But Norton's opinions, no matter how significant, were not the only ones which had discredited the concept of preparation in the second half of the seventeenth century. Another critique, based on an opposite point of view, was published by Giles Firmin thirteen years after the *Orthodox Evangelist*. Firmin criticized preparation not because it cheapened grace but for the barriers it placed in man's way. The

40. Norton, *The Answer*, p. 28.

manner in which Hooker, Shepard, and others had preached the
concept, said Firmin, made the standards of grace too high.
Their demands for preparatory activity not only fenced the
communion table but put salvation beyond the reach of all
ordinary mortals.

✠

Giles Firmin, who was born in 1614 at Ipswich, England,
matriculated at Emmanuel College in 1629, where he studied
medicine as well as divinity. In 1632 he went to New England
with his father and was ordained deacon of the Boston church
under Cotton. In 1638 he was given a grant of land at Ipswich,
Massachusetts, where he married Susanna, daughter of Nathaniel Ward. There he practiced medicine and frequently
heard Norton preach. Soon, however, he returned to England
—leaving his wife and family in America. In 1648 he was appointed to the vicarage of Shalford, Essex; but because he had
preached before he was in orders, the Congregational ministers
were unwilling to impose hands. Subsequently he was ordained
by the Presbyterians, and he had an enthusiastic following until
after the Restoration. In 1662 he was ejected. In his old age he
retired to Ridgewell, Essex, where he again practiced medicine
until he died in 1697.[41]

In America he had known Hooker, Shepard, Bulkeley, and
Davenport, as well as Cotton and Norton. He was present at
the Hutchinsonian Synod, witnessed the trial before the Boston
church, and afterwards wrote a defense of the ministers.[42] "The
sum is this," he said; "when all ways according to the Word had
been tried with Mrs. Hutchinson to recall her, but none would
prevail, the question was put to the Church to manifest consent
to her excommunication. . . . Now I appeal unto all to judge
where was the tyranny in this act?"[43] Yet when all her accusers

41. Gordon, 7, 45–46.
42. John Ward Dean, *A Brief Memoir of Rev. Giles Firmin* (Boston,
1866), p. 7.
43. Giles Firmin, *Separation Examined* (London, 1652), p. 102.

were dead, Firmin took great exception to the theory of conversion that lay at the root of their arguments against her. In *The Real Christian*, published in 1670, he complained that "certain of their books" had caused men trouble, "some in the preparation of the soul for Christ, amongst which are the works of the eminent servants of Christ, Mr. Thomas Hooker and Mr. Thomas Shepard." The trouble, said Firmin, was originally caused by "our ancient divines," among them "Mr. Perkins," with their "description of faith." "I was troubled at them myself at my first reading of them," he confessed, and then "I began to question the truth of those particulars." Once, after a sermon in which Firmin had refuted Shepard's views, "a gentleman and a scholar meeting me gave me thanks. . . . I asked him why. He told me he had a maidservant who was very godly, and reading of that particular in Mr. Shepard's book which I opposed, she was so cast down and fell into such troubles that all the Christians that came to her could not quiet her spirits." Furthermore, Firmin went on, "I have met with several persons who could not be resolved that ever their faith was true, because of that which he had written."[44]

The way to Christ, said Firmin, must be cleared of "stumbling blocks"—in spite of the "eminent divines" who laid the blocks in the way. When the sinner resolves to turn toward the covenant of grace, why should his course be hindered with demands that he be "rightly humbled and prepared for Christ" and "a long time under preparation"? Although some may doubt the truth of their conversion "for want of their sensible experience of these preparative works," still it must be said that preachers who demand "such strong convictions, such dreadful legal terrors, deep sorrows, and humblings" show little regard for anything that might "ease troubled souls." "Now when the awakened sinner in his way to Christ meets with these," Firmin observed, "Oh what work do these make a poor distressed, lost,

44. Giles Firmin, *The Real Christian* (London, 1670), "To the Christian Reader."

undone sinner! . . . Surely the work of regeneration is not so easy, though these things be left out. . . . Why then these blocks must be thrown in the way I know not."[45]

Throughout his critique, Firmin is harder on Shepard than Hooker. He had written to Shepard in the last two years of the Cambridge minister's life and was therefore more closely acquainted with his thought. "Mr. Shepard, both in his book and in his letters to me, is oft up with this," he said; while "Mr. Hooker, though I had heard his doctrine, yet I had not read his book before I had read Mr. Shepard and had seriously considered him." On the question of "legal terrors" and preparative rules, Firmin was particularly against Shepard. Where, he asked, does Scripture put the condition "prepared" in the sense of "great terrors, fears"? If we understand faith as "Mr. Perkins" defines it, then to talk of faith without such preparations is "dangerous indeed." But "how many men have had great humblings, legal terrors, sorrows, in a high degree?" Shepard, said Firmin, demands that we endure these terrors "without God's love," and that man be "content though God will never work grace." This, however, is not the Christian message. Moreover, it fails to assume that the baptized may already be pledged to God: "To say then there is such a rule laid down for preparative works, that every one must pass through before they can be regenerated, or have faith, I cannot be convinced of it, unless you can tell me how infants can be prepared according to Mr. Shepard's method. . . . I marvel what use Mr. Shepard would have us make of baptism . . . I wonder that Mr. Shepard should let such a logical fault slip and not take notice of it . . . Doth not God many times in infancy cast in the immortal seed?"[46] And Firmin continued:

> The reason of my laying this position is this: Reverend Mr. Shepard saith "Many thousands are miserably deceived

45. Ibid., "The Introduction," pp. 1, 3.
46. Ibid., pp. 5–6, 9, 129, 107, 124–25.

about their estates by this one thing, of crooking and wrestling God's rule to Christian experience," *The Sound Believer,* p. 53. Then he gives this caution, "We must not bring rules to men, but men to rules." p. 52 . . . But then what shall we say to all those whom the Lord regenerates in their infancy? I am sure Mr. Shepard, nor Mr. Hooker (who saith, "Certainly God doth work faith in the hearts of all elected infants," *Covenant of Grace Opened,* p. 26, 27) will deny but God doth regenerate some infants.[47]

Firman's main argument, then, is that Shepard, to the detriment of all other aspects of conversion, insists too strongly on rules and legal constraint. Therefore, he attacked the part of Shepard's thought that least resembles Hooker's: "I remember Mr. Hooker, at a meeting of about forty ministers, put that question: What rules they would go by in admission of members to churches? Will you go by the narration of the work of God upon them in conversion? Or will you look at the frame wherewith they make their narration? . . . Mr. Shepard said, More are driven to Christ by the sense of the burden of an hard, dead, blind, filthy heart, than by the sense of sorrows." But in other respects, said Firmin, "I see both the father-in-law, Mr. Hooker, with his son-in-law, Mr. Shepard, go both in the same way."[48]

Where Shepard and Hooker do take man's affective nature into account, Firmin maintains that both, nevertheless, are inconsistent: for while the two depict Israel "now under the work of conversion, turning home to God, and being made willing to come home to God," they at the same time insist that "Israel must be content though God will not receive him."[49] This inconsistency Firmin attributes to the fallacy of the stages of faith, which in themselves, he holds, are a barrier to effectual

47. Ibid., pp. 7–8.
48. Ibid., pp. 86, 107.
49. Ibid., p. 112.

grace. In tracing their origins to Richard Rogers, he pleads that man be allowed to have assurance at all costs:

> Mr. Richard Rogers, in *Seven Treatises,* makes several degrees of faith: 1. the weakest and least measure, when there is no assurance in the believer; 2. when there is some assurance at some time, but in weak degree. . . . Yet he hath set out faith by assurance and said that is the faith which uniteth to Christ. Now how can these things possibly hang together, when as he and so holy Perkins will own many for sound believers, in whom was no assurance, and yet it is that assurance . . . which uniteth to Christ?"[50]

Firmin insists, however, that preparation as such should not be denied, so long as all anxiety is eliminated. The concept itself, he says, is not only "the opinion of Mr. Hooker, Mr. Shepard, or two or three more such rigid men," but can be found in the writings of "the ablist practical divines, besides our divines at the Synod of Dort." On this ground alone it should be allowed to stand, although with certain modifications. It should be allowed to stand if man can be assured of attaining his goal, if the soul can be assured of salvation; but if the heart is torn by agony and doubt, there is nothing to be gained from the process. Indeed, if the truth of the matter be known—in spite of all the preparationists might say—the "Real Christian" is the baptized child, not the man who must turn toward God or struggle with his conscience. "When Mr. Hooker preached those sermons about the souls preparation for Christ," Firmin recalled, "my father-in-law, Mr. Nathaniel Ward, told him, 'Mr. Hooker, you make as good Christian before men are in Christ as ever they are after'; and wished, 'would I were but as good a Christian now as you make men while they are preparing for Christ.' "[51] Because Firmin himself longed for what he called "a sure persuasion of my heart," he could not

50. Ibid., p. 191.
51. Ibid., pp. 230, 19, 153.

accept the notion of conditional requirements. Let the heart be prepared, he maintained, but let it be free from tyrannical demands. Let there be no conditions on which the spiritual life may be said to depend.

Like Norton, then, Firmin was willing to retain preparation; and for this reason, among others, he had taken the side of the ministers in 1637. He had stood with the accusers of Anne Hutchinson. But he wanted to retain the preparatory phase without the anxiety which Hooker, Shepard, and other "such rigid men" thought necessary. He was willing to allow for a general sense of expectation but made no concessions to conditional requirements. Norton, on the other hand, valued these requirements for whatever degree of anxiety they might still arouse. No better system, he believed, could be devised to check the uncontrolled enthusiasm of those who might claim salvation by direct revelation of the Holy Spirit. At the same time, however, the victory of the preparationists in the high tide of the first generation had led to synergistic opinions (in spite of all the founding divines had said to distinguish their views from Arminianism), and Norton, in the tradition of Cotton, was determined to make a sharp division between any act on man's part and the fact of divine election. He therefore cut off the efficacy of the preparatory phase, which was all that Firmin had wanted to retain.

Although nominally a Congregationalist, Firmin had been ordained by the Presbyterians. Most important of all, he held to their sense of continuity between baptism and assurance with little regard for a conscious experience of regenerating work. And this attitude of mind, in competition with Norton's view, anticipates a rival trend in the course theology would run. From Norton's position there is a clear line of development which can readily be traced through the next few generations, through figures such as Increase Mather and Solomon Stoddard down to Jonathan Edwards. It is a line that would continue into the nineteenth century through a series of evangelical revivals.

From Firmin's position, on the other hand, there emerged a
different tradition—one more closely allied to the Presbyterian
attitudes which had put New England on its guard in the 1640s.
It is a line that cannot be so accurately traced in terms of immediate influence, but one that would continue into the next
two centuries as a moving force in the development of a more
"liberal" theology. There would be those, like Firmin, who
professed assurance of faith from birth with little or no sense
of change in the heart; and there would be others, like Norton,
who continued to believe that knowledge of God must come
through sudden transformation.

What needs to be examined, of course, are the conditions
under which these rival notions would begin to thrive and the
reasons for their growing appeal. The members of the second
generation were naturally not pitched to the high key of piety
which had marked the Great Migration to the Bay. However
much they may have sympathized with their elders' views, there
were many among them who could not honestly claim to have
known the unique experience which their parents had described
as a gradual change of heart. As a result, there arose a class of
people virtually set apart from the regenerate community,
people for whom the theories of the founders were far too
strenuous and demanding. As one historian has remarked:

> The original settlers of New England were men of tried
> religious experience. Most of those who occupied positions
> of prominence in the community could give a reason for
> the faith that was in them. They had been sifted out of the
> mass of the Puritans of England. The struggles through
> which they had gone, the type of piety which they had
> heard inculcated, and their efforts to overcome the spiritual
> inertia of the English Establishment, engendered prevail-
> ingly a deep, emotional, introspective faith, which looked
> upon a conscious regenerative work of the spirit of God
> in the heart as essential to Christian hope.[52]

52. Walker, *Creeds*, p. 245.

But the offspring of these immigrants were a whole generation removed from the struggles in England; and by the time they had come "of age," when they were asked to give their own experience of grace, this intensity of feeling had gone. Indeed, less than a decade after the Cambridge Platform had been adopted, the problem consisted not so much in keeping out unworthy applicants for full membership as in inducing external members to strive. The problem also consisted of what to do with the children of these external members, as the ministers extended baptism only to the immediate offspring of the regenerate.

In this crisis a convention of ministers was called, as the church had to go on even if largely composed of unregenerate members; and the convention was asked to devise a means whereby the children of the external members might be kept within the covenant bond. The Massachusetts Court, in the autumn of 1656, had ordered that certain ministers of the Bay, including John Norton, Richard Mather, and "Mr. Bulkeley, if he can come," be prepared "to meet at Boston the first fifth day of June next following [June 4, 1657] to confer and debate the said questions amongst themselves or with such divines as shall be sent to said meeting from the other colonies."[53] Bulkeley, now nearly seventy-four years old, was unable to attend. Connecticut sent the Reverend Samuel Stone, Hooker's successor at Hartford, as one of four delegates. But New Haven, under the influence of John Davenport, refused to appoint a single representative. So far as Davenport was concerned, there was nothing to debate. The baptismal right, he maintained, must always be confined to the children of visible believers, as any extention of the right would open the way for renewed Presbyterian subversion. And he let it be known that the delegates leaving from Connecticut should be treated with scorn, as Robert Child had been handled in 1646.[54]

Ten years earlier, when Child had first challenged the

53. *Records of Massachusetts Bay* (Boston, 1853), 3, 419.
54. Walker, *Creeds*, p. 260.

churches on their discipline, the framers of the Cambridge
Platform had been able to pass over the question of infant
baptism, mainly because the Army Independents had triumphed in England and the threat of Presbyterian rule had
been removed. Robert Child had insisted that all who would
have been considered members of the Church of England at
home should be admitted to the Lord's Supper and their children baptized. But such a practice would have broken down
the theory of visible sainthood. Moreover, it would have eliminated experiential relations with the requirement of preparation as evidence of sainthood. Only at Newbury, where it seems
nothing could be done about it, were such aberrant principles
tolerated. Now, however, the problem had to be faced directly.
External members could not be expelled without cause, nor
could they be admitted to communion: and so it was decided,
when the convention finally met, that they could transmit their
status to the next generation, provided they themselves assented
to the truths of the Gospel and promised fidelity to church discipline, or "owned the covenant." The unregenerate were still
to be barred from communion until such time as they experienced a change of heart; and to this degree the Cambridge Platform was upheld. The notion of preparation was not disputed;
the standards for full church membership were not diminished.
But the churches were now committed to the nurture and care
of a future assortment of people for whom the baptismal tie
might have to stand in perpetuity as their only visible link to
God. In time, therefore, either the tie would have to be accepted
as a substitute for felt experience, and the notion of conversion
altogether discarded, or a more direct and immediate means of
assurance would have to be devised. In short, the unregenerate
might look in one of two possible directions. Either they could
look in Firmin's direction, where a conscious experience of
grace need never be felt; or they could turn to Norton, where
a conscious sense of change might clearly be felt, while they
themselves would have nothing effectual to do on their own.

Norton, to be sure, had retained the preparatory act as a nominal check on enthusiasm, but he had also maintained that "every essential change is in a moment." "Generation," he had said, "is taken improperly for the way and preparation," when in fact it "cannot be effected divisibly and successively, or gradually." God, in the moment of conversion, "works that blessed work in an instant."

Ironically enough, then, just as Norton was about to publish his *Orthodox Evangelist,* which pointed to one possible solution, the way—in a sense—had already been paved for the adoption of his views. At the same time, it should be said, the way had been equally well prepared for the adoption of views similar to Firmin's. Although the older standards were still enforced, and traditional views upheld, the stage had been set for these alternate ways of thinking to take hold. Through the final decision to extend baptism to the children of unregenerate parents, the ministers had forced the churches to retain still another generation of unregenerate members; and these would eventually have to find an easier way to God.

✠

Earlier in the convention, when a final decision had yet to be made, the delegates had been faced with a host of complex issues. In the proceedings themselves, which hint at a strong and articulate opposition, they had first to deal with the established view on the meaning of the covenant relationship. According to the New Testament, the convention acknowledged, it is indeed possible to hold that "The Gospel by Covenant seed intends only the seed of immediate parents in Church Covenant, as appears from I Cor. 7:14" ("else were your children unclean"). Here, the ministers agreed, "The Gospel extends not the external Covenant beyond the immediate parents." But it can also be shown from Scripture, they were quick to point out, that the Apostles "in the work of discipling" clearly expanded the covenant promises to include others. ("Repent

and be baptized . . . for the promise is unto you and to your
children and to all that are afar off, even as many as the Lord
God shall call." Acts 2:38, 39) Furthermore, in the Old Testament there are "Scripture examples of persons both called to,
and entering into Covenant, many of whom could not be looked
upon as . . . fit for all ordinances, Deut. 29:12, 13" ("Thou
shouldest enter into covenant with the Lord thy God . . . that
he may establish thee today for a people unto himself . . . as he
hath sworn unto thy fathers, to Abraham, to Isaac, and to
Jacob."). It follows, then, the convention argued, that "Children in the covenant of Abraham, as to the substance thereof,
i.e. to whom the promises made to Abraham as to the substance
thereof doth belong, are to be baptized." In the opinion of the
majority, the problem could be reduced to one essential issue:
"Either the children in question are to be baptized, or the
Gospel dispensation forbids the application of the seal unto
children regularly in the Church covenant, unto whom the
Mosaical dispensation commanded it to be applied." In other
words, according to the weight of biblical argument, the children of unregenerate parents have as great a right to the covenant promises—sealed in baptism—as do the children of the
regenerate. To the objection that "the child ought not to be
baptized . . . if the parent though a Church member owning
the Covenant . . . is not admitted to full communion," the
majority answered: "Benjamin an infant, but an hour old, is
as truly a son as Reuben, a man of twenty-two years of age. The
child is baptized by virtue of his own membership, and not by
virtue of his parents membership." Because the promise made
to Abraham belongs to the child, the child is baptized "by
virtue of that promise"; and it then becomes his duty, on coming
of age, "to examine himself" and to be "subject to the examination of others" before he can be accepted into full church membership.[55]

55. "The Results of 1657," in Walker, *Creeds*, pp. 292–98.

As early as 1634 a "godly grandfather" of the Dorchester church had requested baptism for a child born to one of his own unregenerate progeny. When the matter was presented to the Boston church for an opinion, John Cotton had decided in the grandfather's favor. "We do profess it to be the judgment of our church," he wrote, "that the grandfather, a member of the church, may claim the privilege of baptism for his grandchild, though the next seed, the parents of the child, be not received themselves into Church Covenant."[56] But Cotton, who held to a distinctly low conception of baptism, had little regard for the efficacy of the seed. The best seed that had been sown, he maintained, could be unfruitful; and so it mattered not at all if the children of unregenerate parents were taken into the outward covenant through baptism. What mattered was whether or not on coming of age they could convince their examiners of the "certain and infallible signs of their regeneration." When at last his opponents objected on the grounds that in time the churches would be entirely composed of natural and carnal members, Cotton had answered, "This argument putteth a fear where no fear is." He was convinced that the established requirements for full communion would prevail. "Though all the infants of the church members be baptized," he had said, "yet none of them are received into communion at the Lord's Table . . . until they do approve themselves by public profession before the church."[57]

Hooker, on the other hand, had taken the opposite point of view, declaring that baptism, precisely because of the covenant relationship involved, must be limited to the immediate offspring of regenerate parents. "The parent," he argued, "enters

56. Cotton's decision was written down in a letter dated December 16, 1634, and can be found in Increase Mather, *First Principles of New England* (Cambridge, 1675), pp. 2–4.

57. Cotton, *A Treatise*, pp. 204, 208, 115–20; *Grounds and Ends of Baptism*, pp. 159, 161–62. For an extensive discussion of Cotton's views on baptism, see above, pp. 134–38.

into covenant for himself and his seed, so that children are within the convenant because they came from parents within the covenant."[58] Although Hooker had confessed that at times he was moved by "secret desire and inclination" to give way on this point (because it did seem "harsh" and "uncharitable"), he continued to insist that where the parents, "though godly," were "yet unwilling to come into church fellowship," he had no other choice but to defend the essential "nature and truth of Church Covenant."[59] Because he took the covenant relationship seriously, he had wanted its full significance recognized by each successive generation; while for Cotton it was unimportant if the parents of a child happened not to be "convinced of the necessity of Church Covenant."[60]

Hooker's stand had been generally accepted throughout most of New England in the first period of settlement. Those who agreed with his views contended that no child without parents in full communion could be baptized; and this practice was enforced by the Cambridge Platform in 1648. Soon, however, the tide of opinion had begun to turn in Cotton's favor; and in time there were many who agreed that the terms of baptism should be enlarged. Thomas Shepard, just before his death in 1649, had openly declared his support for the larger principle. By 1650 the Reverend Samuel Stone of Hartford had done the same, although his church—founded by Hooker—had been thoroughly committed to the established way from the start.[61] Six years later, when the convention was called by the General Court, the issue had reached the point where a clear decision had to be made; and at last a majority was willing to break with the past.

With a large number of external members on their hands,

58. Hooker, *A Survey of the Sum of Church Discipline*, Part 3, pp. 18, 12; Part 1, p. 58.
59. Ibid., Part 3, p. 12.
60. Cotton's decision, printed in I. Mather, p. 3.
61. Letter to Richard Mather, dated June 6, 1650; I. Mather, p. 9.

most of the delegates were eager to extend the covenant, and with it the promises. But they were willing to do so only as a matter of expediency. They had been forced, as it were (by sheer weight of numbers), to recognize the deepest possible roots in the covenant bond; so that in spite of their extension of the promises and their concern with scriptural support, they did not assume, any more than Cotton had assumed, that the covenant link brought conversion any closer. Nor did they assume that the promises themselves might evoke an efficacious response. Although Cotton's more radical views were never openly expressed, namely that baptized infants are "children of wrath," and so in conversion "all confidence that they had in Abraham's covenant is burnt up," nevertheless these notions lurked in the shadows. John Norton, who frequently spoke to the Convention, had published his *Orthodox Evangelist* that same year: and five years later, when another meeting was called, what had lurked in the shadows gradually came to light.

✠

The convention of 1657, it should be recalled, did not have the status of a synod; and so nothing was done officially to impose its recommendations on the churches. But in 1660, when political events in England had restored the monarchy to power, the Congregational Way was once again threatened by hostile forces at home; and the Massachusetts Court, as in 1646 and 1656, was determined to establish uniformity of practice. Accordingly, in December 1661, it was decided that a synod should convene at Boston the following March, and that the delegates should be urged to act quickly. At this meeting, for the first time since 1646, it was up to the assembled ministers to make a comprehensive statement on church discipline. Furthermore, unlike the delegates of 1657, they were obliged to describe this discipline with particular concern for details.

Just prior to the opening of the Synod, the Court had presented to the elders of the Bay a list of questions for their

consideration. These were resolved in *The Answer of the Elders,*
which the Synod followed in reaching its final decision. In this
document the relationship of external members is clearly defined in keeping with the recommendations of 1657. Moreover,
in accordance with the Cambridge Platform, the concept of
preparation is fully acknowledged. But where the Cambridge
Platform had recognized preparatory activity as an integral
part of "God's manner of working upon the soul," the Synod of
1662 established no direct relationship between "heart preparation" and effectual conversion. As stated by the Synod, "The
term House of Israel doth according to Scripture use fitly express and take in both parents and children. . . . But mere membership is not sufficient for full communion. . . . In the Old
Testament more was required to the adult person eating the
Passover than mere membership: Repentance, 2 Chron. 30:6
. . . heart preparation for it, verse 19."[62] Although the requirement of preparation stands—indicating that candidates must
still give a full account of the conversion experience—it stands
undefined. Nowhere is the efficacy of preparation stated. And
the reason might be that it was John Norton who led the Synod
to its final decision. In the document of 1662 those in external
covenant are pledged by their adherence to church discipline
to do all in their power to lead a religious life and seek a
Christian hope. But nowhere are they told that these efforts will
have the least effect on their spiritual condition. Indeed, while
candidates are fully expected to prepare for grace, it would
seem that they were no longer expected to prepare as the founders had demanded.[63]

✠

President Charles Chauncy of Harvard, Increase and Eleazer
Mather (sons of Richard Mather), and John Davenport of New
Haven, all denounced what later came to be called the "Half-

62. In Walker, *Creeds,* pp. 320, 327.
63. Walker, *Creeds,* p. 306.

way Covenant." Although Richard Mather, together with Norton, was one of the leading exponents of the new principle, Mather's sons took a firm stand against it. They had made it their business, in fact, to keep Davenport informed of the Synod's proceedings. In May of 1662, at the close of the second session, Eleazer Mather had written to Davenport: "There was scarce any of the Congregational principles but what were layen at by some or other of the assembly; as relations of the work of grace . . . profession of faith and repentance not to be required of such as were baptized in the church, in reference to the baptism of their children";[64] and Davenport, fearing that all the established precedents were about to crumble, sent back his firm objections. But when Increase Mather tried to read these opinions before the assembled delegates, Norton intervened, and Mather was forced to change his tactics. "I have your writings still in my hands," he later wrote to Davenport; "I offered the synod to read them, but Mr. Norton advised them not to suffer me; whereupon I let them have a copy of them which was generally transcribed. I have given in your . . . testimony unto the general court, with a preface subscribed by Mr. Chauncy . . . my brother, and myself, in the name of others of the dissenting brethren in the synod, wherein we declare that we fully concur with what is inserted by yourself in those papers."[65]

Davenport believed that once the churches were composed entirely of unregenerate members, "it required but one step more to make such persons members in full communion, though professing to be total strangers to any such thing as a work of grace in the heart." He therefore refused to baptize the children of those who "by their personal right" could not demonstrate "some ground for . . . their fitness for regular Church membership."[66] In New Haven, of course, he was free to oppose the

64. May 4, 1662, in Hutchinson, *History of Massachusetts, 1,* 224.
65. October 21, 1662, in Hutchinson, *1,* 224.
66. M'Clure, *Lives,* p. 286; Davenport, *Another Essay,* p. 28.

new practice, as the decision of the Synod applied only to the churches in Massachusetts. But in the Bay there were opposing congregations as well, and their refusal to comply created a continuous controversy. Meanwhile, as controversy raged, the Boston church was deprived of both its teacher and pastor. Norton died a year after the Synod's close, followed by Wilson in 1667: and now Davenport was called from New Haven to be installed as copastor with the Reverend James Allen. But no sooner had they been ordained, in December of 1668, than twenty-eight members withdrew. Not one of these could continue under the New Haven minister, they said, because of his opposition to the Synod's findings.

When Davenport ministered in England and Holland, he had freely extended the baptismal right to the offspring of those who merely "professed" their faith. In keeping with the practice of Puritan divines before the founding of the Bay, he had not required that parents relate "a work of grace in the heart." But in New England, where experiential tests were made a part of the established way, he would not go back on what the founders had prescribed and so brought schism to the very church he had once exhorted to "walk by the same rule" and "mind the same thing." Unlike Cotton, he could never be persuaded that those who objected to the wider practice "putteth a fear where no fear is." Until he died of apoplexy in 1670, he remained convinced that the halfway measures would eventually open the communion table to all.

✝

With the advent of the Halfway Covenant, then, both Norton's and Firmin's views had a clear opportunity to thrive. On the one hand, Norton's theory of conversion had made its mark. Experiential tests had been adjusted to fit his doctrinal stance. On the other hand, "it required but one step more" to make baptized children "members in full communion, though professing to be total strangers to any such thing as a work of grace in the heart." Indeed, as the seventeenth century came to a close, the halfway basis of baptismal right was no longer, in fact, so strictly upheld. In many churches applicants were admitted to external covenant, and their children baptized, without regard to birth membership and without experiential relations. Thus, it was reasoned, if a man could be baptized without parents in covenant, and without a conscious experience of grace, he should also be admitted to the Lord's Supper.

As early as 1677 the Reverend Solomon Stoddard of Northampton had introduced the practice of allowing professing Christians to take communion and to enjoy the privileges of full membership without "evidence" of grace. Candidates were admitted to communion not as a sign of their having achieved grace but as preparation for grace. Stoddard's practice, which spread widely, was soon to be adopted by most of the churches in western Massachusetts. At the same time, however, it was opposed by those who still upheld the original standards of the Halfway Covenant. In particular, Stoddard was challenged by Increase Mather, "the leading voice of the East."

Mather, who in 1675 had with great reluctance dropped his opposition to the halfway measures, now vigorously invoked their authority with all the energy at his command; for he was willing to admit that they at least gave adequate protection to the Supper. In 1677, when Stoddard began his practice, Mather had cried out before the General Court: "I wish there be not teachers found in our Israel that have espoused loose large principles here, designing to bring all persons to the Lord's Supper . . . though they never had experience of a work of regeneration in their souls."[67] Two years later, when the practice had increased considerably, Mather petitioned the Court to call a general synod, as he hoped that such a gathering would help to reaffirm the standards of the past. With eighteen signers supporting him, he submitted his petition on May 28, 1679, asking

67. I. Mather, *A Call from Heaven to the Present and Succeeding Generations* (Boston, 1679), p. 84.

that his colleagues in the ministry be required to reassert "ye same faith and order of the Gospel in which these Churches were at first established, and of which our fathers witnessed a good confession in such an Assembly at Cambridge in the year 1648, and afterwards left upon record unto us in ye platform of discipline and other writings."[68]

Stoddard, interestingly enough, was among the signers, perhaps because he sensed that an open debate on the issue might be to his advantage. And to a large extent he was right. He knew full well, of course, that he could never persuade the delegates to condone the practice of "open communion," as the churches in eastern Massachusetts were adamant against it. Yet in spite of this opposition, he was able to convince the majority to make mere profession of faith, and not the relation of a personal experience of grace, the requisite for church membership. According to Stoddard's own account:

> Some of the elders in the Synod had drawn up a conclusion, that persons should make a relation of the work of God's Spirit upon their hearts in order to coming into full communion. Some others of the elders objected against it, and after some discourse it was agreed to have a dispute on that question, whether those professors of religion as are of good conversation are not to be admitted to full communion . . . Mr. Mather held the negative; I laboured to make good the affirmative. The result was that they blotted out that clause of making a relation of the work of God's Spirit, and put in the room of it the making a profession of their faith and repentance; and so I voted with the rest, and am of the same judgment still.[69]

In its final report, the Synod took no notice of the 1648 provision that candidates declare "God's manner of working upon the soul," nor did it remark on the 1662 requirement

68. "Petition to the Legislature," Walker, Creeds, pp. 414–15.

69. Solomon Stoddard, An Appeal to the Learned (London, 1709), pp. 93, 94.

that none should be admitted to full communion without "heart preparation for it." Instead, the elders simply stated that applicants for membership give "a personal and public profession of their faith and repentance."[70] Although the Cambridge Platform was subscribed to "in substance," and the Halfway Covenant upheld, the notion of preparation—whether effectual or ineffectual—was no longer officially mentioned as a part of the New England Way. This was the decision of the Reforming Synod, as handed down in 1679.

The Synod, to be sure, may not have taken its decision too seriously. In spite of Stoddard's triumph, there were numerous churches in eastern Massachusetts that continued in the established way. Nevertheless, the wording of the document would indicate a major break with Puritan experientialism. When the majority of the Synod had refused to accept Mather's principle, Stoddard knew that he had made great progress for his own cause: and Mather, in turn, was equally convinced that the way had been cleared for condoning the use of open communion in place of experiential knowledge as requisite to full standing in the church. In this respect, at least, the petition for a synod had worked in Stoddard's favor.

It was not long, in fact, before Stoddard openly proclaimed that all men of "competent knowledge" may come to the Supper, "though they know themselves to be in a natural condition." "This Ordinance," he said, "has a proper tendency of its own nature to convert men."[71] Yet in 1714, when Stoddard published *A Guide to Christ,* Mather wrote a preface in which he wholly endorsed the author's views on the preparatory phase as such. Apart from the use of communion, the two were in total accord.[72]

---

70. "The Results of 1679," Walker, *Creeds,* p. 433.

71. Solomon Stoddard, *The Doctrine of Instituted Churches* (London, 1700), p. 281; *An Appeal to the Learned,* p. 2.

72. For an incisive account of the Mather-Stoddard controversy that clarifies the points on which they differed, see Edmund S. Morgan, *Visible Saints,* pp. 146–49.

"That preparation for Christ is necessary," said Mather in the preface, "is an undoubted truth." But whether or not there is any preparatory work which is "saving before faith" is another question. "My learned tutor Mr. Norton," he declared, "has elaborately proved the negative": and here he referred to the *Orthodox Evangelist* as the work that had shaped his thoughts on the subject.[73] Mather, who studied under Norton's tutorship from 1651 to 1656, had delivered his first sermon in 1657—the year the *Orthodox Evangelist* was published. Since then he had been on his guard against the heresies that had originally aroused his tutor's concern. And Stoddard, although he offered communion to the unregenerate, had likewise denounced both Arminian and Antinomian subversion. Therefore, Mather could say that Stoddard also followed Norton's rules.

Man, said Stoddard in the text, can neither effect his own conversion nor achieve salvation through direct revelation. "There is no necessity of any preparation before the infusion of grace," he asserted, as "men when prepared can do nothing to help God in planting grace in them." Nevertheless, he went on, "there is an absolute necessity that men be prepared before the exercise of faith." If the "principle" of preparation were denied, he argued, this would give "a deadly wound to religion," as men would neglect the Word as well as their duties toward God. Indeed, the proof of the necessity of preparation, he maintained, "has been left on the record by Hildersam, Perkins, Sibbes, Preston, Hooker, Shepard, and others of like stamp." Moreover, "experience" shows that ministers who have "an interest in the hearts of others" should exhort to preparation. Yet "we now hold," said Stoddard, that such activity "can have no relationship to God's intentions."[74]

Thus Mather and Stoddard, in spite of their differences,

73. Increase Mather, "To the Reader," in Solomon Stoddard, *A Guide to Christ* (London, 1714), p. i.
74. Stoddard, *A Guide to Christ*, pp. 1–7.

were at one with Norton. Both spoke for preparation as a barrier to enthusiasm; yet both also deprived it of its efficacy in
order to reduce the dangers of Arminian error. Although Stoddard had discarded experiential relations as the requisite for
church membership and had extended communion to sinners,
this practice did not alter his notion of conversion. Like Norton,
he held that the experience itself should be contracted into a
moment in time. "This change," he said, "is made at once on
the soul, it is wrought in the twinkling of an eye."[75] Unlike
Norton, however, he questioned the ability of the church to
discern saving grace, or "visible signs" of sainthood, no matter
how convincing the testimony. Although his "business," he said,
was "not at all to direct the churches to admit any that were
not to rational charity true believers," he could not accept what
he considered to be impossible standards of charity.[76] All rigid
demands for "proof," he maintained, served only to discourage
the faithful. Therefore, rational charity should depend upon
professions of faith and repentance, not upon relations of the
experience of grace. In short, he was able to encourage the
unregenerate while assuming the highest standards of unspoken
piety.

✛

This return to the sanctity of the inner life, immune from
the probings of others, gave rise to a genuine sense of spiritual
release. What is more, it allowed for a freedom of religious
thought hitherto unknown in New England. Because the Halfway Covenant had gone to the roots of the covenant bond and
had emphasized baptismal ties, Stoddard was able to work with
external covenanters in terms of their continuing relationship.
Because he chose to treat them as potentially saved, they in turn
were free from excessive pressure, or from any compulsion to
respond with an experience of grace. Visible saints, said Stod-

75. Ibid., p. 8.
76. Stoddard, *An Appeal to the Learned*, pp. 2–3.

dard, fall into two categories, "such as make a profession of the true religion, together with those that do descend from them, till rejected by God";[77] and both categories, he insisted, should be freely admitted to communion. In other words, by refusing to erect spiritual tests, Stoddard committed himself to a new and revolutionary principle: that baptized members, no matter what the status of their immediate parents, should always be given the full benefit of the doubt. Although he held to Norton's theory of conversion, he had clearly opened the way for Firmin's views to take hold.

Rigid dogmatism, he had come to realize, had little in common with the temper of the times. Throughout the latter half of the seventeenth century the colonists had been faced with urgent practical matters which left them few moments for prescribed notions of religious experience. The prosperity that the first half century had brought to New England had been interrupted when King Philip's War, an Indian uprising which took a heavy toll in lives and property, had started in 1675. In addition, Boston had suffered two great fires, one in 1676 and another in 1679, which had virtually destroyed the business district of the town. During this same period the government of Charles II had threatened to restrict the liberties of the people and to impose the Anglican Prayer Book on their ministers. As a result, the settlers were mainly concerned with preserving their freedom and economy, while the clergy struggled to preserve the ritual structure of the churches; and indifference to the inner life became more and more pronounced.

This indifference soon gained increased support with the founding of the Brattle Street Church in the last year of the century. In 1699, as Stoddardean methods were spreading, William and Thomas Brattle gathered a body of worshipers with the express purpose of doing away with a public declaration of religious experience. William Brattle, who in 1696 had

77. Stoddard, *The Doctrine of Instituted Churches*, p. 6.

been ordained pastor of the church in Cambridge, preached
sermons that were later described as "calm, and soft, and
melting." The baptized, he said, had only to proclaim themselves ready for full standing in the church, as a conscious
experience of grace had neither to be known nor felt.[78] Brattle,
together with John Leverett, Simon Bradstreet, and others in
this movement, was openly sympathetic to the sacramental
views of Solomon Stoddard. Like Stoddard, he was also opposed
by Increase Mather and by all who in strictness of conscience
could not give up the original standards of the Halfway Covenant. In 1700, as an effort to stem the tide, Mather had warned
the Brattle Street Church that "If we espouse such principles
as these, namely that churches are not to enquire into the
regeneration of those whom they admit unto their communion;
that admission to sacraments is to be left wholly to the prudence
and conscience of the minister; that explicit covenanting with
God and with the church is needless . . . that all professed
Christians have right to baptism . . . we then give away the
whole Congregational cause at once."[79] But in spite of Mather's
warning, the tide continued to turn; and by 1728, at a church
meeting in Westfield, Massachusetts, it was possible for the
elders to vote that "Those who enter full communion may have
liberty to give an account of a work of saving conversion or
not. It shall be regarded by the church as a matter of indifference."[80] Until 1748, when Stoddard's grandson Jonathan
Edwards restored the requirement of experiential relations, this
freedom from scrutiny made church admissions virtually auto-
matic.

✠

78. Manuscript notes taken on Brattle's sermons by John Leverett (Massachusetts Historical Society Library) and by John Hancock (Harvard University Library) provide adequate insights into Brattle's doctrinal stance.
79. Increase Mather, *Order of the Gospel* (Boston, 1700), p. 8.
80. Quoted in Walker, *Creeds*, p. 282 n.

A general tone of laxity, then, seemed now to prevail; and so it remained to be seen whether the country would altogether follow this trend. Would New England, so to speak, continue in the Brattle Street Way, inevitably to adopt a theology of grace more consistent with the new practice? Or would an effort be made to recover and revamp the more immediate sense of grace still to be found in Stoddard's thought? The issue, to be sure, was never this clearly defined; yet it was, nevertheless, genuinely real: for the same period of spiritual calm which had accompanied the rise of Stoddardean freedom had also ignited a reactionary flame of religious zeal. Under the influence of George Whitefield, the English revivalist who preached in America from 1739 to 1741, various pastors in New England had begun to encourage a type of spirituality which resembled the teachings of the founding divines. In time this reaction spread through the middle colonies and came to be known as the "Great Awakening." The notion of divine election as a conscious sense of change in man's relationship to God again became a point to be examined in the religious experience. By 1744, in fact, Jonathan Edwards was convinced that his grandfather's methods were wrong.

It is not intended here to attempt a thorough examination of Edwards' theology, which is exceedingly complex. Nor will an effort be made to describe in detail developments of the eighteenth and early nineteenth centuries. Rather, in bringing this study to a close, our purpose is to show that while the concept of preparation was no longer discussed in the language of seventeenth-century divines, it nevertheless remained an issue which could not be entirely dismissed. Although it ceased to exist as a technical source of controversy, in that New England as a whole was no longer committed to an orthodox way, it lay at the roots of continuing rival attitudes; and Edwards' views set the tone for the evangelical frame of mind.

Edwards, who succeeded Stoddard at Northampton in 1729, had at first continued the practice of open communion. For almost twenty years he made no sharp distinction between the converted and the unconverted. He simply assumed, as had Stoddard, that if God alone is able to distinguish the regenerate from the unregenerate, then experiential tests are meaningless. But as the years went by he gradually began to alter his views; and when at last he had revised his position, he had come to the conclusion that visible sainthood may and ought to be discerned—although not in the manner the founders had prescribed.

Unlike the first generation divines, Edwards did not demand a close relation of "beginnings." Rather, in examining applicants, he assumed that "they themselves should suppose the essential things belonging to Christian piety to be in them." At Northampton, where he finally abolished open communion in December 1748, he required that candidates "profess the great things wherein Christian piety consists"; and true piety, he maintained, "may be determined without entering into any controversies about the nature of conversion," as only "the more essential things which belong to it ought to be professed." In other words, Edwards assumed that candidates who could discern the nature of piety were already amongst the elect. He therefore had little use for the nominal and ineffectual preparatory phase which Stoddard and Mather, through the influence of Norton, had retained as a prelude to assurance. He had come, in fact, to assert as strong a Reformed position on election and grace as can be found in New England thought. Because "the unregenerate have not the Spirit of God dwelling in them in any degree," and because "none but real Saints possess that experience which is truly spiritual," it naturally follows, said Edwards, that a "profession of true piety" is sufficient visible proof. "Assurance," he explained, "is not to be obtained so much by self-examination as by active piety"; and "true piety is what persons ought to look at in themselves as the qualification that is proper ground for them to proceed upon in coming to the visible Church of Christ and taking the privileges of its members."[81] According to his own interpretation of Scripture,

> When the Apostle directs professing Christians to try them-
> selves (I Pet. 1:7), using the word indefinitely as properly
> signifying the examining or proving a thing whether it be
> genuine or counterfeit, the most natural construction of
> his advice is that they should try themselves with respect
> to their spiritual state and religious profession, whether
> they are disciples indeed, real and genuine Christians, or
> whether they are not false and hypocritical professors.[82]

For Edwards, as for Zwingli and Calvin, the eternal decrees
seemed to take precedence over experiential regeneration. He
therefore began with the fact of election and then enjoined the
Saints to "try" their faith by the "fruits" of the Spirit. Through
a series of twelve "signs" he helped them to test the authenticity
of their faith and to perceive the nature of true piety. By the
"sense of the heart" he meant the ability to promote and cherish
grace, not the ability to discern its first invasion of the soul. Thus
religious sorrow and brokeness of heart were not, in his mind,
preliminary steps to conversion but distinguishing marks in the
character of a Saint. Where the earliest Puritan divines had
looked to "conversion" as the beginning of "hope," as the start
of a process leading toward possible assurance of election, Edwards saw conversion as one of the many "signs" of election. In
brief, he distinguished between the nature of true piety and
the process whereby that piety is revealed. Only those to whom
the sense of the heart already belonged could possibly exhibit
the signs.[83]

81. Jonathan Edwards, *An Humble Inquiry into the Rules of the Word of
God, Concerning the Qualifications Requisite to a Complete Standing and
Full Communion in the Visible Christian Church* (Boston, 1749), pp. 7, 36,
49; *The Treatise on Religious Affections* (New York, 1836), pp. 100, 107.
82. Edwards, *An Humble Inquiry*, p. 78.
83. See Jonathan Edwards, *Religious Affections*, ed. John E. Smith (New
Haven, 1959), "Editor's Introduction." See also Perry Miller, *Jonathan
Edwards* (New York, 1949). As Miller has pointed out, by 1740 Edwards had

Edwards, then, had found what he believed to be a far more secure, less doubt-ridden way to God than that which even Norton had devised. Moreover, he had found a doctrine that allowed him at last to take a firm stand on the sacraments. By June of 1750 he had been dismissed from the Northampton church for denouncing his grandfather's use of the Supper. He had also been taken to task for his refusal to comply with the theory of baptismal right as laid down in the Halfway Covenant. "No religious honors to be obtained any other way than by real religion are much worth contending for," he had announced; therefore, "it is no honor at all to a man to have merely the outward badges of a Christian without being a Christian indeed." The Halfway measures, he maintained, not only encouraged false security in those who remained outside the church but discouraged true piety in those who might otherwise be known as genuine saints. It would be far better, said Edwards, "if baptism were denied to all children whose parents did not profess godliness, and in a judgment of rational charity appear real Saints"; for experience has shown that "the contrary practice has a natural tendency to quiet the minds of persons, both in their own and their children's unregeneracy."[84] In keeping with Norton and Stoddard, Edwards discarded the concept of gradual assurance, or conversion

---

given up "trying to force himself through the stages marked out by seventeenth-century scholasticism" and had confessed that his own conversion did not conform to "those particular steps, wherein the people of New England, and anciently the Dissenters of Old England, used to experience it." At the same time, he had turned away from criticizing the Arminians and had begun to criticize his followers who had become too enthusiastic. In reacting against the excesses of emotionalism, writes Miller, he came, "like the first Puritans, to believe that a public confession was . . . the most reliable test for brotherhood." However, "He still rejected the scholastic metaphysics out of which the founders had devised their argument for profession, and he did not want to set up again the complex theology of the covenant" (pp. 207, 215).

84. Edwards, *An Humble Inquiry*, pp. 129, 130.

through efficacious stages. But unlike them, he would not extend the covenant seal as a measure of pure expediency.

✛

Edwards' views, although rejected by many, launched a new
system of theology as well as a new era in the history of New
England divinity. It was an era that found the clergy split and
the churches in disorder. Above all, it was an era out of which
numerous approaches to doctrine and discipline emerged. Although Edwards had retained the covenant tie between regenerate parents and child, by 1793 the Reverend Cyprian Strong
of Portland, Connecticut, had gone so far as to deny this covenant standing altogether. The baptized, he declared, have no
essential right to the seal, as their baptism is nothing more than
an outward sign or "token" of their parents' faith. "As to the
children or natural offspring of believers," wrote Strong, "although I am firmly persuaded that they are the proper subjects
of baptism, yet I apprehend there is great reason to question
whether the institution be at all founded on the idea of their
being in covenant; yea, whether there be any such covenant
relation existing . . . whether the natural seed of believers as
such are in any proper sense of the word in covenant." These
children, he maintained, "have not a real title to the blessings
of the covenant of grace"; nor can they be said to have an interest in the covenant until such time as they can claim a title
to the "peculiar and essential blessings of the new covenant," or
show themselves to be truly pious.[85]
  Strong was opposed by those who took an extreme stand for
the opposite point of view, among them Moses Hemmenway,
preacher at Wells, Maine. Hemmenway, who in 1781 had already begun to fear for what he called "the divine right of

  85. Cyprian Strong, *An Inquiry Wherein the end and design of Baptism
are particularly Considered* (Hartford, 1793), pp. 9, 10, 16.

baptism," argued that infants, no matter what the covenant standing of their parents, are "capable not only of the outward sign of baptism but also of having an interest in the blessings and grace of the new covenant and coming under its bonds." Most important of all, the baptized are "members by right" before they are "members by admission" and so "belong to the visible church that they may, under its watch, instruction, and discipline, be trained up in the nurture and admonition of the Lord."[86]

Hemmenway, moreover, had his own conception of "nurture," as well as his own idea of what it means to have sufficient interest in the covenant for access to full communion. "Though we grant that none have a right of access but those who may and ought to profess religion," he declared, "yet we allow not that true saints only may and ought to be professors." In point of fact, said Hemmenway, "There is another kind of holiness spoken of in Scripture besides that of the heart," namely, the holiness of those who "assent to, approve, and acquiesce in the Gospel." Therefore, in coming to communion, "it is not required of any one to profess that he has complied savingly with the covenant of grace." Indeed, those who simply profess religion "may and ought to come to communion," as their very uncertainty and doubt gives "a certain right of access." Although they themselves might never know "grace in the heart," they should not for this reason be rejected, as the church is obliged to admit "all who appear to be professors of true religion and not scandalous." In many such cases, to be sure, the minister and elders "may not believe the sincerity of an unexceptional professor"; but "so long as a man's profession appears sound and unexceptional . . . the unfavorable opinion of a church or any of its members is no sufficient reason for their refusing to receive him. He is evidently a visible Saint what-

86. Moses Hemmenway, *A Discourse on the Nature and Subjects of Christian Baptism* (Boston, 1781), pp. 27, 28, 45.

ever his heart may be, or whatever it may be suspected or thought."[87]

By 1800, in spite of the Edwardsean reaction, this trend toward "liberalism"—in both ecclesiastical discipline and notions of "heart piety"—had set the tone for important future developments. In fact, this lack of concern for experiential testing emerged not only in nineteenth-century Unitarianism but in the full-blown Transcendentalism of Ralph Waldo Emerson. Though Emerson was a long way from Hemmenway, he avowed in 1842 what might be called militant indifference to prescribed experientialism. "Do not cumber yourself with fruitless pains to mend and remedy remote effects," he wrote; "Let the soul be erect, and all things will go well." But where Hemmenway had been satisfied if a man were judged regenerate, "whatever his heart may be," Emerson was not indifferent to the true spiritual condition of the heart. Rather, in the tradition of Giles Firmin, he professed what can only be described as innate antinomianism, or absolute assurance from birth. "The Transcendentalist," said Emerson, "adopts the whole connection of spiritual doctrine. . . . Thus the spiritual measure of inspiration is to the depth of the thought." In action "he easily incurs the charge of antinomianism by his avowal that he, who has the Lawgiver, may with safety not only neglect but even contravene every written commandment."[88] Like Hemmenway, Emerson was determined to eliminate all anxiety in man's relationship to God; but like Firmin, he was convinced that there should be no disparity between the motions of the heart and the actual condition of the soul. Therefore, to the mind of the great Transcendentalist, no distinction could be made between preparation and assurance, as both were one and the same. Man prepared not for a first "evidence" but for more assurance, easily

87. Moses Hemmenway, *Remarks on the Scriptural Qualifications for Admission and Access to the Christian Sacraments* (Boston, 1794), pp. 47, 30, 27, 5, 46, 36.

88. Ralph Waldo Emerson, *Works* (2 vols. Boston, 1909), *1*, 316–17.

come by; so that all of life was preparation, all of life, assurance.

Emerson, of course, voiced no New England consensus in 1842. By then he had left the church, and his views were rejected by many of his former colleagues in the Unitarian ministry.[89] Moreover, orthodoxy in New England was still committed to conversion and revivals. Lyman Beecher, who in the 1820s had led a wave of reaction against Unitarianism, aimed at a continuous revival. By 1826 he had been called from his Connecticut parish at Litchfield to organize a new evangelical church on Hanover Street in Boston; and for the next six and a half years, until he answered a call to Ohio in 1832, led the first movement of this kind in Massachusetts since the period of the Great Awakening. But if Beecher was successful in his time, he was hardly an apostle of the future. Although he helped to preserve the evangelistic strain, even there the lines were breaking. Horace Bushnell, who by the 1840s had cast off the orthodoxy of the day, was rethinking the matter of baptism and Christian nurture. As pastor of the North Church at Hartford, he denounced the theory that children should be excluded from the covenant until their piety had been fully established. Furthermore, he protested against all dogmatic notions of conversion and firmly denied that it was possible to describe religious experience in the precise language of contemporary theology. "The child," he said, "is to grow up a Christian and never know himself as being otherwise." When Bushnell had reassessed the needs of the time, he came to the conclusion that "the aim, effort, and expectation should be, not as is commonly asumed, that a child is to grow up in sin to be converted after he comes to mature age; but that he is to open on the world as one that is spiritually renewed, not remembering the time when he went through a technical experience."[90]

Bushnell had entered the ministry in 1833, a year after Emer-

89. William R. Hutchison, *The Transcendentalist Ministers* (New Haven, 1959), chap. 6.
90. Horace Bushnell, *Christian Nurture* (Hartford, 1848), p. 8.

son had broken with the church and with the ministry in general. Although first and last a churchman, he had soon felt the need to revise the truths of religion and to translate the doctrines of the church into terms which could be intuitively understood. Therefore, like Emerson, he had gradually turned his back on the doctrinal camps and had groped his way toward another vision of the inner life. "Every man's life," said Bushnell, "is shaped by his love. . . . Hence it is that so much is said of the heart in the Gospel, and of a change of the heart." But the meaning of this change, he explained, "is not that Christianity proposes to give us a new organ of the soul, or to extract one member of the soul and insert another. . . . Equally plain is it that the change is not to be effected by waiting for some new creating act of God to be literally passed on the soul." Rather, those who are properly nurtured in Christ grow up in his care, and so "remember no time when they began to love him."[91] Bushnell, of course, spoke to the conservative mind of the church, while Emerson was concerned with a far more secular audience. But as Bushnell's disciples would soon be multiplying, it is clear that Emerson did, in fact, speak for New England's future. "The heart," said Emerson, is "the ark in which the fire is concealed, which shall burn in a broader and universal flame."[92] It was an image of the heart that the founding divines would not have understood.

91. Horace Bushnell, *Sermons for the New Life* (New York, 1866), pp. 118–19, 244. For a recent examination of Bushnell's thought, see Barbara M. Cross, *Horace Bushnell: Minister to a Changing America* (Chicago, 1958).
92. Emerson, *Works, 1,* 337.

Epilogue

From the writings of Giles Firmin it is possible to date the beginnings of an era in which Puritanism finally degenerated into moralism and sentimentalism. This, perhaps, is the tradition in which we now stand. From John Norton it is possible to look back, through Cotton to Calvin to Zwingli, to the position taken by the chief architects of Reformed theology. Here is the tradition from which preparation made its departure. Here is the dogma from which it struggled to be free.

The notion of the "heart prepared" emerged from under the shadow and tyranny of the doctrine of divine coercion. Man, said its exponents, must be allowed to desire. He must look to God with expectation; he must want to be reconciled with his creator before the moment arrives. If God, in the work of conversion, proceeds immediately from legal terrors to saving grace, then man is simply wrenched by the Law into a state of salvation. He cannot experience the transformation; he cannot anticipate; his own consciousness is not involved. But if God proceeds by degrees, then man, under the Law, may look to his heart before uniting to Christ. "Therefore also now the Lord saith, turn you unto me with all your heart" (Joel 2:12).

Preparation thus evolved within a complex pattern of conflicting attitudes. Through the doctrine of the Holy Spirit the Puritans arrived at their conclusion that conversion may hap-

pen by degrees. Through covenant theology they brought to
bear the great Prophetic exhortations to return to God: "Break
up your fallow ground, for it is time to seek the Lord, till he
come and rain righteousness upon you" (Hosea 10:12). Both the
gradual workings of the Holy Spirit and the extreme emphasis
on covenant ideals were fundamentally opposed to the basic
tenets of Reformed theology. Both contradicted the dogmatic
stand that anything done on man's part diminishes God's
sovereignty. Yet the ultimate convictions behind Reformed
dogmatics remained at the core of Puritan thought.

Richard Greenham was among the first to state the problem
as a major concern for Puritan spirituality. Man, he said, must
come to God through "voluntary submission," not "violent
subjection"; and Richard Rogers was the first to enumerate the
"works" of the Spirit to which man may respond without excessive constraint. In the writings of Rogers' successors, preparatory activity ranged up and down the scale of efficacy.
Arthur Hildersam was the first to elaborate the stages; but
their efficacy remained unclarified. For William Perkins, man
under legal constraint was a "reprobate"; but in the "beginnings of composition" he was a "child of God." Richard Sibbes
carried on Rogers' concern with man's responses to the interior
workings of the Spirit. With Sibbes, man in preparation, although "reprobate," was able to "entertain" the Spirit and to
prepare for God's descending love. Then, with John Preston
and William Ames, the efficacy of baptism provided a new
starting point for preparatory activity. Baptized covenanters,
under the work of the Law, were all but fully regenerate.

With Thomas Hooker, Thomas Shepard, Peter Bulkeley,
and John Davenport there was little agreement on the efficacy
of baptism. Davenport, in keeping with Cotton's views, put it
lowest on the scale; and Bulkeley put it highest. Hooker and
Shepard were both concerned with severe conviction of conscience under the Law, and Shepard was more concerned with
legal terrors than Hooker; but Bulkeley denied the efficacy of

the Law altogether. The baptized, he said, had only to turn to God of their own volition. This was covenant theology in its purest form.

Indeed, the real significance of covenant theology, as it passed from Bullinger to the Puritans, was not that it solved anything, not that it made room for a halfway point between predestinarian and pelagian convictions. Quite to the contrary. Although it stemmed from a branch of Reformed thinking which wanted to avoid scholastic definitions and mechanical metaphors, its real significance was its conscious ambivalence. On the one hand it emphasized the inner reformation of the heart as the basis of man's salvation. It said that man must enter the covenant "voluntarily," that the disposition of the heart determines the spiritual condition. On the other hand it said that God remains arbitrary, that His will cannot be forced; so that whatever gestures it made toward solving the paradox of God's omnipotence and man's responsibilities were bound to be self-contradictory. If it emphasized biblical prescription over the written creeds, those creeds were never entirely discarded; and the trained theologian, caught in the middle, was left to shift for himself.

While every student of Puritan thought owes a profound debt of gratitude to the late Professor Perry Miller, his interpretation of covenant theology has tended to restrict the Puritan imagination and to distort certain concepts. According to Professor Miller, the biblical notion of a covenant between man and God put man in a bargaining position with his maker. God would do His part if man did his. As this "contractual" idea appealed to the Puritans, it naturally followed that they should conceive of preparing themselves for salvation. Under covenant with God, they could know the terms before the contract had been sealed. In Miller's estimation,

by putting the relationship between God and man into contractual terms, they found themselves blessed with the

corollary that the terms could be known in advance. If a
Sovereign proposes conditions, there must be a moment
in time, however infinitesimal, between absolute depravity
and concluding the bond. If election be a flash of lightning
which strikes without warning, men cannot place themselves in its path, nor cultivate anticipatory attitudes, but
when it comes as a chance to take up a contract, they must
first of all learn what is to be contracted.[1]

It is hard to see, however, how covenant theology was intended to supply a bargaining basis for man's relationship with
God. If God granted a compact out of His own free will, it was
meant as a sign of both His divine authority and His mercy.[2]
Man was not in a position to haggle for his rights; he could
neither negotiate with God nor prepare for grace on the basis
of negotiations. What is more, the idea of preparation was never
discussed, in early Puritanism at least, as a term in a contract.
To say that preparation derived solely from contractual bargaining is an oversimplification which both negates the significance of the interior life and diminishes the range of Puritan
religious thought. Nor does it do justice to the role of religious
experience as a guide to theological formulation. Moreover, it
misinterprets the Puritans' fundamental adherence to the doctrine of divine sovereignty.[3]

Perry Miller has also maintained that "Regeneration through
covenant meant that men could make themselves ready, at
least by studying the nature of covenants."[4] He has implied,

1. Miller, *The New England Mind*, 2, 55.
2. See John D. Eusden, *Puritans, Lawyers, and Politics in Early Seventeenth-Century England* (New Haven, 1958), pp. 28–50.
3. For remarks by Peter Bulkeley that directly contradict Miller's thesis,
see above, Chap. 4, pp. 120–21, where Bulkeley insists that man must not
"give laws unto God," and that "Faith offers nothing to stand in exchange
for the mercy offered."
4. Miller, 2, 55.

in other words, that preparation was little more than a clever way out from under predestinarian dogma. But for a genuine understanding of the concept within the covenant framework, we must try to see its function as something more than this. It is not intended here simply to argue with Miller's views on covenant theology but to emphasize the fact that preparation must be seen within the whole complex of the religious imagination—as part of a growing consciousness in Puritanism of the entire range of biblical prescription, as part of an ongoing examination of the facts of regeneration as the Puritans severally experienced it.

The men who spoke for preparation, particularly in New England, were determined to defend it against all comers. Hooker and Bulkeley were especially concerned that man should have a part to play of his own. They did not believe, as did their opponents, that God's omnipotence was diminished by such activity. Because they held their ground against John Cotton and the antinomians, their doctrine survived its first and most serious challenge in the New World; and they in turn were able to set the course theology would run. But if the form and structure of their doctrine survived, it was Davenport's point of view, not Bulkeley's, Hooker's, or even Shepard's, which came to stand most clearly for the New England Way; and Davenport's limitations, together with Cotton's equally influential rigidity on the subject of church membership, combined to turn the concept into a formidable barrier to communion. Then, with a resurgence of the strict Reformed tradition, championed by John Norton, the notion of conversion through efficacious stages was overthrown. The halfway measures and the Reforming Synod formally documented the process.

In the end, preparation in its rigid forms became inadequate to the situation and needs of the Puritan churches. It created not only religious difficulties, in terms of Giles Firmin's objections, but ecclesiastical difficulties, in terms of a changing attitude toward church membership: and with the rise of Stoddardean practices it was dealt a mortal blow. In its more imaginative forms, however, it contributed to a broader realm of religious experience and so remained enthroned in the New England heart.

Bibliography

The titles in the bibliography are listed alphabetically under two headings: *Sources* and *Secondary Works*. As the place and date of publication, when known, are indicated after each title, it has not seemed necessary to discuss variants in editions or other bibliographical minutiae.

The titles listed under *Secondary Works*, whether cited in the text or not, are those which have provided essential background knowledge for dealing with the original sources. Harry A. Wolfson's *The Philosophy of the Church Fathers* (Cambridge, 1956), and *Religious Philosophy* (Cambridge, 1961) have been extremely useful in clarifying relevant views of early Christian thinkers. They contain detailed examinations of orthodox primitive Christianity and illuminate Augustine's relation to that tradition. Anders Nygren's *Agape and Eros* (3 vols. London, 1932, 1938) provides a basic understanding of Augustinian piety and makes important distinctions between Hellenic and New Testament conceptions of divine love. Nygren points to what the Roman, Lutheran, and Reformed churches each derived from that piety.

Two books of the same title, *Reformed Dogmatics*, one by Heinrich Heppe (London, 1950) and the other by Louis Berkhof (2 vols. Grand Rapids, 1932), give an essential introduction to Reformed theology. Scholars of Puritan thought often begin in the late sixteenth century and tend to neglect the earlier Reformed background. But the full implications of Puritan attitudes cannot be seen without some consideration of early Reformed theology.

N. P. Williams in *The Grace of God* (London, 1930), traces the doctrine of grace and its meaning for conversion from earliest Christian times through Reformed interpretations. And Philip Schaff in *The Creeds of Christendom* (3 vols., New York, 1877), presents a detailed record of how the doctrine was interpreted by the Reformed churches of Western Europe. Schaff's historical commentary is invaluable.

The influence of Continental Reformers on English churchmen has been outlined by Frederick J. Smithen in *Continental Protestantism and the English Reformation* (London, 1927). Smithen's account, together with the *Zurich Letters* and *Original Letters Relative to the English Reformation* (Parker Society, Cambridge, England, 1842, 1846), illuminates the exchange of ideas in the period leading up to the beginnings of Puritanism; and William Haller's *The Rise of Puritanism* (New York, 1938) contains a highly sensitive analysis of Puritan spirituality. Haller's description of the "Spiritual brotherhood" points to the values shared by the early Puritan leaders, while Geoffrey Nuttall in *The Holy Spirit in Puritan Faith and Experience* (Oxford, 1946) discusses the deeper theological problems which concerned them. Here the doctrine of the Holy Spirit, with its significance for the Puritan concept of conversion, is clarified in full detail.

George E. Ellis, in *The Puritan Age and Rule in the Colony of the Massachusetts Bay, 1629–1685* (Boston, 1888), gives a good analysis of the practical problems of early settlement which has withstood the test of time; and Williston Walker, in *The Creeds and Platforms of Congregationalism* (New York, 1893), and *A History of the Congregational Churches in the*

United States (New York, 1897), provides a running commentary on church polity which has yet to be surpassed. Walker's *Creeds and Platforms* contains the major public statements on conversion drawn up in early New England. His comments are as valuable as the documents themselves.

Perry Miller is one of the few contemporary writers who has discussed the concept of preparation as a problem in Puritan thought. His article " 'Preparation for salvation' in Seventeenth-Century New England" (*Journal of the History of Ideas*, Vol. 4, No. 3, June [1943], pp. 253–86) first stated the social implications of the concept for Puritan society in America. In *The New England Mind; from Colony to Province* (Cambridge, 1953), he emphasized the importance of preparation for the Antinomian Controversy. He has also treated the subject in "The Marrow of Puritan Divinity" (1935), reprinted in *Errand into the Wilderness* (Cambridge, 1956).

Edmund S. Morgan's *Visible Saints: The History of a Puritan Idea* (New York, 1963) is a pioneer work to which this study owes more than can be adequately expressed. In tracing the origins of experiential relations as a requirement for full church membership, Mr. Morgan has revised all previous assumptions. Had he not been kind enough to share his findings while this manuscript was in progress and before his own book had been published, the present work would have suffered immeasurably.

Finally, the articles in *The Dictionary of National Biography* (Oxford, 1950) and *Dictionary of American Biography* (New York, 1943) have provided more than adequate sketches of the leading Puritan divines; while Martin Buber's *Two Types of Faith* (New York, 1961) has provided the main intellectual channel through which their thought has been approached. Buber's discussion of the disparity between Hebraic and Pauline notions of man's relationship to God is still open to criticism, but there can be little doubt that the Puritan mind was torn between two extremes rooted in this very issue.

I. *Sources*

Adams, Charles Francis, ed. *Antinomianism in the Colony of Massa-chusetts Bay, 1636–1638,* Boston, The Prince Society, 1894. (A collection of documents.)

Ames, William, *The Marrow of Sacred Divinity,* London, 1642.

―――― *Works,* London, 1643.

Baillie, Robert, *A Dissuasive from the Errors of our Time,* London, 1645.

Bulkeley, Peter, *The Gospel-Covenant, or the Covenant of Grace opened,* London, 1646; 2d ed., London, 1653. (Both editions contain a preface by Thomas Shepard.)

Bullinger, Heinrich, *Decades,* ed. Parker Society, 5 vols. Cambridge, England, 1849.

―――― *Decades, Fifty Godly Sermons,* London, 1587.

Bushnell, Horace, *Christian Nurture,* Hartford, 1848.

―――― *Sermons for the New Life,* New York, 1866.

Calvin, John, *Commentary on the Psalms,* trans. Arthur Golding, Oxford, 1840.

―――― *Institutes of the Christian Religion,* trans. John Allen, 2 vols. Philadelphia, 1936.

―――― *Letters,* ed. Jules Bonnet, 4 vols. Boston, 1857.

Clarke, Samuel, *The Lives of Sundry Modern English Divines,* London, 1651.

Clemens, Titus Flavius, *Works,* ed. and trans. G. W. Butterworth, New York, 1919.

Colonial Society of Massachusetts, *Publications,* Boston, 1920.

Cotton, John, *Christ the Fountain of Life,* London, 1651.

―――― *The Churches Resurrection,* London, 1642.

―――― *A Copy of Letter,* with the questions propounded to such as are admitted to the Church-fellowship, 1641.

―――― *The Covenant of God's Free Grace,* London, 1645.

―――― *The Grounds and Ends of the Baptism of the Children of the Faithful,* London, 1647.

―――― *Of the Holiness of Church Members,* London, 1650.

―――― *Sixteen Questions of Serious and Necessary Consequences,* London, 1644.

―――― *A Treatise of the Covenant of Grace,* London, 1671.

―――― *A Treatise of Faith,* no date.

―――― *The Way of the Congregational Churches Cleared,* London, 1648.

―――― *The Way of Life,* London, 1641.

Davenport, John, *Another Essay for the Investigation of the Truth*, Cambridge, 1663.
────── *An Answer of the Elders of the Several Churches in New England*, London, 1643.
────── *The Knowledge of Christ*, London, 1653.
────── *The Power of Congregational Churches*, London, 1672.
────── *The Saints Anchor-Hold*, London, 1682.
Downame, John, *Guide to Godliness*, London, 1622.
Edwards, Jonathan, *An Humble Inquiry into the Rules of the Word of God, Concerning the Qualifications Requisite to a Complete Standing and Full Communion in the Visible Christian Church*, Boston, 1749.
────── *Treatise Concerning Religious Affections* (1746), ed. John E. Smith, New Haven, Yale University Press, 1959.
────── *The Treatise on Religious Affections*, New York, 1836.
Emerson, Ralph Waldo, *Works*, 2 vols. Boston, Houghton, Mifflin and Co., 1909.
Firmin, Giles, *The Real Christian*, London, 1670.
────── *Separation Examined*, London, 1652.
Forbes, John, *How a Christian Man May Discern the Testimony of God's Spirit*, London, 1616.
Goodwin, Thomas, *Works*, ed. John C. Miller, 12 vols., Edinburgh, 1861–66.
Great Britain, Public Record Office, Colonial Record, 1637. Class 1, Vol. 9, No. 72, Library of Congress Microfilm, Ac. 10,741, Reel 4.
Greenham, Richard, *Works*, London, 1612.
Hall, Joseph, *Works*, London, 1863.
Hemmenway, Moses, *A Discourse on the Nature and Subjects of Christian Baptism*, Boston, 1781.
────── *Remarks on the Scriptural Qualifications for Admission and Access to the Christian Sacraments*, Boston, 1794.
Hildersam, Arthur, *The Doctrine of Fasting and Prayer, and Humiliation for Sin*, London, 1633.
────── *CLII Lectures upon Psalm LI*, London, 1635.
────── *Lectures upon the Fourth of John*, London, 1629.
Hooker, Thomas, *The Application of Redemption*, London, 1659.
────── *The Covenant of Grace Opened*, London, 1649.
────── *The Faithful Covenanter*, London, 1644.
────── *The Souls Humiliation*, London, 1638.
────── *The Souls Implantation*, London, 1637.
────── *The Souls Preparation for Christ*, London, 1632.
────── *The Souls Vocation or Effectual Calling*, London, 1638.

———— *A Survey of the Sum of Church Discipline,* London, 1648.

———— *The Unbelievers Preparing for Christ,* London, 1638.

Knappen, M. M., ed. *Two Elizabethan Puritan Diaries,* Chicago, The American Society of Church History, 1933. (Contains diaries of Richard Rogers and Samuel Ward.)

Lechford, Thomas, *Plain Dealing,* London, 1642.

Martyr, Peter, *Commentaries on the Epistle of Paul to the Romans,* London, 1558.

———— *The Common Places,* London, 1583.

Mather, Cotton, *Magnalia Christi Americana* (1702), 2 vols. Hartford, S. Andrus and Son, 1855.

Mather, Increase, *A Call from Heaven to the Present and Succeeding Generations,* Boston, 1679.

———— *First Principles of New England,* Cambridge, 1675.

———— *Order of the Gospel,* Boston, 1700.

Norton, John, *The Answer,* trans. Douglas Horton, Cambridge, Harvard University Press, 1958. (Translated from the Latin edition of 1648.)

———— *The Orthodox Evangelist,* London, 1657.

Parker Society, ed., *Original Letters relative to the English Reformation,* Cambridge, England, The University Press, 1846.

———— *Zurich Letters,* Cambridge, England, The University Press, 1842. (Both the *Original Letters* and *Zurich Letters* contain correspondence between Continental Reformers and English divines.)

Pemble, William, *Works,* Oxford, 1659.

Perkins, William, *A Golden Chain,* London, 1597.

———— *Works,* 3 vols. London, 1626.

Preston, John, *The Breastplate of Faith and Love,* London, 1632.

———— *The New Covenant, or Saints Portion,* London, 1630.

———— *Remains,* London, 1637.

Rogers, Richard, *Seven Treatises,* London, 1610.

Schaff, Philip, ed., *The Creeds of Christendom,* 3 vols. New York, Harper and Brothers, 1878.

———— ed., *Nicene and Post-Nicene Fathers.* Vol. 5, New York, 1887. (Contains Augustine's "On the Gift of Perseverance.")

Shepard, Thomas, *Autobiography,* ed. Nehemiah Adams, Boston, 1832.

———— *Certain Select Cases Resolved,* London, 1648.

———— *The Church Membership of Children and Their Right to Baptism,* London, 1662.

———— *Meditations and Spiritual Experiences,* London, 1749.

―――― *The Parable of the Ten Virgins,* London, 1660.

―――― *The Sincere Convert,* London, 1646.

―――― *The Sound Believer,* London, 1645.

―――― *Subjection to Christ,* London, 1657.

Sibbes, Richard, *Works,* ed. Alexander Grosart, 7 vols. Edinburgh, 1862–64.

Stoddard, Solomon, *An Appeal to the Learned,* London, 1709.

―――― *The Doctrine of Instituted Churches,* London, 1700.

―――― *A Guide to Christ,* London, 1714.

Strong, Cyprian, *An Inquiry Wherein the End and Design of Baptism Are Particularly Considered,* Hartford, 1793.

Thomas Aquinas, Saint, *Summa Theologica,* trans. Fathers of the English Dominican Province, 3 vols. New York, 1947.

Twisse, William, *A Treatise of Mr. Cottons Clearing Certain Doubts Concerning Predestination, Together with an Examination Thereof,* London, 1646.

Tyndale, William, *An Answer unto Sir Thomas More's Dialogue,* ed. Parker Society, London, Cambridge University Press, 1850.

―――― *Prologue upon the Epistle of St. Paul to the Romans,* 1533.

―――― *Works,* ed. Thomas Russell, London, 1831.

Wheelwright, John, "Fast-day Sermon," in *John Wheelwright, his writings,* ed. Charles H. Bell, Boston, Prince Society, 1876.

Winthrop, John, *The History of New England from 1630 to 1649,* ed. James Savage, 2 vols. Boston, Little, Brown and Co., 1853.

―――― *Journal,* ed. James Hosmer, 2 vols. New York, C. Scribner's Sons, 1908.

―――― *Winthrop Papers,* 1631–37, Vol. 3, Massachusetts Historical Society, Boston, 1943.

Wits, Herman, *The Economy of the Covenants between God and Man,* 3 vols. New York, 1798.

Zwingli, Huldreich, *The Latin Works,* ed. S. M. Jackson, trans. H. Preble, W. Lichtenstein, L. A. McLouth, 3 vols. New York, G. P. Putnam's Sons, 1912.

―――― *Opera,* ed. M. Schuler and J. Schulthess, 3 vols. Zurich, 1828–42.

II. *Secondary Works*

Adams, Charles Francis, *Three Episodes of Massachusetts History,* 2 vols. Boston, Houghton, Mifflin and Co., 1892.

Ahlstrom, Sydney E., "Theology in America: A Historical Survey," in *Religion in American Life,* ed. James Ward Smith, Vol. 1, Princeton University Press, 1961.

Albro, John A., *The Life of Thomas Shepard,* Boston, 1870.

Andrews, Charles M., *The Colonial Period of American History,* Vol. 2, New Haven, Yale University Press, 1936.

Berkhof, Louis, *Reformed Dogmatics,* 2 vols. Grand Rapids, Wm. B. Eerdman, 1932.

Brauer, Jerald C., "Reflections on the Nature of English Puritanism," *Church History,* 23 (1954), 99–107.

Brown, John, *The English Puritans,* London, Cambridge University Press, 1912.

——— *Puritan Preaching in England,* New York, C. Scribner's Sons, 1900.

Brown, W. Adams, "Covenant Theology," *Encyclopaedia of Religion and Ethics,* ed. James Hastings, 12 vols. New York, C. Scribner's Sons, and Edinburgh, T. & T. Clark, 1908–22, Vol. 4, pp. 216–24.

Browne, Edward H., *An Exposition of the Thirty-Nine Articles,* New York, 1870.

Bruce, F. F., *The English Bible; a History of Translations,* New York, Oxford University Press, 1961.

Brunner, Emil, *The Mediator: a Study of the Central Doctrine of the Christian Faith,* trans. Olive Wyon, London, Macmillan, 1934.

——— *Revelation and Reason,* Philadelphia, The Westminster Press, 1946.

Buber, Martin, *Two Types of Faith,* New York, Harper and Brothers, 1961.

Burrage, Champlin, *The Early English Dissenters,* 2 vols. London, Cambridge University Press, 1912.

Citron, Bernhard, *New Birth: a Study of the Evangelical Doctrine of Conversion in the Protestant Fathers,* Edinburgh, University Press, Clarke, Irwin, 1951.

Clark, Henry W., *History of English Nonconformity,* 2 vols. London, Chapman and Hall, Ltd., 1911–13.

Colie, Rosalie L., *Light and Enlightenment; a Study of the Cambridge Platonists and the Dutch Arminians,* London, Cambridge University Press, 1957.

Collins, Joseph B., *Christian Mysticism in the Elizabethan Age,* Baltimore, The Johns Hopkins Press, 1940.

Cragg, C. R., *From Puritanism to the Age of Reason: a Study of Changes in Religious Thought within the Church of England, 1660–1700,* London, Cambridge University Press, 1950.

——— *Puritanism in the Period of the Great Persecution, 1660–1688,* London, Cambridge University Press, 1957.

Cremeans, Charles Davis, *The Reception of Calvinistic Thought in England,* Urbana, University of Illinois Press, 1949.

Cushman, Robert E., "Faith and Reason in the Thought of St. Augustine," *Church History, 19* (1950), 271–94.

Davies, Horton, *The Worship of the English Puritans,* London, Dacre Press, 1948.

Davis, Joe Lee, "Mystical Versus Enthusiastic Sensibility," *Journal of the History of Ideas, 4* (1943), 301–19.

Dean, John Ward, *A Brief Memoir of Rev. Giles Firmin,* Boston, 1866.

De Jong, Peter Y., *The Covenant Idea in New England Theology,* Grand Rapids, Wm. B. Eerdman, 1945.

Dictionary of American Biography, ed. Dumas Malone, 20 vols. New York, C. Scribner's Sons, 1943.

The Dictionary of National Biography, ed. Leslie Stephen and Sidney Lee, 22 vols. London, Oxford University Press, 1950.

Dillenberger, John (with Claude Welch), *Protestant Christianity,* New York, C. Scribner's Sons, 1954.

Dorner, I. A., *History of Protestant Theology,* trans. G. Robson and S. Taylor, Edinburgh, T. & T. Clark, 1871.

Ellis, George E., *The Puritan Age and Rule in the Colony of the Massachusetts Bay, 1629–1685,* Boston, Houghton, Mifflin and Co., 1888.

Elwood, D. J., *The Philosophical Theology of Jonathan Edwards,* New York, Columbia University Press, 1960.

Emerson, Everett H., "Calvin and Covenant Theology," *Church History, 25* (1956), pp. 136–42.

——— "Thomas Hooker and the Reformed Theology: the relationship of Hooker's conversion preaching to its background." Doctoral dissertation, Louisiana State University, 1955.

Eusden, John D., *Puritans, Lawyers, and Politics in Early Seventeenth-Century England,* New Haven, Yale University Press, 1958.

Fisher, George Park, *History of the Christian Church,* New York, C. Scribner's Sons, 1888.

Foster, Frank Hugh, *A Genetic History of New England Theology,* Chicago, University of Chicago Press, 1907.

Frere, Walter H., *The English Church in the Reigns of Elizabeth and James I,* London, Macmillan, 1904.

Gairdner, James, *The English Church in the Sixteenth Century,* London, Macmillan, 1902.

Gaustad, Edwin S., *The Great Awakening in New England,* New York, Harper and Brothers, 1957.

George, Charles H. and Katherine, *The Protestant Mind of the English Reformation, 1570–1640,* Princeton University Press, 1961.

Gilson, Etienne, *Reason and Revelation in the Middle Ages,* New York, C. Scribner's Sons, 1938.

——— *The Spirit of Mediaeval Philosophy,* New York, C. Scribner's Sons, 1940.

Goen, C. C., *Revivalism and Separatism in New England, 1740–1800: Strict Congregationalists and Separate Baptists in the Great Awakening,* New Haven, Yale University Press, 1962.

Haller, William, *The Rise of Puritanism,* New York, Columbia University Press, 1938.

Haroutunian, Joseph, *Piety versus Moralism; the Passing of the New England Theology,* New York, H. Holt & Co., 1932.

Heppe, Heinrich, *Reformed Dogmatics,* ed. Ernst Bizer, trans. G. T. Thomson, London, Allen & Unwin, 1950.

Hodge, Charles, *Systematic Theology,* London, 1880.

Hodgson, Leonard, *The Grace of God in Faith and Philosophy,* London, Longmans, Green, and Co., 1936.

Howard, Leon, *Literature and the American Tradition,* New York, Doubleday, 1960.

Hubbard, William, *A General History of New England,* Massachusetts Historical Society, Boston, 1848.

Hutchinson, Thomas, *The History of the Colony of Massachusetts,* 2 vols. London, 1765.

Hutchison, William R., *The Transcendentalist Ministers,* New Haven, Yale University Press, 1959.

Kirk, Kenneth E., *The Vision of God,* London, Longmans, Green, and Co., 1932.

Kittel, Gerhard, *Bible Key Words,* New York, Harper and Brothers, 1951.

Knappen, M. M., *Tudor Puritanism,* Chicago, University of Chicago Press, 1939.

Kroner, Richard, *The Religious Function of the Imagination,* New Haven, Yale University Press, 1941.

Levy, Babette May, *Preaching in the First Half Century of New England History,* The American Society of Church History, 1945.

Lindsay, Thomas M., *History of the Reformation,* 2 vols. Edinburgh, T. & T. Clark, 1907.

Loane, Marcus L., *Masters of the English Reformation,* London, Church Book Room Press, 1954.

McAdoo, H. R., *The Structure of Caroline Moral Theology,* London, Longmans, Green, and Co., 1949.

McKee, William W., "The Idea of Covenant in Early English Puritanism," Unpublished dissertation, Yale University, 1948.

McLelland, Joseph C., *The Visible Words of God; an exposition of the sacramental theology of Peter Martyr Vermigli, A.D. 1500–1562*, Grand Rapids, Wm. B. Eerdman, 1957.

MacKinnon, James, *The Origins of the Reformation*, London, Longmans, Green, and Co., 1939.

Manning, B. L., *The People's Faith in the Time of Wyclif*, London, Cambridge University Press, 1919.

Marchant, Ronald A., *The Puritans and the Church Courts in the Diocese of York, 1560–1642*, London, Longmans, Green, and Co., 1960.

M'Clure, A. W., *The Lives of John Wilson, John Norton, and John Davenport*, Boston, 1846.

Michaelson, Robert S., "Changes in the Puritan Concept of Calling or Vocation," *New England Quarterly, 26* (1953), 315–36.

Miller, Perry, *Errand into the Wilderness*, Cambridge, Harvard University Press, 1956.

———— "Jonathan Edwards on the Sense of the Heart," *Harvard Theological Review, 41* (1948), 123–45.

———— *The New England Mind: the Seventeenth Century*, Cambridge, Harvard University Press, 1939.

———— *The New England Mind; from Colony to Province*, Cambridge, Harvard University Press, 1953.

———— *Orthodoxy in Massachusetts*, Cambridge, Harvard University Press, 1933.

———— " 'Preparation for Salvation' in Seventeenth-Century New England," *Journal of the History of Ideas, 4* (1943), 253–86.

Moffat, James, *Grace in the New Testament*, New York, Harper and Brothers, 1932.

Møller, Jens G., "The Beginnings of Puritan Covenant Theology," *The Journal of Ecclesiastical History, 14* (1963), 46–67.

Morgan, Edmund S., *The Puritan Dilemma: The Story of John Winthrop*, Boston, Little, Brown, 1958.

———— *Visible Saints: The History of a Puritan Idea*, New York University Press, 1963.

Mosse, G. L., *The Reformation*, New York, Henry Holt & Co., 1953.

Mueller, Gustav E., "Calvin's *Institutes of the Christian Religion* as an Illustration of Christian Thinking," *Journal of the History of Ideas, 4* (1943), pp. 287–300.

Murdock, Kenneth B., "Clio in the Wilderness: History and Biography in Puritan New England," *Church History, 24* (1955), 221–36.

——— *Increase Mather; the Foremost American Puritan,* Cambridge, Harvard University Press, 1925.

——— *Literature and Theology in Colonial New England,* Cambridge, Harvard University Press, 1949.

Nuttall, Geoffrey, *The Holy Spirit in Puritan Faith and Experience,* London, Oxford University Press, 1946.

——— *Visible Saints, The Congregational Way, 1640–1660,* London, Oxford University Press, 1957.

Nygren, Anders, *Agape and Eros,* Part I, trans. A. G. Herbert, Part II, trans. Philip S. Watson, 3 vols. London, Society for Promoting Christian Knowledge, 1932–39.

Oman, John, *Grace and Personality,* London, Cambridge University Press, 1931.

Parker, T. H. L., *The Doctrine of the Knowledge of God; a Study in the theology of John Calvin,* Edinburgh, Oliver & Boyd, Ltd., 1952.

Pollard, A. F., *Cambridge Modern History,* Vol. 2, London, Cambridge University Press, 1903.

Porter, H. C., *Reformation and Reaction in Tudor Cambridge,* London, Cambridge University Press, 1958.

Pourrat, Pierre, *Christian Spirituality,* 3 vols. London, Burns, Oates and Washbourne, Ltd., 1922.

Reilly, Bart M., *The Elizabethan Puritan's Conception of the Nature and Destiny of Fallen Man,* Washington, D.C., Catholic University of America Press, 1948.

Rice, Eugene F. Jr., "John Colet and the Annihilation of the Natural," *Harvard Theological Review, 45* (1952), 141–63.

Schaff, Philip, *The Creeds of Christendom,* 3 vols. New York, Harper and Brothers, 1878.

——— *History of the Reformation,* 2 vols. New York, C. Scribner's Sons, 1892.

Schneider, H. W., *The Puritan Mind,* New York, H. Holt & Co., 1930.

Scott, John, *The History of the Church of Christ,* London, 1828.

Simpson, Alan, *Puritanism in Old and New England,* Chicago, University of Chicago Press, 1955.

Singleton, Charles S., *Dante Studies 2,* Cambridge, Harvard University Press, 1958.

Smith, John E., *Reason and God,* New Haven, Yale University Press, 1961.

Smith, Lacey Baldwin, "The Reformation and the Decay of Medieval Ideals," *Church History, 24* (1955), 212–20.

Smithen, Frederick J., *Continental Protestantism and the English Reformation,* London, J. Clarke & Co., Ltd., 1927.

Trinterud, L. J., *The Forming of an American Tradition; A Reexamination of Colonial Presbyterianism,* Philadelphia, Westminster Press, 1949.

——— "The Origins of Puritanism," *Church History, 20* (1951), pp. 37–55.

Underhill, Evelyn, *Mysticism,* London, Methuen & Co., Ltd., 1930.

Walker, George Leon, *Some Aspects of the Religious Life of New England,* New York, Silver, Burdette Co., 1897.

——— *Thomas Hooker; Preacher, Founder, Democrat,* New York, Dodd, Mead, & Co., 1891.

Walker, Williston, *The Creeds and Platforms of Congregationalism,* New York, 1893.

——— *A History of the Congregational Churches in the United States,* New York, The Christian Literature Co., 1897.

——— *Ten New England Leaders,* New York, Silver, Burdette Co., 1901.

Whitley, W. T., ed., *The Doctrine of Grace,* London, Macmillan, 1932. (Contains essays on theology by contemporary British churchmen.)

Willey, Basil, *The Seventeenth Century Background; Studies in the Thought of the Age in Relation to Poetry and Religion,* London, Chatto & Windus, 1934.

Williams, John Bickerton, *Letters on Puritans,* London, 1843. (A theological critique of various Puritan thinkers.)

Williams, N. P., *The Grace of God,* London, Longmans, Green, and Co., 1930.

Wolfson, Harry A., *The Philosophy of the Church Fathers,* Cambridge, Harvard University Press, 1956.

——— *Religious Philosophy,* Cambridge, Harvard University Press, 1961.

Wood, Thomas, *English Casuistical Divinity during the Seventeenth Century,* London, Society for Promoting Christian Knowledge, 1952.

Wright, Louis B., "William Perkins: Elizabethan Apostle of 'Practical Divinity,'" *Huntington Library Quarterly, 3* (1940), 171–96.

Ziff, Larzer, *The Career of John Cotton, Puritanism and the American Experience,* Princeton University Press, 1962.

Index

Ab Ulmis, John, and Traheron-Hooper dispute over Calvin's and Bullinger's views, 44 n.

Adams, Nehemiah, views on Thomas Shepard's admissions practices, 102

Agricola, Johannes, antinomian doctrine of, 140

Ahlstrom, Sydney E., ix, 5 n.

Ames, William: and John Preston, 74; and Preston, Richard Sibbes, and Arthur Hildersam, 79; life of, 79–81; and William Perkins, 79–80; and Congregationalism, 80–81; theology of conversion, 81–83; and Bullinger, 82; and church membership, 80–81, 83–84; views on baptism, 81–82, 84–85, 87; compared with Preston, 85; and Hooker, 88, 89; final estimate of, 218

Anabaptists. *See* Church Membership

Andrewes, Lancelot, 5

Andrews, Charles M., on Thomas Hooker's removal, 142 n.

Anglicanism, and condition of church before Restoration, 5 and n.

Antinomianism, 90; Thomas Shepard's congregation preserved from, 103; Shepard's brief flirtation with, 107, 109–10, 140, 146, 152; definition, origins, and significance of, 140–41; John Cotton denies responsibility for, 148; critical charges against proponents of, 151; as "Quakerism," a threat to New England after *1650*, 177; John Norton's fear of, 178, 183; and Ralph Waldo Emerson, 214; final estimate of, 221

Appolonius, William, and John Norton's *The Answer*, 159

Aristotelian revival, and Scholastic views on preparation, 24–27

Arminianism: discussed at Synod of Dort, 125–29; growth in Lincolnshire, 131; Thomas Shepard warns John Winthrop against, 144–45; as threat to New England after *1650*, 176–77; John Norton's antipathy to, 176–77, 180, 183, 189; as avoided by Increase Mather and Solomon Stoddard, 205; and Jonathan Edwards, 210 n.

Arminius, Jacobus, views at Synod of Dort, 125–26

Augustine, Saint: and mystical preparation, 15; and Pelagian Controversy, 22–24; and conception of the will, 23, 123–24, 124 n.; and prevenient grace in Puritan thought, 123–24; essential books on, 223

Baillie, Robert, and church membership in Massachusetts, 162

Ball, John, and Thomas Shepard, 104 n.

Baptism: meaning in covenant theology, 12–13; Puritan views on, 13; and regeneration, 21, 74–75, 75 n., 87; in Paul and the early church, 43 n., 75 n., 118 n.; Bullinger and Zwingli differ on, 36; Calvin follows Zwingli, differs from Bullinger on, 43; in John Preston, 77–78; in William Ames, 81–82, 84–85; in Thomas Hooker, 91–93, 99–100; in Thomas Shepard, 105–06, 111–12; Shepard and Hooker compared on, 110; in Peter Bulkeley, 117–18, 118 n., 120–21; Hooker, Shepard, and Bulkeley compared on, 123; and covenant notions, 123–24; in John Cotton, 134–36, 138, 156; debates on, 157, 159; William Vassall and Robert Child's petition to the General Court on, 162–63; and the Synod of 1646–48, 163–64; in Cambridge Platform, 166–67; in John Davenport, 173; in Giles Firmin, 186–87, 188, 189; problem of, after Cambridge Platform, 191; and ministerial convention of 1657, 192, 193–97; controversy over, Cotton's and Hooker's opinions on, 195–96; and Synod of 1662, Halfway Covenant on, 197–201, 205; in Solomon Stoddard, 205–06; position of William Brattle on, 207; position of Jonathan Edwards on, 211; position of Cyprian Strong on, 212; position of Moses Hemmenway on, 212–14; position of Horace Bushnell on, 215; final estimate of, 218–19

Baptists. See Church Membership

Baynes, Paul, 66

Beecher, Lyman, and evangelical revivals, 215

Berkhof, Louis, 223

Bible, vii, viii; "true sense" discussed, 5; and Holy Spirit, 10

Bible, Geneva: and marginal notes, viii; and marginalia on Proverbs, 9 n.; commentary on Isaiah in, 93 n.

Boston, Lincolnshire, 131, 132

Boston, Mass., 132, 133, 140, 145; Thomas Hooker, John Cotton, and Samuel Stone sail for, Cotton remains at, 90; Hooker returns to, 91; sympathy of, for John Wheelwright, 147; Synod of 1662 at, 197; burning of, 206; Hanover Street Church in, 215

Bradford, William, 168

Bradstreet, Simon, 207

Brattle Street Church: founding of, 206; Increase Mather's warning of, 207; and theology of grace in New England, 208

Brattle, Thomas, 206

Brattle, William: views on church membership and baptism, 206–07, 207 n.; influence of Solomon Stoddard on, 207; opposed by Increase Mather, 207

Brierly, Roger, and "Grindletonians," 147

Browne, Robert, 80

Buber, Martin, 225

Bucer, Martin: and Peter Martyr's doctrine, 31–32; influence on John Cotton, 178

Bulkeley, Peter, 87, 88; and Thomas Hooker and Thomas Shepard, 114, 115–16, 123; and The Gospel Covenant, 114–15; life of, 115–16; on baptismal efficacy, 117–18, 118 n., 120–21; influence of Bullinger on, 119–20, 121–22; compared with Richard Rogers and Shepard, 120–21; compared with Hooker and Shepard on baptism, 123; compared with John Cotton on conversion, 129, 138, on baptism, 135;

ordination of, 147; appointed to Hutchinsonian Synod, 149; and Cambridge Platform, 166–67; and John Davenport, 170, 176; and Giles Firmin, 184; and ministerial convention of *1657*, 191; final estimate of, 218–19, 221

Bullinger, Heinrich: influence on English Reformation, 31, 32–33, 35; theology of conversion, 35–39; succeeds Zwingli and differs on baptism, 35–36; and Peter Martyr on predestination, 39; differs from Calvin on baptism, 43, on preparation, 44, on predestination, 44 n.; influence on Richard Greenham, 55; Arthur Hildersam compared with, 60; influence on William Perkins, 65; influence on John Preston and William Ames, 74–75, 82; influence on Thomas Shepard, 113; influence on Peter Bulkeley, 119–20, 121–22; and significance of covenant theology, 219

Bushnell, Horace: reaction to orthodoxy and position on baptism, church membership, and conversion, 215–16; compared with Ralph Waldo Emerson, 215–16

Calvin, John: and Zwinglian tradition, 2; influence on English Reformation, 30–33; *Institutes* required reading at Oxford and Cambridge, 33, 65; differs from Zwingli and Peter Martyr on preparation, 41–42; follows Zwingli on baptism, 43; differs from Bullinger on baptism, 43, on preparation, 44, on predestination, 44 n.; tradition of, in Richard Greenham, 48–49, 51; where Greenham departs from, 55; views modified by Arthur Hildersam, 60; influence on William Perkins, 65; influence on John Preston, 75–76; views on church membership, 84; influence

on Thomas Shepard, 113, 123; and Peter Bulkeley, 122; convictions reasserted by William Pemble, 128; influence on John Cotton, 130, 132, 133, 139, 145, 178; influence on John Norton, 181, 183, 217; and Jonathan Edwards, 210

Cambridge, Mass. *See* Newtown

Cambridge Platform, 104, 164–67, 167 n.; and John Davenport, 169–70; aftermath of, 191–92, 196, 198; and Synod of *1679*, 201–03

Cambridge University: and beginnings of Puritanism, 4, 5; Calvin's Catechism ordered to be used at, *Institutes* becomes textbook at, 32–33; Richard Greenham at, 48; Richard Rogers at, 51; Arthur Hildersam at, 57; William Perkins at, 61–62; Richard Sibbes at, 66; John Preston at, 75; William Ames at, 79–80; Thomas Hooker at, 88–89; Congregationalism at, 88; Thomas Shepard at, 102; Peter Bulkeley at, 115; John Cotton at, 130; John Norton at, 177; Giles Firmin at, 184

Cartwright, Thomas: and strict Puritans, 4; challenges church authorities, 4; and Presbyterian attitudes in England, 4, 158

Chaderton, Laurence: influence on Puritan divines, 56–57; influence on William Perkins, 61; and John Preston, 76; and Thomas Hooker, 88

Charles I, 5, 76; and Westminster Assembly, 159

Charles II, and Anglican Prayer Book, 206

Chauncy, Charles, and Halfway Covenant, Synod of *1662*, 198–99

Chelmsford, Essex: Thomas Hooker invited to, 89; Hooker's ministry at, 102

Child, Robert: and William Vassall, petition to General Court, 162–

64; and Cambridge Platform, 164–65; and aftermath of Cambridge Platform, 191–92

Children: in covenant theology, 12; extension of baptism to, 191, 192, 193–97; and position of John Cotton on baptism, 134–36; and position on Jonathan Edwards on baptism, 211; and positions of Cyprian Strong and Moses Hemmenway on baptism, 212–13; and Horace Bushnell on Christian nurture, 215

Church of England: repudiated by Separatists, 80; considered to be "true Church" by William Ames and Congregationalists, 80; Puritan divines ordained ministers of, 87; and ecclesiastical polity in New England, 160; and Robert Child, 192

Church Membership: preparation a prerequisite for, 20; limitations on, 21; restricted to elect by William Ames, lack of admissions tests for, 80–81, 81 n.; assurance of salvation not required for, 83–84; and Baptists and Anabaptists, 84; position of Thomas Hooker on, 90–91, 100–01; Robert Stansby's letter on, 90–91; position of Thomas Shepard on, at Dorchester, 101–02; Peter Bulkeley and Shepard compared on, 115–16; Hooker and John Cotton at odds on, 133–34; Cotton's restrictions on, 143–53; debates on, 157; and position of the baptized in English and American Puritanism, 158; and qualifications for in New England, 159–70; Hooker's and Cotton's final conflict on, 161–62; William Vassall and Robert Child's petition to the General Court on, 162–64; Synod of 1646–48 on, 163–64; Cambridge Platform on, 164–67; in Plymouth, Connecticut, and

New Haven, 168–69; position of John Davenport on, 170, 173–74; position of John Norton on, 183; problem of, after Cambridge Platform; 191; and ministerial convention of 1657, 191–97; and Synod of 1662, Halfway Covenant on, 197–201; in Synod of 1679, 202–03; position of Solomon Stoddard on, 201–03, 205; position of William Brattle on, 207; vote of Westfield Church on, 207; position of Jonathan Edwards on, 207, 208–12; position of Cyprian Strong on, 212; position of Moses Hemmenway on, 212–14; position of Horace Bushnell on, 215–16; final estimate of, 221; significance of Edmund S. Morgan's research on, 225

Clement of Alexandria, and preparation, 22

Colet, John, influence on English Reformation, 29–30, 30 n.

Congregationalism: and Church of England and Separatists, 80; and Church admissions, 80–81, 83–84; and Cambridge University, 88; and Westminster Assembly, 91; defended by Thomas Hooker, 91; defined in Cambridge Platform, 104; and English Presbyterianism, 158–60; and English Independents, 159 n., 164; and Giles Firmin, 184, 189; threatened by Restoration, 197; and Synod of 1662, 199

Connecticut, 90, 104, 212; church practices in, 81 n., 100–01, 168; delegates to Synod of 1646–48, 163; and ministerial convention of 1657, 191

Contrition: in preparatory process, 18; views of Peter Martyr on, 33–34; Thomas Hooker first preaches on, 89; in Hooker's theology of conversion, 96–98, 109; in Thomas

Shepard's theology of conversion, 108

Cotton, John, 19–20, 88, 159; sails with Thomas Hooker and Samuel Stone, 90, 132; part played in Hooker's removal to Hartford, 90–91, 133–34, 142 n.; and Thomas Shepard, 103; and William Pemble, 129; compared with Richard Sibbes, 129; compared with Hooker, Shepard, and Peter Bulkeley, 129, 138; life of, 130–31; influence of Calvin on, 130, 132, 133, 139, 145; influence of William Perkins on, 130, 132; influence of Sibbes on, 130–32, 131 n.; and John Preston, 131; early doctrine of conversion, 131–32; criticized by William Twisse, 131; later doctrine of conversion, 133–40; criticizes Hooker, 133–34; on baptism and church membership, 134–38; compared with Bulkeley on baptism, 135; compared with Zwingli and Peter Martyr on conversion, 139; and antinomianism, 140–41; and Anne Hutchinson, 141, 145; opposes John Wilson, 143, 145; questioned by ministers, 145–46; defends John Wheelwright and refuses to attend Bulkeley's ordination, 147; threatens to move to Quinnipiac, 148, 172–74; denies responsibility for antinomianism, 148; position on Hutchinsonian "errors," 150–51; in civil trial of Anne Hutchinson, 152–54; in church trial of Anne Hutchinson, 154–55; doctrine of conversion after trials, 155–56; opposition to Presbyterian sympathizers, 161; final conflict with Hooker on church admissions, 161–62; attacked by English Presbyterians and Robert Baillie on church admissions, 162 and n.; and Cambridge Platform, 166–67; influence on John Davenport, 170–71; compared with Davenport on baptism, church admissions, and conversion, 170, 173–75, 176; compared with John Norton on conversion, 178–81, 182–83; and Giles Firmin, 184; opinion on baptism controversy, 195–97, 200; as link in strict Reformed tradition, 217; final estimate of, 218, 221

Court of High Commission: Hooker summoned by, 89; and John Cotton, 132

Covenant theology: and experiential religion, 11; and the Pauline message, 11–12; and reprobate children, 12; preserve of Puritans, avoided by Anglicans, 13 n.; Thomas Shepard caught in dilemma of, 105; full flowering in Peter Bulkeley, 114, 119–20; and Hebraic prescription, 123; and John Cotton's doctrine of conversion, 138; and Jonathan Edwards, 210 n.; final estimate of, 218–21

Cranmer, Thomas: influence on English Reformation, 30–31; martyrdom of, 32

Davenport, John, 148, 159; and church admissions in New Haven, 168–70; influence of Richard Rogers on, 169; compared with John Cotton, Thomas Shepard, Thomas Hooker, and Peter Bulkeley, 170; life of, 170–72; influence of Richard Sibbes, John Preston, and John Cotton on, 170–71; and baptism controversy in Holland, 171, 200; and the Antinomian Controversy, 171–72; compared with Cotton on baptism, church admissions, and conversion, 170, 173–75, 176; compared with Hooker on church admissions, conversion, and baptism, 169–70, 175–76; compared with Shepard on baptism, 176; compared with John Norton on conversion, 178–81; and Giles Firmin, 184; and ministerial convention of *1657*, 191; and Half-way Covenant, Synod of *1662*, 198–200; and baptism controversy in Boston, 200; death of, 200; final estimate of, 218, 221

Davies, J. G., and Pauline views on baptism, 118 n.

Dod, John: influence on Puritan divines, 56–57; and John Preston, 76

Dorchester Church: rôle of Thomas Shepard in gathering of, 101–02, 113; and position of John Cotton in baptism controversy, 195

Dry Drayton, Cambridgeshire, 48, 51, 61

Dudley, Thomas, 142; and cross-examination of John Cotton, 153

Eaton, Theophilus, 171

Edward VI, and English Protestant-ism, 31

Edwards, Jonathan: reaction to Stoddardean practices, 207, 208–09; compared with founding di-vines on experiential relations and conversion, 209–10, 210 n.; compared with Zwingli and Calvin on regeneration, 210; dismissal from Northampton and opposi-tion to Halfway Covenant, 211; compared with John Norton and Solomon Stoddard on conversion, 211–12; influence on New England theology, 212

Elizabeth, viii, 3, 4, 32, 61

Ellis, George E., 224

Emerson, Everett H., on Calvin's conception of conversion, 41 n.

Emerson, Ralph Waldo: Transcen-dentalism of, indifference to pre-scribed experientialism, 214; com-pared with Moses Hemmenway, 214; compared with Giles Firmin,

214; antinomianism of, 214; and Unitarian ministry, 215, 216; com-pared with Horace Bushnell, 215–16

English Church: position of Puri-tanism within, 6; Joseph Hall delegate of, at Synod of Dort, 125–26

English churchmen, vii, 2; and Re-formed theology, 3; early emphasis on divine sovereignty, 3; relation-ship to radical Puritans, 4; agree-ment with Puritans on doctrine, 5 n.; position on predestination, 6; position on salvation, 15; essential books on influence of Continental Reformers on, 224

English Reformation: second phase of, 4; first phase of, 13; influence of Continental Protestantism on, 29–31; influence of John Wycliffe on, 29 and n.; influence of John Colet on, 29–30; influence of Henry VIII, Myconias, and Thomas Cranmer on, 30–31; in-fluence of Peter Martyr, Bullinger, and Calvin on, 33

Firmin, Giles: and John Norton, Thomas Hooker, Thomas Shep-ard, Peter Bulkeley, and John Cotton, 183–84; life of, 184; criti-cism of Hooker and Shepard by, 185–89; criticism of William Per-kins by, 185–86, 188; criticism of Richard Rogers by, 188; compared with Norton, 189–90; and trends in New England theology, 189–90, 192–93; and Halfway Covenant, 200; and Solomon Stoddard, 206; and Ralph Waldo Emerson, 214; final estimate of, 217, 221–22

General Court: petition of Thomas Hooker to, 90; John Wheelwright censured by, 147; charge of, against Anne Hutchinson, 152;

petition of William Vassall and Robert Child to, 162–64; Synod of *1646–48* called by and Declaration issued by, 163; requests John Davenport to settle in Massachusetts, 172; and ministerial convention of *1657*, 191, 196; and Synod of *1662*, 197–99; petition and speech of Increase Mather to, Synod of *1679*, 201–02

Goodwin, Thomas, and Philip Nye, 67

Gospel, and the Law in conversion, 15–16

Gray's Inn, London, 66

Great Awakening, 124, 208, 215

Greenham, Richard, 5; and application of covenant ideas, 13; life of, 48; theology of conversion, 48–51; compared with Richard Rogers on preparation, 51–52, on conversion, 52–55; and William Perkins, 61, 63; compared with Thomas Shepard, 110, 112–13; final estimate of, 218

Halfway Covenant, 198–201; standards upheld by Increase Mather, 201–03; and Synod of *1679*, 202–03; and church practice of Solomon Stoddard, 205; and founding of Brattle Street Church, 207; opposition of Jonathan Edwards to, 211; final estimate of, 221

Hall, Joseph, and Synod of Dort, 125–28, 129

Haller, William, 224

Hancock, John, 207 n.

Hankridge, Sarah, second wife of John Cotton, 131

Hartford, Conn.: Thomas Hooker goes to, 90–91; church admissions at, 100

Harvard College, ix; and Thomas Shepard, 103–04; and Peter Bulkeley, 116

Haynes, John, 142

Hebrews: prophetic message of, vii; tradition of, in Church Fathers, 23; exhortations of, in Arthur Hildersam, 59; and circumcision as antetype of baptism, in Thomas Hooker, 92, in covenant theology, 123; and conception of the will as opposed to Augustinian notions, 23, 123–24, 124 n.; and relationship to God as opposed to Pauline notions, 225

Hemmenway, Moses: position on baptism, church membership, 212–14; compared with Ralph Waldo Emerson, 214

Henry VIII, influence on English Reformation, 30–31

Heppe, Heinrich, 223

Herbert, George, 5

Hildersam, Arthur, 5, 56; concern with covenant, 13–14; life of, 57; theology of conversion, 57–61; compared with Richard Rogers, 58, 61; compared with Bullinger, 60; modifies Calvin, 60; and William Perkins, 61; compared with Perkins, 63–65; compared with Richard Sibbes, 71; compared with Thomas Hooker, 94; influence on Solomon Stoddard, 204; final estimate of, 218

Hobart, Peter, 161

Holland: and English nonconformists, 86; Thomas Hooker and William Ames in, 89; Arminian Remonstrance addressed to Estates of, 125; John Davenport escapes to, 171; baptism controversy in, 171; Davenport resigns his post in, 171

Holy Spirit: doctrine of, 9–11; Calvin's views on, 41–42; in Paul's teachings on baptism, 43 n., 75 n., 118 n.; in Richard Rogers, 52–55, 65; in William Perkins, 65; renewed interest of Puritans in, 65–66; as principle of actions in con-

---

version, 65–66; in Richard Sibbes, 67–74; as principle of actions in Sibbes, 73; in John Preston, 76–78; in Thomas Hooker, 92, 95, 99; in Peter Bulkeley, 120; in Arminian Remonstrance, 125; in Joseph Hall, 126; in John Cotton, 130–31, 132, 133, 135–36, 139; in New England Puritanism, 146; in fast day sermon of John Wheelwright, 146–47; in Hutchinsonian "errors," 150; in civil trial of Anne Hutchinson, 152–53; in Cotton after Antinomian Controversy, 156; in John Davenport, 173–75; in John Norton, 179, 180–81, 181–82, 189; in Solomon Stoddard's account of Synod of 1679, 202; in Jonathan Edwards, 209–10; final estimate of, 217–18; Geoffrey Nuttall on, 224

Holy Trinity, Cambridge, 66

Hooker, Joanna: daughter of Thomas Hooker, 89; second wife of Thomas Shepard, 104

Hooker, Susanna, wife of Thomas Hooker, 89

Hooker, Thomas, 86, 87, 158; criticized by John Bickerton Williams on doctrine of grace, 88; life of, 88–91; and John Preston, Laurence Chaderton, William Perkins, Richard Sibbes, and William Ames, 88, 89; sails with John Cotton and Samuel Stone, 90, 132; views on church membership and removal from Massachusetts, 91–93, 99–100; doctrine of Holy Spirit in, 92; conversion of, 93–94; compared with Arthur Hildersam, 94; on Paul's conversion, 94; compared with John Preston, 96; theology of conversion, 96–101; compared with Richard Sibbes, 99, 108; influence on Thomas Shepard, 102–03; compared with Shepard on baptism and conversion, 105–06, 107–

10, 114; and Peter Bulkeley, 114, 115; compared with Shepard and Bulkeley on baptism, 123; compared with Cotton, 129, 138; criticized by Cotton, 133–34; opposes antinomians, 142; opposes calling Hutchinsonian Synod, and acts as moderator, 148–49; opposes Presbyterian sympathizers, 161; final conflict with Cotton on church admissions, 161–62; and Cambridge Platform, 166–67; compared with John Davenport on church admissions, conversion, and baptism, 169–70, 175–76; compared with John Norton, 178–81; and Giles Firmin, 183–84; criticized by Firmin, 185–89; opinion on baptism controversy, 195–96; influence on Solomon Stoddard, 204; final estimate of, 218–19, 221

Hooper, John, and dispute with Bartholomew Traheron over Calvin's and Bullinger's views, 44 n.

Horrocks, Elizabeth, first wife of John Cotton, 131

Hubbard, William, views on Thomas Hooker's removal, 91

Humiliation, doctrine of: in preparatory process, 18; in Richard Greenham, 49–51; in Richard Rogers, 53–55; in Arthur Hildersam, 58–61; in William Perkins, 65; in Richard Sibbes, 70–71; in John Preston, 77; in William Ames, 81; in Thomas Hooker, 89, 98; in Thomas Shepard, 108; in Peter Bulkeley, 119, 121; criticized by Giles Firmin, 185–86

Hutchinson, Anne, 19, 91, 115; theory of conversion, 141; and Thomas Hooker, 141; and John Cotton, 141, 145, 150, 152–55; accuses clergy of teaching doctrine of works, 145; and John Wheelwright, 142, 145, 150; civil trial of, 152–54; church trial of, 154–55; revelational views of, 155 n.; excommunication, banishment, and death of, 156–57; comments of Giles Firmin on church trial of, 184, 188

Hutchinsonian Synod: attended by Thomas Hooker, 91; Peter Bulkeley and Hooker appointed moderators of, 115; suggested by Thomas Shepard, supported by John Cotton, and opposed by Hooker, 148–49; held at Newtown, 149–50; "errors" confuted at, 149–50; adjourned, 152; and John Davenport, 171–72; Giles Firmin at, 184

Hutchinsonians, 20; John Winthrop's arguments against, 144–45; "errors" confuted at Synod, 149–51; refusal to accept Synod's conclusions, 152

Independents: and Westminster Assembly, 159 n., 160 n., 164; and New England Congregationalism, 159 n., 160 n., 164; and Oliver Cromwell, 162; and triumph over Presbyterians, 192

Ipswich, Mass.: John Norton at, 178; Nathaniel Ward at, 178, 184; Giles Firmin at, 184

Israel, viii; and its covenant, 12; meaning for New England, 86; in Richard Mather's defence of Dorchester church, 101–02; analogous with external covenanters, 123; in John Cotton as opposed to Hosea, 134, 138; in Giles Firmin's criticism of Thomas Hooker and Thomas Shepard, 187; "House of," in Synod of 1662, 198; in Increase Mather's speech to the General Court, 201

James I, 76; and Joseph Hall, 126

Jewel, John, letter to Peter Martyr, 32

Jews: significance of Peter's exhortation to, 3; meaning for New England, 86; and "sealed" as term for circumcision, 118 n.

King Philip's War, 206

Laud, William, 5; and John Preston, 76; and nonconformists, 86; and exiled divines, 87; Thomas Hooker deprived of lectureship by, 89; Thomas Shepard suspended by, 102; Bishop of York alerted by, 103; Peter Bulkeley suspended by, 115; defied by John Davenport, 171

Law: and preparation, 15–17; uses of, in Pauline theology of conversion, 15–16; as "schoolmaster" in Paul's thought, 27–28; in New England theology, 18; and the Gospel in Patristic thought, 22; as problem in Puritan thought, 47, 61; in Richard Greenham, 50–51; in Richard Rogers, 53, 65; in Arthur Hildersam, 57–58, 60; in William Perkins, 64–65, 130; and the Spirit, 65; and the Gospel in Richard Sibbes, 69–70; in John Preston, 76–77; in William Ames, 81–83; in Thomas Hooker, 94, 97; in Thomas Shepard, 106–08, 110, 111, 113; in Peter Bulkeley, 122; in Joseph Hall, 129; and John Cotton, 130, 132; and the Gospel in Cotton's thought, 135–37, 136 n.; and antinomianism, 140–41, 151, 153; in Cotton after Antinomian Controversy, 156; in John Davenport, 170, 175; in John Norton, 179, 181, 182; criticized by Giles Firmin, 186; final estimate of, 217–19

Leverett, John, 207, and n.

Luther, Martin: influence on English Reformation, 30–31; and Johannes Agricola, 140; Anders Nygren on, 223

Lydia's conversion, biblical example of: in Reformed theology, 27–28;

in Richard Rogers, 54–55; in Richard Sibbes, 72–73; in Thomas Hooker, 95; in Thomas Shepard, 109; in Peter Bulkeley, 121

Marsh, H. G., on Pauline views on baptism, 43 n., 75 n.
Martyr, Peter: influence in England, 31–33; views on conversion, 33–35; and Bullinger on predestination, 39; and Richard Greenham, 55; and John Preston, 78–79; and Peter Bulkeley, 122; and John Cotton, 139, 178; influence on John Norton, 181, 182, 183
Massachusetts: church practices in, 80–81, 81 n., 84, 90–91, 100, 101–02, 159–67, 199–200, 201–03; Thomas Shepard's influence on, 104–05
Mather, Cotton: on John Cotton, 130, 150–51; on Thomas Hooker and William Ames, 89; on Hooker's conversion, 93–94; on Peter Bulkeley, 114, 115
Mather, Eleazer, and Halfway Covenant, Synod of 1662, 198–99
Mather, Increase, 195 n.; and Halfway Covenant, Synod of 1662, 198–99; opposition to Solomon Stoddard, 201–03, 203 n.; speech of and petition to General Court, 201–03; position at Synod of 1679, 202–03; Stoddard's views on preparation endorsed by, 203–04; influence of John Norton on, 204; compared with Stoddard and Norton, 204–05; warning to Brattle Street Church, 207; reaction of Jonathan Edwards to, 209
Mather, Richard, 131, 159; and first gathering of Dorchester church, 101–02; letter to Thomas Shepard, 101–02; and ministerial convention of 1657, 191; and Halfway Covenant, Synod of 1662, 198–99
Miller, Perry: on Calvin's concep-

tion of conversion, 40 n.; views on covenant theology, 120 n., 219–21; on Thomas Hooker's removal, 142 n.; on John Cotton and the antinomians, 141; on Jonathan Edwards' conversion and church practice, 210 n.; works on concept of preparation, 225
Ministerial Convention of 1657, 191–97
Morgan, Edmund S., ix; views on church membership, 81 n., 225; on Mather–Stoddard controversy, 203 n.; research acknowledged, ix, 225
Myconias, influence on English Reformation, 30–31

Newbury, Mass.: Thomas Parker and James Noyes at, 161; and Presbyterian subversion, 192
New Haven, Conn., 148; church practices in, 81 n., 168–70; John Cotton considers moving to, 155, 173–74; delegates to Synod of 1646–48, 163; and ministerial convention of 1657, 191; and John Davenport, 155, 168–70, 173–74, 198, 199, 200
New Testament: contradictory exhortations in, 3; and fulfillment of the Old, 12; and the Law as interpreted by Paul, 15–16; in Richard Sibbes, 71–72; and baptismal regeneration, 75 n.; and infant baptism, 193; and divine love, 223
Newtown, Mass.: Thomas Hooker at, 90–91, 103–04, 133, 142; Samuel Stone at, 90; Thomas Shepard at, 90–91, 103–04, 142; Hooker's removal from, 90–91, 142 and n.; Harvard College founded at, 103–04; Hutchinsonian Synod appointed by General Court and held at, 147, 149
Northampton, Mass., Jonathan Edwards dismissed from, 211

Norton, John: and Thomas Shepard, 103, 177; and *The Answer*, 159 and n.; and *The Orthodox Evangelist*, 177, 178, 193, 197, 204; life of, 177–78; and Richard Sibbes, 178; and John Cotton, 178; theology of conversion, 178–81, 182–83; compared with Thomas Hooker, Shepard, John Davenport, and Cotton, 178–81, 182–83; influence of Peter Martyr, Calvin, William Perkins, William Pemble, and John Preston on, 181 and n., 182, 183; compared with Richard Rogers and Sibbes, 182; and Giles Firmin, 183–84; compared with Firmin, 189–90; compared with Cotton, 189; and Increase Mather, Solomon Stoddard, and Jonathan Edwards, 189–90; and ministerial convention of *1657*, 191, 192–93, 197; and Synod of *1662*, Halfway Covenant, 198–99, 200; death of, 200; influence on Increase Mather, 204; compared with Mather on conversion, 204–05; compared with Stoddard on conversion, 204–05, 206, 211; reaction of Edwards to, 209; compared with Edwards on conversion, 211–12; as link with strict Reformed theology, 217, 221

Nuttall, Geoffrey, 224

Nygren, Anders, 223

Old Testament, 7; contradictory exhortations in, 2–3; and the Law as interpreted by Paul, 15; and Bullinger's use of prophetic exhortations, 36–37; in Richard Sibbes, 71–72; the circumcised as antetypes of the baptized, 93; and covenant exhortations, 123; and Reformed thought in John Cotton, 138; in ministerial convention of *1657*, 194; in Synod of *1662*, 198

Oxford University: influence of John Colet on, 29–30; Peter Martyr lectures at, 31; Calvin's Catechism ordered to be used at, 32–33; Calvin's *Institutes* becomes textbook at, 33; William Pemble at, 128; John Davenport at, 170

Paget, John, and baptism controversy with John Davenport, 171

Parker, Thomas, Presbyterian sympathizer with James Noyes at Newbury, 161

Parliament: and Charles I, Westminster Assembly, and Commissioners for Plantations, 159–60; *Apologetical Narration* submitted to, 160 n.; appeal of William Vassall and Robert Child to, 162–64

Patristic theology, and preparation, 22–24

Paul: Reformed understanding of, 2; paradox in preaching on conversion, 3; Puritan interpretations of, 7; and Damascus conversion, 7; and preparation, 8; on covenant with Abraham, 11–12; on efficacy of the "seed," 12; on function of the Law, 15; conversion as interpreted by Zwingli, 16; on Fall of man, 23; conversion as interpreted by Thomas Aquinas, 25–26; doctrine of repentance in Reformed theology, 27–28; doctrine of repentance in Bullinger, 37; teachings on baptism, 43 n., 75 n., 118 n.; conversion as interpreted by Thomas Hooker, 94–95

Pelagianism: Augustine's struggle against, 22–24; and English divines at Synod of Dort, 127–28; and covenant theology, 219

Pemble, William: views on Synod of Dort, 128; and John Cotton, 129; influence on John Norton, 181

Perkins, William, 5; on "Puritans" and "Precisians," 6; on use of covenant, 14; life of, 61–62; theology of conversion, 62–65; com-

pared with Richard Rogers and
Arthur Hildersam, 63–65; influence of Richard Greenham on,
63; influence of Calvin on, 65;
influence of Bullinger on, 65; and
Richard Sibbes, 66; compared
with Sibbes, 67, 69, 74; and
Thomas Hooker, 88; compared
with Thomas Shepard, 106; influence on John Cotton, 130, 132;
influence on John Norton, 181; as
criticized by Giles Firmin, 185–86,
188; influence on Solomon Stoddard, 204; final estimate of, 218
Peter: emphasis on repentance and
the promises, 3, 28; in Cambridge
Platform, 166
Plymouth, Mass.: church practices
in, 81 n., 168 and n.; William Vassall of, 162; delegates to Synod of
1646–48, 163; John Norton at,
178
Preparation: biblical passages for
and against man's participation
in, 8–9; ambiguous biblical passages on, 9; Geneva and authorized
Bibles on, 9 n.; and Reformed
theology, 9, 28–29, 217; emphasis
on voluntarism in, 14; and the
Law, 15–18; contrition and humiliation in, 18, 19; as an ability
on man's part, 20–21; as a barrier
to grace, 20–21, 87–88; in Patristic
and Scholastic thought, 22–27; in
Peter Martyr, Bullinger, and Calvin, 33–45; denied by William
Tyndale, 34–35; first described by
Bullinger, 38; biblical exhortations to, retained by Calvin, 41–42;
differences between Bullinger and
Calvin on, 44; in *Thirty-Nine
Articles* and Council of Trent,
45–46; four considerations of, in
Puritan thought, 47; in Richard
Greenham, 50–51; differences between Greenham and Richard
Rogers on, 51–52, 54; in Arthur

Hildersam and Rogers, 61; in William Perkins, 63–64; in Richard
Sibbes, 67, 71–74; and baptismal
regeneration, 74–75, 85, 87; in
John Preston, 76–78; in William
Ames, 81–83; and divine constraint, 87; Thomas Hooker first
preaches on, 89; Hooker and John
Cotton at odds on, 90; in Hooker,
95–96, 98, 100–01; in Thomas
Shepard, 105, 108–09, 113–14;
Shepard and Hooker compared
on, 109; in Peter Bulkeley, 118–21,
123; validity questioned, 124; examined at Synod of Dort, 125–28,
129; rejected by William Pemble,
128; in Cotton, 129, 131–32, 145;
denied by antinomians, 141; in
Shepard's letter to John Winthrop, 144; attacked by John
Wheelwright, 146–47; as requirement for settlement in Bay, 148;
denied at Hutchinsonian Synod,
civil trial, and church trial, 149–
51, 153, 154–55; issue not resolved
by banishment, 157; in Hooker's
and Cotton's final debate on
church admissions, 161–62; and
Cambridge Platform, 164–67, 198;
as criticized and altered by John
Norton, 177, 179–83, 189–90; as
criticized by Giles Firmin, 185–90;
and ministerial convention of
1657, 192; in Synod of *1662*, Halfway Covenant, 198; in Solomon
Stoddard, 201, 204–05; not mentioned by Synod of *1679*, 203; in
Increase Mather, 204–05; remains
an issue in New England theology,
209; discarded by Jonathan Edwards, 209; in Ralph Waldo Emerson, 214–15; final estimate of, 217–
22
Presbyterianism: and Thomas Cartwright, 4, 158; and New England
Congregationalism, 158–60; sympathizers in Massachusetts and

convention of *1643*, 161; and Synod of *1646–48*, 164, 176; John Davenport's objections to, in Holland, 171; and Giles Firmin, 184, 189–90; and ministerial convention of *1657*, 191–92

Preston, John, 74–75, 79; life of, 75–76; and John Cotton, 75, 79, 131; and John Donne, 76; and Laurence Chaderton, 76; and Richard Sibbes, 76; and Charles I, 76; and Arthur Hildersam, 76 and n.; and William Laud, 76; and John Dod, 76; theology of conversion, 76–79; compared with William Perkins, 76–77; compared with Richard Greenham, Richard Rogers, Hildersam, and Sibbes, 77; views on baptism, 77–78, 87; compared with Zwingli and Peter Martyr, 78–79; compared with William Ames, 85; and Thomas Hooker, 88; compared with Hooker, 96; influence on Thomas Shepard, 106–07; influence on John Davenport, 170; influence on John Norton, 181; influence on Solomon Stoddard, 204; final estimate of, 218

Prophetic exhortations: and covenant theology, 218; final estimate of, 218

Protestantism: radical wing under Thomas Cartwright, 4; restoration under Elizabeth, 4; influence on English Reformation, 29–31; favored by Somerset and Edward VI, 31

Puritanism, definition of, 3–6

Quinnipiac, John Cotton considers moving to, 148, 172–73

Reformed dogmatics: and Puritan thought, 2; and English churchmen, 2; and biblical passages on preparation, 9; rigid discipline derived from, 17; final estimate of,

218; essential books on, 223

Reformed theology: and biblical prescription, viii; and English churchmen, 2, 3; early influence in England, 4, 5, 31; extent to which Puritans followed general approach of, 5–6; extent to which preparation could be reconciled with, 9; and doctrine of the Holy Spirit, 10; and infant baptism, 12; and bondage under the Law, 16; and Patristic and scholastic thought, 22–27; and the nature of the "calling," 27–29; as interpreted by Peter Martyr, Bullinger, and Calvin, 33–45; William Perkins reasserts basic tenets of, 62; Calvinist strain in, 65; John Preston recalls basic tenet of, 79; and preparation in New England, 124; and Arminian doctrine, 126; link of John Norton to, 183, 217; final estimate of, 218; essential books on, 223–24

Rogers, Richard, 5, 10; life of, 51; influence of Richard Greenham on, 51; differs from Greenham on preparation, 51–52, on conversion, 53–54; theology of conversion, 52–55; compared with Arthur Hildersam, 58, 61; compared with William Perkins and Hildersam, 63–65; influence on Thomas Shepard, 106–07, 113; compared with Shepard and Peter Bulkeley, 120–21; influence on John Davenport, 169; and John Norton, 182; as criticized by Giles Firmin, 188; final estimate of, 218

Saints: knowledge of, 10; and double covenant, 21; and Jonathan Edwards, 210–11

Schaff, Philip, 224

Scholastic theology: and preparation, 22, 24–27; abandoned by John Colet, 29–30

Separatists: and Church of England, 80; church practices in England and New England, 81 n.

Shepard, Thomas, 86, 87, 89, 158; as criticized by John Bickerton Williams on doctrine of grace, 88; organizes church at Newtown, 90, 103; and first gathering of Dorchester church, 101–02, 113–14; life of, 102–04; and John Norton, Thomas Hooker, and John Cotton, 103; compared with Hooker on baptism and conversion, 105–06, 107–10, 114; compared with William Perkins, 106; conversion of, 106–08; and Laurence Chaderton, 106; influence of John Preston on, 106–07; influence of Richard Rogers on, 106–07, 113; compared with Richard Greenham, 110, 112–13; influence of Calvin and Bullinger on, 113, 123; and Peter Bulkeley, 114, 115–16, 120–21; compared with Hooker and Bulkeley on baptism, 123; compared with Cotton, 129, 138, 152; opposes antinomians, 142; letter to John Winthrop, 144; suggests Hutchinsonian Synod, 148; admonishes Anne Hutchinson, 155; on Cotton's repentance, 156; and Cotton's policy of church admissions, 161; and John Davenport's policy of church admissions, 170; compared with Davenport on baptism, 176; compared with John Norton on conversion, 178–81; and Giles Firmin, 183–84; as criticized by Firmin, 185–89; and baptism controversy, 196; influence on Solomon Stoddard, 204; final estimate of, 218–19, 221

Sibbes, Richard: life of, 66–67; theology of conversion, 67–74; compared with William Perkins, 67, 69, 74; compared with Arthur Hildersam, 71; and Richard Rog-

ers, 72; and Thomas Hooker, 88; compared with Hooker, 99, 108; compared with John Cotton, 129; influence on Cotton, 130–32, 131 n.; influence on John Davenport, 170; and John Norton, 178, 182; influence on Solomon Stoddard, 204; final estimate of, 218

Smithen, Frederick J., 29 n., 224

Spiritual brotherhood: beginnings at Cambridge University, 4; Richard Greenham first great teacher of, 48; John Dod "chief Holy man" of, 56–57, 76; and imagery of Richard Sibbes, 99; William Haller on, 224

Spirituality: as distinguished from dogma, 5 n.; and dogma, 55–56; sense of regenerative process in, 83

Stansby, Robert, letter to John Wilson on Thomas Hooker's removal, 90–91, 142 n.

Stoddard, Solomon: church practice of, 201, 205–06; opposed by Increase Mather on "open communion," 201–03, 203 n.; influence on Synod of 1679, 202–03; endorsed by Mather on preparation, 203–04; views on preparation, 204; influence of Hildersam, Perkins, Sibbes, Preston, Hooker, and Shepard on, 204; compared with Mather on conversion, 204–05; compared with Norton on conversion, 204–05, 206, 211; position on baptism, 205–06; and Giles Firmin, 206; influence on Brattle Street Church, 207; and theology of grace in New England, 208; reaction of Jonathan Edwards to, 207, 208–09; compared with Edwards on conversion, 211–12; final estimate of, 222

Stone, Samuel: sails with Thomas Hooker and John Cotton, 90; and ministerial convention of 1657,

191; and baptism controversy, 196

Strong, Cyprian: opposition to covenant notions, 212; position on baptism, 212

Synod: of Dort, 80, 125–28, 129, 188; of *1637, see* Hutchinsonian Synod, of *1646–48,* 163–67; of *1662,* 197–200; of *1679,* 165, 201–03

Tauteville, Margaret, first wife of Thomas Shepard, 103

Thirty-Nine Articles, on preparation, 45–46

Thomas Aquinas, Saint: and Aristotelian premises in preparation, 24–27; on infallibility, 56; views opposed by John Cotton, 145–46; views distinguished from Puritan doctrine, 145–46

Traheron, Bartholomew, and dispute with John Hooper over Calvin's and Bullinger's views, 44 n.

Transcendentalism, 214

Trent, Council of, on preparation, 45–46

Twisse, William, and John Cotton, 131

Tyndale, William, 6; and the covenant, 13; Zwingli's theology adopted by, 34; views on conversion, 34–35

Unitarianism, 214, 215

Vane, Henry: and Anne Hutchinson, 142; and John Wilson, 143; protests censure of John Wheelwright, refuses to attend Peter Bulkeley's ordination, dropped from office, 147; letter from John Winthrop to, 148; returns to England, 149

Vassall, William, and petition to General Court, 162–64

Walker, Williston, 224–25

Ward, Nathaniel, 88, 178; father-in-law of Giles Firmin, 184, 188; views on Thomas Hooker's doctrine of grace, 188

Ward, Susanna, daughter of Nathaniel Ward and wife of Giles Firmin, 184

Weld, Thomas: and Thomas Shepard, 102; Hutchinsonian "errors" published by, 149–51, 149 n.; testimony at Anne Hutchinson's church trial, 154

Westfield, Mass., vote of church on experiential relations at, 207

Westminster Assembly: gathering of, 159; and Independency in England, 159 n., 160 n.

Westminster Confession, and Synod of *1646–48,* 164

Wheelwright, John, 19; opposed by John Winthrop and John Wilson, 142–43; and Anne Hutchinson, 142, 145, 150; fast day sermon of, 146–47; censured by General Court and refuses to attend Peter Bulkeley's ordination, 147; civil trial of, 152–54; banishment and death of, 156–57

Whitefield, George, and Great Awakening, 208

Williams, John Bickerton: criticism of Thomas Hooker's doctrine of grace, 88; criticism of Thomas Shepard's doctrine of grace, 88, 108, 113–14

Williams, N. P., 224

Wilson, John: and William Ames, 88–89; letter from Robert Stansby to, on Thomas Hooker's removal, 90–91, 142 n.; and John Cotton, 132, 133; opposes antinomians with John Winthrop, 142; speech recalled by Winthrop, 143; accused of teaching covenant of works, 143–44; rebuked by Cotton, 145; death of, 200

Winthrop, John: and John Cotton, 133, 156; and John Wilson, 133,

142–44; opposes antinomians, 142–45; letter from Thomas Shepard to, on preparation, 144; reelected Governor of Massachusetts and supports law against strangers, 147–48; letter to Henry Vane from, 148; "errors" of Hutchinsonians collected by, 149; opinions of Anne Hutchinson condemned by, 154

Wits, Herman, views on Synod of Dort, 127–28

Wolfson, Harry A., 124 n., 223

Wycliffe, John, influence on English Reformation, 29 and n.

Zwingli, Huldreich: emphasis on God's inscrutable will, on inability of man to cooperate in conversion, 2; on Paul's conversion, 8; on the Law in Paul's conversion, 16; on faith and repentance, 28; influence on English Reformation, 30–31; succeeded by Bullinger, 32, 35–36; views on conversion accepted by Peter Martyr, 34; theology adopted by William Tyndale, 34–35; differs from Bullinger on baptism, 36; differs from Calvin on conversion, 41; anticipates Calvin on baptism, 43; and John Preston, 78–79; and Peter Bulkeley, 122; and John Cotton, 139; and Jonathan Edwards, 210; and John Norton, 217

About the Authors

Norman Pettit's ancestor Thomas Pettit came to the Massachusetts Bay Colony in John Winthrop's first fleet. Pettit is the editor of Jonathan Edwards's *Life of David Brainerd* in the Yale Edition of *The Works of Jonathan Edwards* and, with George Hunston Williams, of *Thomas Hooker: Writings in England and Holland, 1626–1633*. He is professor of English at Boston University. He received an A.B. from Harvard (1954), a B.A. and M.A. from Oxford (1956, 1959) and a Ph.D. from Yale University (1963), from which he won the Egleston history prize for *The Heart Prepared*.

David D. Hall is professor of history at Boston University. He is the editor of *The Antinomian Controversy, 1636–1638: A Documentary History* (Wesleyan 1968) and author of *The Faithful Shepherd: A History of the New England Ministry in the Seventeenth Century*.